How to Disagree Better

Julia Minson

Avery
an imprint of Penguin Random House
New York

AVERY

an imprint of Penguin Random House LLC
1745 Broadway, New York, NY 10019
penguinrandomhouse.com

Copyright © 2026 by Julia Alexandra Minson
Penguin Random House values and supports copyright. Copyright fuels creativity, encourages diverse voices, promotes free speech, and creates a vibrant culture. Thank you for buying an authorized edition of this book and for complying with copyright laws by not reproducing, scanning, or distributing any part of it in any form without permission. You are supporting writers and allowing Penguin Random House to continue to publish books for every reader. Please note that no part of this book may be used or reproduced in any manner for the purpose of training artificial intelligence technologies or systems.

Avery with colophon is a registered trademark of Penguin Random House LLC

Most Avery books are available at a discount when purchased in quantity for sales promotions or corporate use. Special editions, which include personalized covers, excerpts, and corporate imprints, can be created when purchased in large quantities. For more information, please e-mail specialmarkets@penguinrandomhouse.com. Your local bookstore can also assist with discounted bulk purchases using the Penguin Random House corporate Business-to-Business program. For assistance in locating a participating retailer, e-mail B2B@penguinrandomhouse.com.

Book design by Angie Boutin

Library of Congress Cataloging-in-Publication Data

Names: Minson, Julia author
Title: How to disagree better / Julia Minson.
Description: New York : Avery, an imprint of Penguin Random House, [2026] | Includes bibliographical references and index.
Identifiers: LCCN 2025044285 (print) | LCCN 2025044286 (ebook) | ISBN 9780593855003 hardcover | ISBN 9780593855027 epub
Subjects: LCSH: Interpersonal conflict | Conflict management | Interpersonal relations
Classification: LCC BF637.I48 M567 2026 (print) | LCC BF637.I48 (ebook)
LC record available at https://lccn.loc.gov/2025044285
LC ebook record available at https://lccn.loc.gov/2025044286

International edition ISBN: 9798217183081

Printed in the United States of America
1st Printing

The authorized representative in the EU for product safety and compliance is Penguin Random House Ireland, Morrison Chambers, 32 Nassau Street, Dublin D02 YH68, Ireland, https://eu-contact.penguin.ie.

To anyone who has ever disagreed with me. Thank you.

Contents

Introduction: Why Do We Need a Book About Disagreement? *ix*

1
Disagreement, Conflict, and What's Wrong with Everyone Around You *1*

2
Discovering the Receptive Mindset *19*

3
It's Not the Thought That Counts *47*

4
The Awesome Power of Signaling Learning Goals *67*

5
Asking the Right Questions *89*

6
Listening with Your Words *109*

7
The H.E.A.R. Framework—Showing Receptiveness While Making Your Point *129*

8
What's Your Story? *153*

9
The Courage to Speak with Receptiveness *177*

10
Building Your Receptiveness Muscle *205*

11
Building Receptive Relationships, Teams, and Communities *223*

Conclusion *239*

Acknowledgments *245*

Notes *249*

Index *261*

Introduction

WHY DO WE NEED A BOOK ABOUT DISAGREEMENT?

WHEN FACED WITH A PROBLEM (HOW DO WE SET OUR HOUSEhold budget? How do we turn our children into competent adults?) or a crisis (How do we handle a global pandemic? What costs must we cut to offset the declining revenue?), humans deploy a unique strategy that has yielded brilliant results since the dawn of time. Regular people, like you and me, put our heads together, debate, brainstorm, and consider possible approaches to whatever predicament we are facing. We generate ideas, flesh out the good ones, reject the bad, revise our understanding of what the problem really is, and update the emerging approach as the situation evolves. We follow this process in our homes, in our workplaces, and in our communities, confident that sharing insights borne out of our unique experiences will ultimately lead to sensible solutions, shared progress, and flourishing societies.

Yet, despite literally millennia of practice, expressing our views honestly and clearly, hearing opposing views from others, and navigating through the mess of contradictory ideas toward a common goal do not come easily. Having our ideas challenged and engaging with different perspectives advanced by others can lead to brilliant insights, yes, but also to discomfort, frustration, resentment, and withdrawal. So some problems go unsolved. Good ideas get lost. Bad ideas waste time. Trust gets eroded. Relationships become strained. We ruminate and resent. We think of the last time that speaking up cost us a relationship (or a job), and we keep our mouth shut. We come to think of disagreement as a very risky gamble, one that is generally not worth it. So much for novel solutions and human flourishing.

But it does not have to be this way. Disagreeing well is a skill like any other. We may not be very good at it now, but we can improve. Eventually, we can be great at it. By disagreeing more effectively we can help humanity thrive, yes, but we can also have more engaged, honest, and productive conversations at work and at home. Investing some time and effort to learn to disagree with authenticity and grace can be the gift that keeps on giving in every facet of your life because disagreement is not the problem. Lack of skill at disagreeing is.

THINK BACK TO your morning. Unless you've been in a state of meditative bliss or under anesthesia, there is a high chance that in that time you experienced one or more disagreements with a fellow human.

It may have started at home, when your teenager woke up with a headache and wanted to skip school. While you happen to believe that whatever she will miss in class is less important than her health, your spouse maintains that coddling your children and allowing them to skip school teaches bad discipline. In nearly twenty years of marriage the two of you are yet to feel truly simpatico about how to raise your children, and this morning was no exception.

When you got to work, you might have been forced to sit

through another meeting where your colleagues pushed for an idea that you considered to be doomed from the start. You have seen this idea fail before and you were already frustrated with having your objections ignored. Hearing it again made you seriously question your colleagues' competence and why you even work at this company. And while you are normally not shy about speaking up, having the same bad arguments rehashed again makes you feel like you should just go along with the bad idea to avoid having to have this meeting again for the tenth time. Why do you care? It's not your company anyway.

To help yourself endure the endless meeting, you checked your phone, only to find that a childhood friend sent you a political meme. Not only did you not find the meme funny, but receiving it reminded you of the ever-growing gap in how you and your friend have come to see the world. Thinking about your differing worldviews made you a little sad, and more than a little irritated, not only with your friend but also with the half of the country that seems to share your friend's views.

It's not even lunch, and you're annoyed with your spouse, your colleagues, and your friend. Your children have probably learned more about how two people fight about parenting than about their own health or responsibilities. Your time at work has been wasted and a bad idea is likely to be implemented. Years of friendship have been called into question over a three-second nonverbal exchange.

A typical American experiences approximately 6.2 memorable disagreements every week. Not surprisingly, that number is related to how many people they interact with on a daily basis. The more humans, the more opinions, the more disagreement. Beyond the actual disagreement, people spend another 3.7 hours a week ruminating about and regretting their disagreements.

Every disagreement—at home, at work, or online—presents

us with a set of choices. At first glance, the choices seem to boil down to confronting the person we disagree with and risking an escalating conflict, or "letting it go" and enduring mounting frustration as we continue to bite our tongue. Because neither of these options is particularly attractive, even just thinking about our disagreements (forget actively engaging with them!) takes a psychological toll.

Should I have said it? Should I say it tonight? Should I say it differently? Should I never say it again? These questions swirl in our minds, distract us from our work, cost us sleep, and account for hundreds of hours of therapy.

As a social psychologist, I have spent my career fascinated with how disagreement can go badly and how we can do it better. Members of other species don't know how to disagree. They may fight, but they don't have the cognitive capacity or linguistic ability to articulate a set of beliefs, recognize the presence of different ones, and then make a choice to act on that disagreement or ignore it. Some animals live in communities, but those communities are based around safety and reproduction, not around a desire for new ideas and creative stimulation.

By contrast, when we humans go to extensive effort to surround ourselves with other people, we do this for safety and reproduction, yes, but also because we hope that they will teach us something new, interesting, and potentially delightful based on their divergent knowledge and life experiences. Because of this, thinking about disagreement presents a fascinating contradiction. While most people find disagreement uncomfortable, it is in fact what we are signing up for when we choose to live in communities. It is also absolutely crucial for learning and sound decision-making. And while disagreements can be destructive to relationships, some of the closest, most exciting, and most fulfilling relationships are based on the unique (and often different) perspectives that the participants bring to each interaction.

WHY DO WE NEED TO DISAGREE?

The spring after I received my PhD and began working as a lecturer at the University of Pennsylvania, my grandfather—a towering figure in my life and the patriarch of our immigrant family—needed triple bypass surgery to treat his heart disease. But despite the top-notch medical care he received, his recovery at home was slow. He was weak and short of breath, looking pale and constantly complaining. With Easter around the corner, my grandmother and I spent hours strategizing about how to make him comfortable during brunch and considering which seat would offer him the best view of my toddler daughters hunting for Easter eggs. We were confident that time with the kids would lift his spirits and fix whatever ailed him.

My Canadian American mother-in-law was skeptical of our plans. "Grandpa is really not doing well. Maybe he should stay home, sweetie," she suggested mildly but repeatedly. But I dismissed her concerns. Of course Grandpa had to come to Easter brunch! How could he possibly miss the egg hunt? What kind of terrible family would we be if we did not find a way to include my grandparents?

To be honest, in the back of my mind, I assumed that my mother-in-law didn't really want my grandparents at brunch. As elderly Russian Jewish immigrants with broken English and galloping anxiety about anything and everything kid-related, they were sometimes difficult to take. I interpreted my mother-in-law's expressions of concern as a polite way of trying to avoid having to deal with all their eccentricities at a family gathering that was far more important in her culture than in ours. I assumed that Grandma and I would eventually find a way to make Grandpa comfortable and that my mother-in-law was exaggerating the strain that simply coming to brunch would put on him. Boy, was I wrong.

Grandpa never made it to brunch. He collapsed in our tiny powder room right after making the herculean effort of climbing our front porch steps. Apparently, the whole time when he was complaining about being short of breath, he literally couldn't breathe. His lungs had filled with fluid that his compromised heart could not pump away. Instead of eating brunch and hunting for Easter eggs, we scrambled to get Grandpa back into the car. I then drove at breakneck speed to the ER at Penn Presbyterian Hospital, while he hallucinated in the back seat and my grandmother made frantic calls to his surgeon. Later, when the dust settled, I learned that my mother-in-law had recognized the symptoms of heart failure but did not want to argue with me since I was so hell-bent on having my grandparents over for Easter. She did not want to be rude and contradict me directly when it came to my house and my family. I really wish she had.

My next week was spent running back and forth between home, office, and Penn Presbyterian where my grandfather recovered after having liters of fluid pumped out of his lungs, and my grandmother watched over his care like a frazzled, Russian-speaking hawk. There, she argued with the nurses, complained about the quality of the food and the insufficiency of the television channels, and demanded to know why nothing ever happened on schedule. Several days in, she called me at work, distraught. The hospital had run out of visitor cots, and she was not going to be able to spend the night in Grandpa's room. What if he needs to get up at night? What if the nurses couldn't understand him? What if in the confusion he took the wrong medication? She was in a full-blown panic, so I ran to the hospital to solve the problem of the cots. Surely in a massive urban teaching hospital we would be able to find one more spare cot to accommodate a tiny old lady.

However, the conversation with the nurse manager revealed that the problem wasn't the lack of cots. It was my grandmother.

Apparently, the nursing staff did not appreciate being questioned and contradicted at every turn, so they came up with an elegant solution—no cot equals no Grandma.

For the next hour I swore up and down to the nurse manager that my grandmother would behave. I then had to explain to Grandma that she needed to give the nurses a break if she wanted to stay in Grandpa's room. And in the end, a cot magically appeared and relative peace was restored.

Over the years, I have considered these events many times. Upon reflection, neither my grandmother nor my mother-in-law nor I handled our respective roles effectively. But who—my unfailingly polite mother-in-law or my constantly argumentative grandmother—was closer to expressing the "right" amount of opposition? What did I contribute to the mess by being so committed to having Easter the way we always had it in the past? Or by attributing my mother-in-law's expressions of concern for my grandfather's health to a selfish desire to have an easier, entirely English-speaking meal? Why did the nurses make up a story about the shortage of cots instead of talking to my grandmother? Next time there is a crisis that requires the input and support of multiple people with different views, how could we leverage their perspectives more effectively?

Scholars across many social science disciplines know that disagreement is necessary for everything from making good individual decisions, to running innovative and agile companies, to governing democratic societies. The crux of the argument is that every human endeavor that is the slightest bit complex requires ideas, insights, information, and expertise from more than one individual. On one hand, this idea of bringing together people with different perspectives to solve complex problems seems obvious: One person is unlikely to have all the necessary knowledge or be able to see a given situation from multiple perspectives. We assemble teams of experts, seek advice from our friends and relatives, and base entire societies on the faith that if we put our heads together new ideas will emerge. But of course, one consequence of this approach is that the people who we invite to collaborate on a decision or a solution to a problem will, by virtue of having something unique to say, inevitably disagree with each other. And rather than advancing our thinking, those disagreements often lead to drama.

To be fair, many of us appreciate people who are reliably honest with their views. We recognize that disagreement provides valuable information and creative stimulation, and we value the relationships that are built around authentic debate. If we are in the right mental space, we may even welcome disagreement.

In addition to appreciating *others* who are willing to disagree, we ourselves often initiate disagreements because of a deep-seated need to be authentic and honest. If a friend loved a movie that we thought was stupid, or is about to buy a gym membership we know they'll never use, we often can't just smile and go along, even if in retrospect it might have been wise to do so. Keeping silent while holding an opposing view feels inauthentic and cowardly. So instead, we bravely step into the breach, pointing out the plot holes in the movie and our friend's lineup of unused fitness gadgets. We do this partially in the hope that our opinions will help those we care about, but we also do it because we feel a deep-seated need for self-expression.

Active, vocal, and frequent disagreement comes with many benefits. If we want to run innovative organizations, participate in thriving economies, or simply just have interesting conversations in which we feel authentic and validated, we need to be able to say what we came to say. Indeed, a variety of disasters, ranging from the Easter brunch that almost killed my grandfather to a host of corporate and public policy fiascos, can be traced back to people failing to disagree effectively. And yet, every day people avoid disagreement. Why?

WHY IS DISAGREEMENT SO HARD?

A few years ago, a student and I ran a very simple study. Participants read a list describing a variety of different activities and imagined spending about twenty minutes engaging in each one. The activities were all familiar and ranged from ones we expected to be pleasant (eating tacos from a food truck) to less so (taking a load of laundry to the dry cleaner). Embedded in the list were several activities where the participant imagined interacting with another person who had a particular point of view on a controversial policy topic. For example, some people were asked to imagine riding in a taxi with a driver who expressed strong pro-immigration views or being at work happy hour and talking to a person who opposed gay marriage.

Unbeknownst to participants, the online questionnaire was engineered to present them with every possible combination of setting (taxi, happy hour, etc.), topic (gay marriage, immigration, the death penalty), and point of view (support or oppose). Our goal was simple—we wanted to get some sense of just how unpleasant disagreement on these topics was.

Of the activities in our study, the one that was rated to be the most enjoyable was taking a warm bubble bath—on a 7-point scale, this activity was rated to be a 5.8. The bubble bath outperformed eating tacos, going out for happy hour, and exercising. Some of the lowest-performing activities included getting a dental cleaning (2.6 out of 7—sorry, dentists!) and paying one's bills (2.8). However, of these many activities, spending twenty minutes talking to somebody we strongly disagree with turned out to be the clear loser. Averaged across topics and scenarios, having a discussion about a policy disagreement ended up being the lowest-ranked of all the scenarios we came up with, including having your teeth scraped with a sharp metal object!

Many readers might find the results of this study obvious. Of course disagreement is unpleasant! Who wants to have a conversation with a person who is expressing views that you believe to be based on ignorance, stupidity, or a fundamental lack of human decency? That conversation is likely to be awkward and frustrating, and could potentially lead to conflict. However, I find these results fascinating.

First, the magnitude of our distaste for engaging with opposing views is striking, suggesting that our participants largely overlooked the many potential benefits of learning about opposing views. For example, the conversation could prove to be informative, stimulating, or at the very least memorable. You could imagine coming home and regaling your family with your taxi driver's argument and getting a second interesting conversation out of the first one. You could imagine reading more about the issue later and fact-checking the claims that your counterpart made. Whether they were right or wrong, you would become a more informed person as a result. You could also imagine having no emotional reaction to the conversation at all. After all, what does it matter what your taxi driver thinks about immigration or what your colleague thinks about gay marriage? They are not setting policy or marrying you, so let them believe whatever they want!

The fact that people dread these conversations suggests that we are not considering the benefits but mostly focusing on the costs. What are the costs that we are so worried about?

The first and most cited potential cost of disagreement is conflict. Although many people use the terms "disagreement" and "conflict" as synonyms, they are not. For example, you have probably had many disagreements in your life about trivial things: whether chocolate cake is better than vanilla (of course it is!), whether composting is worth the trouble (maybe . . .), or whether getting an eyebrow ring is ever a good idea (no!). However, most of these disagreements probably didn't turn into big fights loaded with negative emotions and leading to long-term relational damage. That seems sensible—why would you fight about something that is of so little consequence? If other people want to eat subpar cake or put holes in their faces, so be it.

You have also probably had disagreements about things that have consequences, but not to you or not right now. Whether aliens exist and whether having children is a fundamentally terrible idea are both very important questions. However, in my personal case, I expect no alien encounters in my immediate future, and there is no getting rid of my three children. So I am unlikely to get into a serious conflict over a disagreement that, although important in the abstract, has no impact on my present behavior or my likely life outcomes.

Disagreement is far more likely to turn into conflict when two things are true at the same time: 1) the topic is important, and 2) your counterpart's opinions impact your own life and choices. The presence of these two conditions often leads the disagreeing parties to start working to change each other's minds. You try to persuade each other. You resist the other's attempts at persuasion. You attack; the other person parries and retaliates. Suddenly, you're on a battleground, and as you reach an impasse, your frustration mounts. You become irritated, then bewildered, then angry. You start wondering why this person refuses to listen to reason and how you even got here in the first place. After all, you were just trying to help them make better decisions.

TRYING TO WIN AN ARGUMENT IS A GOOD WAY TO START A FIGHT

From ancient Greeks to modern litigators, people have sought to resolve disagreements through better and better debate. Countless books and blogs have touted the five keys to persuasion or the six ways to win an argument. However, few people have ever measured the success of these techniques in the wild. What sounds good in a philosopher's head might fail in the real world. What works in a courtroom might backfire at the dinner table. And the tools that have been scientifically validated often don't fit the problems most of us face. People who disagree on topics that matter to them—how to run their business, raise their children, or reform immigration policy—are unlikely to be nudged into capitulation by small tweaks to their decision-making environment that might be effective in the context of advertising or fundraising.

The problem is exacerbated by the fact that most of us have only a vague notion of how the dynamics of disagreement really work. We imagine a battlefield where the most logical, just, and useful ideas win out. Or we imagine ourselves as naturally gifted and wise wordsmiths who always seem to know the right thing to say, the right way to say it, and the right time to do so. Yet, how many times have you tried pointing out hypocrisy, appealing to emotion, overwhelming someone with a flood of facts, or citing an authority, only to end up even farther apart from your partner than when you started? How often have you felt confident that you've torn the opposing argument apart only to be accosted with another speech? How many times have you walked away convinced that the other person simply doesn't *want* to hear you? Experiences like these at home, at work, and in our civic spaces make many people avoid disagreement altogether, convinced that discussing the opposing perspective will never lead to anything good and will often end in heartache.

Trying to persuade someone on the other side of a disagreement is a fool's errand. As we chase a fantasy from high school debate or our favorite courtroom drama, our counterpart only becomes further entrenched in their beliefs and grows more committed to persuading *us*. But just because we shouldn't try to convince someone they are wrong doesn't mean we can or should avoid disagreements entirely. Remember, our counterpart might have information that's interesting or even lifesaving.

Thus we are faced with a conundrum. How do we leverage the decision-making and creativity-enhancing benefits of disagreement, while avoiding the relational pitfalls? How do we debate the important policy issues of the day, the design parameters of a new product, or the family vacation plans with vigor, authenticity, respect, and empathy? How do we surround ourselves with people who will disagree with us and not come out emotionally battered and exhausted? How can we disagree better?

PRACTICING RECEPTIVENESS— A BETTER WAY TO DISAGREE

I have always found people and their conflicts interesting. Even as a very young child, I enjoyed nothing more than huddling in the corner of the couch as adults discussed work, relationships, and neighborly squabbles. If I sat quietly enough, there was a good chance that they would forget about my presence and spill something truly juicy.

When I turned eleven, knowing how to navigate disagreement became more of a survival necessity than an idle hobby. That year, my Ukrainian Jewish mother married my American stepfather, relocating us from Ekaterinburg, Russia, to Denver, Colorado. Four days after taking off from the Sheremetyevo International Airport in Moscow, I found myself navigating a public school in the Denver suburbs, ashamed of my hand-me-down clothes and my rudimentary English. Eastern European Jews are famously bold in their approach to disagreement, but the family arguments I had witnessed before suddenly seemed quaint when compared to this rocky melding of cultures, parenting styles, and the epic battles with my new American stepsiblings. Ten years later, my life changed again. I married my husband, Ryan, and was warmly welcomed into his conservative, military, and *very* American family. More disagreements and more learning followed.

After twenty-five years of marriage, my husband and I continue to disagree. A lot. But now our debates are often joined by our three daughters, whose strong opinions are bolstered by evidence from TikTok and the varied and colorful experiences of their friends. On any given day, our kitchen is crowded with local teenagers, visiting friends, current and former colleagues, graduate students, and visiting relatives. These people come from different states, different countries, different political persuasions, and different generations. Our discussions are boisterous and loud and feature opposing opinions about everything from how best to store tomatoes to reproductive rights. Having moved across the United States four times, bought and sold eight homes, made countless career decisions, advised hundreds of students, helped parents through short- and long-term illness, and cared for an entire parade of pets, I feel like there are few difficult topics left that we have not wrestled with.

If you watch enough people go through enough disagreements, you might notice that different people take different approaches. At one extreme, there are people who tend to relish disagreement and are always ready to leap in with the full force of their intellect and their vocal apparatus. Every conversation seems to turn into an argument and many arguments turn into shouting matches. Despite decades of experience, these people are often surprised by this dynamic. It is as if it's never occurred to them that telling somebody that they are dead wrong might not go over well.

At the other extreme are people who seem to want to fully accommodate the beliefs and preferences of others in order to avoid even a hint of discord. Being in their presence is often quite pleasant because there is little psychological friction—all you have to do is say what you want or what you believe and you will get your way. Unfortunately for them, there are two problems with this highly agreeable approach to life. First, the person who is being accommodating is not getting *their* way. They might feel like they are performing a public service by keeping things pleasant, but sooner or later they are likely to get resentful. Second, this person is also not fully contributing to the intellectual capital of the community they are in. They are not offering new ideas, preventing disastrous mistakes, or pushing others to think harder. True, they are not creating drama, but they are also not creating much else. Of course, most of us are somewhere in between these extremes, and our penchant toward conflict varies with the situation we are in.

But if you watch hard enough, you might notice that there is an entirely different approach, one that does not rely on a choice between combat and accommodation. People who follow this path are often slow to express their opinions because they take the time to deeply investigate the opinions of others. When they do say what they think, their views seem to incorporate arguments from multiple perspectives. They rarely feel the need to foist their attitudes on others, but they also don't abandon their own views. They are often fine with disagreement because they realize that there are both merits and flaws to most perspectives. When some sort of decision must be made and agreeing to disagree is not a viable path, these people seem to be able to craft solutions that satisfy all parties because they understand what the parties actually want. I refer to this approach to disagreement as "receptiveness to opposing views."

Receptiveness is both a mindset and a set of behaviors that comes easier to some of us than to others. Nevertheless, irrespective of your natural inclination, it is also a skill at which we can all learn to excel. People who consistently engage with others more receptively have less conflict in their lives and spend less time ruminating about how they should have handled their disagreements better. They have more satisfying conversations even on the most difficult of topics and are viewed more positively by their friends, colleagues, and neighbors. People who are more receptive tend to have more diverse social networks and are more sought out as colleagues and teammates. In other words, they have cracked the code of disagreement. They have learned how to disagree effectively, and by studying them, so can you.

THE RECEPTIVE PATH TO INFLUENCE

A fundamental challenge of navigating disagreement, and one that we will return to over and over in this book, is deciding what you are hoping to accomplish and the likelihood of reaching your goals. Once we recognize that winning the argument is not a realistic goal and admit to ourselves that the other person is unlikely to acknowledge the error of their ways, what is the point of talking to them? As much as I would like to believe that people will take on a self-improvement project like learning about receptiveness for the sake of fostering world peace and relational harmony, I've been around the block a few times and I know better. People like the idea of peace and harmony in theory, but in reality we all just want to get our way.

But what does "getting your way" really mean? When you are arguing with your business partner about their frequent use of the company credit card for lavish business development dinners, you might think that all you need is for them to stop racking up the credit card bills. But in reality, what you are looking for is a reliable thought partner who will help you navigate the myriad decisions about investments, product launches, and hiring for years to come. You want them to respect your views and trust your instincts. If you "win" the battle about business development spending by brandishing the expense report and getting your partner to capitulate, you might lose the war. By trying too doggedly to persuade a person that you are right and they are wrong, you risk making them stop listening to you all together, losing any ability to influence them in the future.

This dynamic plays out in many kinds of relationships. In hopes of getting a short-term win, people give away their ability for long-term influence by coming across as judgmental, dogmatic, and uninterested in their counterpart's perspective and experiences. In some conversations, this approach is more risky than in others. When a doctor tells a patient that their beliefs about vaccines are based on misinformation and endanger everyone around them, they risk the patient walking out, never to be heard from again. The effort of correcting somebody's beliefs with regard to one choice thus results in a loss of influence over all of their future health decisions. Similarly, in the case of public policy, tone-deaf leaders often get voted out, no matter how accurate their analyses and how well-intentioned their policies. As a political strategist once told me, "They never tell you when they stop inviting you to the meetings." Our desire to have the quick win paired with our confidence in the superiority of our arguments and the ultimate justice of our cause blinds us to the collateral damage that we inflict on our relationships and our long-term outcomes.

So what should our goal in disagreement be? I have a simple definition of constructive disagreement:

> A constructive disagreement is any disagreement that increases the parties' willingness to talk to each other again.

In other words, what you are "constructing" is a bridge to the next conversation. You know you are doing well if you are increasing trust, respect, and rapport, not if you are scoring short-term rhetorical points. If you are learning and so are they, even if all you are learning about is the actual source of the conflict, then you are moving in the right direction. This definition recognizes the fundamental fact that no important disagreement about business, public policy, or parenting has ever been settled once and for all in a single argument. Serious disagreements arise from differences in beliefs, attitudes, values, and backgrounds. When people have spent most of their lives believing a fact or holding a value dear, no single conversation will compel them to change their minds. The only consequential thing that a single conversation can do is destroy the chance for future conversations.

So if we want to wield influence, we have to plan for the long term. We have to think about strengthening our relationships with our counterparts and building our reputations as reasonable, trustworthy, well-intentioned people whose views others will willingly seek out. In other words, influence means being the kind of person people want to talk to about their views, not the kind of person who has to beat counterparts into submission to be heard. In the long run, you are much more likely to get your way by strengthening your receptiveness muscle than by honing your persuasion skills.

THE SCIENCE OF DISAGREEMENT

As of this writing, I have spent over twenty years of my life experimentally studying disagreement and conflict: first at Stanford, then at the University of Pennsylvania, and now at Harvard. I chose this career because I knew that behind the pop psychology books and self-help blogs, there was an emerging experimental science slowly uncovering why people argue about topics ranging from the trivial to the profound and what can be done to make these encounters go more smoothly. I wanted to be part of this conversation. I wrote this book to share the science far and wide so everyone with a credit card or a library card could benefit.

Roughly seventy years ago, the field of medicine shifted away from basing its recommendations on the experience of practitioners to basing them on the results of clinical trials. In medicine, it is no longer enough to claim that a process in the body works in a particular way because a doctor had observed a patient (or a hundred patients) and reached a conclusion. The new standard of evidence requires that claims be based on randomized experiments vetted by the scientific community, i.e., empirical, peer-reviewed research. A similar shift is happening in our understanding of human strife. Although evidence-free advice continues to be common, a mounting body of research published in peer-reviewed journals is starting to shift our understanding about why disagreement leads to conflict and what to do about it. Many experiments in this space test simple interventions that improve outcomes by redesigning the process by which the disagreement unfolds or asking participants to change specific behaviors during the interaction. In other words, rather than requiring all those who seek self-improvement to undergo years of therapy, the goal of modern research is to improve outcomes through simple, clearly defined behavioral adjustments that regular people can implement. The promise of this research is that all of us can disagree better: We can express our genuine opinions and engage in thoughtful debate while preserving and even strengthening our relationships. As a result, we can make better decisions while achieving our other long-term goals.

Many of my personal experiences have inspired specific studies that are now part of this peer-reviewed scientific record. At the same time, I am constantly applying the takeaways from the science to my own daily behavior and leveraging it to advise my kids, my students, and my consulting clients—I think of this as "road testing" the research and putting it to work for the world. When the science meets the messy reality of humans in the wild, surprising observations often lead to new studies—and so the cycle of knowledge creation continues.

Some of these ideas are going to feel quite intuitive to many readers. After all, every human in the world is already a highly trained psychologist. All of us have spent decades navigating a world full of other humans, interpreting their behavior and moods, and seeking out mates and collaborators while avoiding making enemies or being ostracized by peers. When the doctor tells you that sleep and hydration are important, you are unlikely to be surprised—your body has been telling you that for decades.

However, some of the ideas in this book will feel quite counterintuitive—or at least they were counterintuitive to me when I first saw the data. An important part of my job is testing popular approaches to conflict, only to find that some don't work at all because the problems they are intended to fix are stubbornly robust or because the way that a solution is implemented often destroys its effectiveness. It's similar to medical doctors finding out through experiments that dieting doesn't work for weight loss, or that being out in the cold does not cause colds—ideas that people believed to be true until they were proven false. By contrast, some ideas long promoted by therapists, mediators, and wise grandmothers wield surprising power and should be used more consistently by all of us.

The first thing we will do is take a closer look at how disagreement becomes conflict. We will then quickly move on to practical tools for managing disagreement more effectively. The focus of our efforts will be on developing our interpersonal skills, intentionally changing how we behave when approaching discussions on thorny topics. In addition to addressing the ways that we can improve as individuals, we will consider the tools that leaders can use to foster cultures of constructive disagreement in organizations and communities. Throughout, I will offer concrete tips and exercises to put the ideas to work in your life.

Because I am a nerd, the discussion will be heavily grounded in the nuances of peer-reviewed research. You will learn about experiments conducted in corporations, on college campuses, with American political opponents, and with participants in the Israeli/Palestinian conflict. These experiments offer clear insights about the tendencies that lead us astray, as well as tested techniques that might give us hope. In addition to the research, I will also share many examples from my personal and professional life. I am hoping that reading about my successes and failures, as well as what I have gleaned from talking to diplomats, mediators, parents, managers, and teenage girls, will make this book more useful to you.

Throughout, the focus will be on helping all of us waste less time and energy on approaches that don't work in order to invest more effort into ones that do. There is no magic solution to navigating every single disagreement, but I am confident that with thoughtful, evidence-based practice we can all get better and reach consistently stronger outcomes in every facet of our lives.

How to Disagree Better

1

DISAGREEMENT, CONFLICT, AND WHAT'S WRONG WITH EVERYONE AROUND YOU

HERE IS A POORLY KEPT AND PERPETUALLY EMBARRASSING SEcret about my academic career—my passion for the science of disagreement did not come from observing the harm that violent conflict sows in the world or studying the academic literature and identifying theoretical gaps that needed filling. My passion for disagreement was primarily fueled by my years as a competitive ballroom dancer, training with, competing with, and regularly fighting with my partner and later husband, Ryan.

I began ballroom dancing as a little girl in Russia. This might seem strange to many American readers, but in Eastern Europe in the eighties, taking ballroom dancing lessons was as common as taking ballet or tap lessons is in the United States. All the little girls wanted to do it, and all the little boys were forced into dancing with their sisters. By the time I had met my husband, I had thousands of hours of training and years of competitive experience under my belt. Ryan, who had never danced a step in his life, wanted to learn to dance because he had grand plans to flirt with a woman he expected to see again at a friend's wedding. I was his teacher.

My husband has an infuriating quality. He is just good at things—not necessarily amazing, but notably above average at almost everything, especially things that require physical coordination and musicality. When it came to dancing, he improved quickly because of his talent and interest—and also because his teacher (soon his girlfriend) had endless time and energy for teaching him. We practiced during every available hour and on every patch of hardwood we could find. I quickly came to realize that I had more fun dancing with this complete beginner than with my competition partner. As weeks turned into months, I decided that I would rather break up the competitive partnership I was involved in and dance with Ryan, even if that meant going back to the basics.

There are several unique aspects to ballroom dancing that make it the perfect microcosm for the study of conflict. First of all, the two partners are in perpetual intimate physical contact. The front of your body is literally plastered to your partner's, meaning that you can feel their most minute movements, down to their breath and their heart rate. Good physical contact improves your ability to lead and follow—to coordinate your movements wordlessly and instantaneously. Indeed, after dancing together for years, I could move my body in response to Ryan's much more quickly than it took my conscious brain to understand what was happening. And when everything worked, when we moved in complete harmony, when we felt in sync with the music and with each other—it was like telepathy. To this day, few experiences I have had compare to this feeling of "oneness."

But of course, it didn't always work. One of us would lose our balance, move too slowly, stretch too far or not far enough, and the other person would get annoyed. And the finely honed sense that allowed us to feel each other's every movement also allowed us to feel each other's every mood. I'd get upset with his tightened grip on my back, he'd get upset that I was upset, and the magic would dissolve in an instant. Left in its place was another couple glaring at each other across several feet of empty dance floor.

Like every dance partnership, when things went badly, we tried to diagnose the cause. Predictably, the cause was the other person. His claim that I had moved too slowly was met with my claim that he had not provided enough momentum. When I said he miscounted the rhythm, he said I was the one who started counting from the wrong measure. When he said I was leaning too far back, I said that he was not counterbalancing enough with his own weight. In fact, every practice, two hours a day, seven days a week, featured a dozen instances where we were both absolutely sure that the other person caused the problem and was simply failing to acknowledge it.

This state of nearly perpetual conflict on the dance floor was especially baffling since we knew each other and the choreography as well as any two people possibly could. We were in love and rarely fought about anything outside of dancing. We had world-class coaches to help us solve our problems, and we were both highly intelligent and analytical people. So how could he be so sure I was to blame and I be so sure that he was? And why did our different perspectives have to lead to so many ugly spats?

My only consolation was that just about everyone around us had the same problem. Observing other dancing couples, ranging from relative beginners to nationally ranked professionals, I saw the same strange phenomenon: Highly trained people who deeply cared about improving their performance were similarly unable to agree on the basic physical facts of which one of them missed the beat or rotated too far.*

In my early twenties, I decided to get a PhD in social psychology, not because I had ambitions to bring peace to the Middle

---

* I later learned that a similar dynamic plays out between bridge partners, tennis partners, and, of course, parents.

East or to restore democracy but because I wanted to figure out how to stop fighting with my dance partner.

PSYCHOLOGICAL CAUSES OF CONFLICT

I applied to graduate school and was fortunate enough to be admitted to Stanford. There, I studied under the legendary psychologist Lee Ross, who at that time was scientifically proving a truth that, while seeming obvious, has profound implications: Most conflict stems from the simple fact that everyone thinks they are right. In his work, Lee argued that most people go around the world believing that their perceptions, experiences, and interpretations of events reflect an objective, knowable external reality. Lee called this phenomenon "naïve realism"—a term borrowed from philosophy and intended to highlight that people "naïvely" believe that their perceptions and judgments are "realistic" in some deep, fundamental sense.

Through many clever experiments, Lee and his students demonstrated how this stance then led to conflict across a broad variety of contexts and topics. Because of naïve realism, any time a person had an opinion (which is basically always) and encountered another person (often), they both entered the conversation with a firm conviction that they "got it." Because both people believed themselves to be fundamentally reasonable and objective, to the extent that their opinions diverged, the seeds of conflict had been sown. As soon as I encountered Lee's work, I realized that I had found my intellectual home. From that time forward, naïve realism and its logical extensions formed the basis of my research program.

In retrospect, it is likely that Lee, who had spent decades working on the conflicts in Northern Ireland and the Middle East, found my desire to apply his theories to squabbles between ballroom dance partners silly. But as an immensely curious person, who found almost all human behavior fascinating, he also recognized what was unique about this particular context: If people who were as close and aligned as Ryan and I were couldn't get past the differences in our perceptions, what hope was there for the rest of the world? Was there some fundamental psychological commonality in conflicts between lovers, colleagues, and nation-states? Indeed, over the years it turned out that competitive ballroom dancing was an excellent laboratory in which to study conflict—a context wherein two parties often saw things fundamentally differently but deeply cared about the outcome and had to reach consensus in order to move forward (or backward, or sideways). I quickly realized that naïve realism was exactly what was causing the issues between Ryan and me.

A unique feature of ballroom dancing is that the partners spend the vast majority of the time facing each other. This means that when Ryan and I passed by a mirror on the wall of the dance studio, I would see my front and his back, but he wouldn't see us at all, because at that moment he would be facing in the opposite direction. As we would move and rotate, our perspectives would shift, but there would literally never be a time when we would both be seeing the world (and ourselves) from the same vantage point. In other words, we would see the same performance, but never at the same time or from the same angle. It turns out that this curious physical arrangement was the perfect metaphor for naïve realism—both partners could grow increasingly certain in their convictions about the quality of their dancing or the source of their mistakes without considering the fact that those convictions might be entirely different if they only saw the world from their partner's point of view.

An important thing to keep in mind is that naïve realism actually serves people quite well, especially in navigating their physical world—a world that even under the simplest circumstances requires humans to make hundreds of tiny judgments every hour.

Thanks to this mindset, we quickly assume that when our feet encounter resistance, they must be on solid ground; when a predator seems very small, it must be very far away; and when green strawberries turn red, they're ready to eat. We thus form the habit of treating our perceptions as accurate reflections of the physical world around us, completely ignoring all the distortion and processing that happens in the split second between sensory contact and the interpretation that our conscious mind imposes on the incoming signal. We do not stop to consider that in a different light, in a different gravity, or with a different set of sensory organs, we would have a completely different experience. Who's got that kind of time? Assuming your views to be basically correct is a pretty effective approach to life—right up until two naïve realists learn that they see the world differently.

Like other cognitive shortcuts—which psychologists often call "cognitive biases"—naïve realism likely persists because it is efficient. Trusting our judgment allows us to make decisions quickly, and the mistakes we make are outweighed by the benefits of this efficiency. The problem is that naïve realism operates largely outside of our awareness and thus shapes our beliefs even in those cases where it might be wise to stop and reconsider. Importantly, just as we don't question our conclusions when it comes to basic sensory experiences, we similarly don't question our conclusions concerning complex and highly disputed social phenomena. In the same way that we mostly forget about the way our sensory organs shape our physical perceptions, we similarly forget about the ways in which our upbringing, our cultural background, our self-interest, our shortsightedness, or our bad mood shape our social judgments. We walk around the world convinced that we are reasonable, objective, sensible people who basically see the world as it is, largely oblivious to the fact that others might see it differently because their views are also being shaped by their backgrounds, personalities, incentives, or moods.

One might argue that all in all, this is not particularly problematic. Everyone has a unique perspective on the world, and we should all live and let live. "You do you"—as my teenage daughters might say. But one other important feature of human psychology gets in the way of us being able to peacefully coexist. Namely, when encountering disagreements, people quickly and automatically make a set of judgments about the *reason* for the divergence in their views. Psychologists call this process "making an attribution"—we are attributing the behavior to some cause or set of causes that gave rise to it. And like most human judgments, the attribution process is far from perfect.

People make attributions for all sorts of social phenomena, not just disagreement. A fundamental task of living in a highly complex society is understanding why other members of the species do whatever they do so that each person can predict the others' behavior with some accuracy. Most of the time, these attributional judgments too are fast and automatic, occurring in the backs of our minds without ever being questioned.

For example, when I see a person waving at another as they walk toward each other, I might attribute that behavior to the fact that they probably know each other and have a friendly relationship. This inference allows me to predict that when they meet, they will probably stop and chat and are unlikely to get into a fistfight. When I see a person hand a cashier money, I attribute the behavior to the fact that the person has taken a product from the store shelf. I can then predict that the cashier is likely to give the customer a receipt and unlikely to break into song. The stories we effortlessly generate about why a particular behavior is taking place allow us to make sense of the world and predict the next act in the play that is unfolding all around us.

However, most attributions we make are extrapolations based on prior patterns we have observed, not deductions based on our observation of the situation at hand. In the end, attributing somebody's behavior to a particular cause is an educated guess that is influenced by the contents of our life experience, our processing capacity, and a variety of cognitive biases. For example, if I see a person angrily kicking their car, I might attribute that behavior to the person's bad temper. What I might not know is that this person is having a very bad day because their dog just died, their partner broke up with them, and they are about to miss a job interview thanks to the broken-down car. In this case (as in many others), I am making a guess based on my previous experience with car-kickers, without knowing all the facts related to this particular instance.

When we encounter disagreement, we follow a similar process. We draw on what we know from our life experience and make an educated guess about why we might be disagreeing. And this is where naïve realism comes into play. If what I have learned from my life experience is that I am a reasonable person who basically "gets it," the most obvious explanation for why we disagree is that something is wrong with *them*.

As it happens, we rarely struggle to generate hypotheses about the shortcomings that lead other people to disagree with us. An obvious possibility that often springs to mind first is that they are simply not aware of all the relevant information. For example, if your colleague is complaining about unusually high expenses, you might say: "No, the expenses for July are not higher than usual. The conference costs are just making them look higher than they really are." In fact, many disagreements start with the assumption that the other person simply made a mistake and once you correct them, they will not only get back to being on the right track but will probably thank you for the valuable information you provided.

But often it does not work out that way. Your counterpart does not think they made a mistake. They know all about the conference expenses and again repeat that you need to rein in department spending. Given that correcting them with accurate information failed to resolve the disagreement, you decide to think a bit harder about why there seems to be a difference of interpretation. Unfortunately, however, you conclude that they simply didn't *understand* the information. Perhaps this individual is not as financially savvy as we had been assuming, or maybe they don't understand the life cycle of a growing business as well as you thought they did. Clearly, you need to explain it again, at greater length and now with data to support your argument.

When this too fails to change your counterpart's mind, you arrive at the final stop in the attribution process. You have provided your counterpart with all of the relevant information and explained it to them in the simplest terms possible. You are confident that anyone with half a brain ought to see it your way by now. So the fact that they persist in their wrongheaded claims suggests that there is some deeper psychological barrier, some bias, that prevents them from agreeing with you. Maybe they are too risk averse? Maybe they are just stubborn and hate changing their mind? Maybe they are a little sexist and don't like a woman telling them they are wrong? Maybe they are an elitist who looks down on anyone without an MBA? Maybe they wanted your job and are still sore that they didn't get it?

Attributions of bias and self-interest can range from merely condescending ("He is just shortsighted") to bordering on paranoid ("He is saying that because he's always hated my guts"). However, in all cases they leave us comfortably continuing to believe our own interpretation of the situation, having neatly disposed with our counterpart's objections as being either irrational or driven by some character flaw.

Of course, people don't like being told that their perspective is stemming from lack of information, lack of intelligence, or bias. When the other person then counters with their version of what is wrong with our thinking and ultimately what is wrong with us, a disagreement about the department budget becomes a conflict about the nature of our relationship, our business acumen, and our level of integrity. This attributional process and its natural consequences are the most fundamental and frequent cause of interpersonal conflict.

HOW UNDERSTANDING NAÏVE REALISM CHANGES OUR UNDERSTANDING OF CONFLICT

The naïve realism perspective offers several simple but often underappreciated insights. First, this view contradicts the common view that people fail to seriously engage with opposing perspectives because they are "threatened" by the potential truths contained therein and what those truths might reveal about the flaws in their own belief systems. Rather than portraying people as insecure and easily threatened, research on naïve realism argues that people are doggedly attached to their convictions because they simply can't see the world any other way. People don't start shouting at each other because they are afraid of being proven wrong; they start shouting because they are frustrated with the others' failure to recognize that they are right. The problem isn't that people need to work on their self-esteem and be less threatened by conflict. The real problem is the opposite: What people need to be working on is a bit of intellectual humility.

Another common myth is that intransigence in conflict comes from a person's psychological need to feel a certain way. "She always needs to be right" is a common lament of frustrated spouses, annoyed friends, and overshadowed younger sisters. The underlying claim is that the "she" in question knows on some level that she might be wrong but is motivated by a powerful psychological need to pretend otherwise. That need might be the above-mentioned insecurity, or a malicious refusal to let someone else "win," or a concern with being seen as weak for backing down.

However, the naïve realism perspective suggests that the person stubbornly failing to change their mind is not secretly questioning her beliefs and faking confidence but is simply interpreting the evidence before her and reaching the only seemingly reasonable conclusion. She is convinced of her correctness and does not understand why another reasonable person would not share her beliefs. Gently telling her that she should not be so defensive is more likely to get your head bitten off than result in persuasion.

A few years ago, I conducted a simple study with Charlie Dorison, a professor at Georgetown University. We asked roughly four hundred research participants about their views on several highly controversial social issues and offered them the opportunity to read arguments for the opposing perspective. Importantly, we told them that they could read arguments that other online participants had found to be "strong arguments based on good evidence" or "weak arguments containing little evidence."

If people are insecure and fail to change their mind because they are afraid of having their fundamental views undermined, they should choose to read the weak arguments. After all, why put yourself through the emotional turmoil of possibly learning that one of your fundamental beliefs is wrong? However, if people are naïve realists who truly believe their views and are constantly confused and annoyed by others' failure to be "reasonable," they might instead choose to read the strong arguments. Reading a high-quality articulation of why the other side believes what they do might go some distance toward restoring your faith in the intelligence of other humans and soothe some of your irritation with those who disagree with you.

And that is exactly what we found. Eighty percent of our participants preferred to read the strong arguments over the weak ones. This pattern remained consistent across the multiple topics we tested and irrespective of how important the participant said the topic was to them. People didn't want to read bad information that would make it easier for them to continue believing whatever they do because they normally don't have any trouble coming up with arguments for their view in the first place. Instead, they were hoping to read something that would inform them. This pattern of results is inconsistent with the idea that people avoid arguments for opposing views because they are afraid to be challenged. Instead, it aligns with the logic of naïve realism and the idea that people avoid arguments for opposing views because they rarely find them compelling but would be open to deeper consideration if something interesting came their way.

The research on naïve realism also sheds new light on the emotions people are likely to feel when confronted with disagreement. If consideration of opposing perspectives leads people to question their convictions, and if they avoid doing so to protect their egos, they ought to report emotions related to fear and anxiety when forced to consider the other side. By contrast, the theory of naïve realism suggests that rather than feeling fear and anxiety, people are more likely to feel anger and irritation. After all, if you know you are right, and the other side is failing to budge, who wouldn't eventually get annoyed? Charlie and I decided to find out which set of emotions is more common.

In a series of experiments, we asked people to consider the emotions they and their opposing counterparts feel when considering arguments for the opposing view. As you might expect by this point in the chapter, participants reported far more anger and irritation than threat and anxiety when considering their *own* emotions. Interestingly, however, when considering their disagreeing counterparts, participants expected *those other people* to feel threatened and anxious. Whereas our participants did not expect their confidence to falter at all as a result of considering opposing perspectives, they expected their counterparts to experience feelings of threat, anxiety, and uncertainty as they came to question their beliefs. In other words, while we see ourselves as in possession of the truth, we seem to think that other people simply can't handle it.

DOES NAÏVE REALISM ALWAYS LEAD TO CONFLICT?

Naïve realism is hard to get around. First, as the saying goes, the fish doesn't know it's in water. The vast majority of the time we don't notice the influence of our culture, upbringing, gender, religion, social position, life history, and recent alcohol intake on our interpretation of the disagreements we are in. Indeed, when people in studies are instructed to carefully consider the biases that influence their own thinking and the thinking of disagreeing others, they consistently conclude that the other person is more subject to bias than they themselves are. This phenomenon is called "the bias blind spot" and has been extensively documented across a variety of disagreements and populations by Princeton professor Emily Pronin and her colleagues. So even when explicitly confronted with opposing perspectives and a list of biases that might lead to distorted reasoning, people point the finger at their counterpart and gamely continue to assert that they themselves are being objective.

Consider a belief you hold and one on which you disagree with somebody in your life. Take a minute to review your reasons for holding that belief. Then take a minute to review your counterpart's reasons. Odds are, no matter how hard you introspect, you are not going to find that you hold your belief because you are too insecure, too biased, or too underinformed to change your mind. However, when you consider your counterpart's view, that is exactly the attribution you are likely to make. It is difficult to unsee the evidence of your senses and life experience. After all, if you thought your belief was incorrect, you would have changed your mind by now!

Adding to the challenge is the fact that people are "cognitive misers." In other words, people consistently pick the path of least resistance when it comes to exerting mental effort. The late Nobel Prize winner Daniel Kahneman wrote extensively about our tendency to use "fast and frugal" mental strategies for most judgment and decision-making tasks. Assuming that we are fundamentally accurate in our perceptions and that therefore there must be something wrong with those who disagree is faster and takes less work than pausing to question our convictions and deeply interrogate all the evidence.

While naïve realism is almost ever present, people's need to act on it by asserting the superiority of their beliefs varies with the context. Remember that situations where disagreeing parties struggle to live and let live usually feature two factors: 1) the outcomes of the disagreement are important, and 2) the people who disagree are in some way interdependent so that their beliefs and decisions impact those of the other person.

Let's unpack these ideas. First, not surprisingly, trivial topics have a lesser chance of turning into conflict than consequential topics (although some people manage). For example, where we will go to dinner is less important than which house we will buy. While I am willing to occasionally indulge your terrible culinary taste and your resultant desire to eat slimy mollusks, I am not willing to indulge your desire to purchase a house in a flood zone (lovely river views notwithstanding).

Second, when people feel that another person's decisions and attitudes will impact their own lives, they are less likely to go along with what they consider wrongheadedness. If a person on another continent thinks women shouldn't be allowed to make management decisions, I would disagree, but I'd be far less motivated to try to change their mind than if this person were a country mate who could vote on policies that affect me and other women I care about. I would be even less tolerant if this person worked with me and tried to stop me from making decisions in my own workplace. And I would be absolutely furious if they were part of my family where their beliefs would both reflect on me and impact my own life decisions. Ironically, this logic implies that we extend the most tolerance to faraway people we don't know, while reserving our greatest indignation for neighbors, colleagues, and family members.

In sum, the disagreements most likely to lead to conflict involve two people who think they are right (i.e., most of us!) engaged in important decisions on which we feel interdependent. Situations where none of these factors are present (trivial arguments where each person is free to make their own decisions, and everyone realizes that there is no "right way") are the least likely to fuel drama. Situations where naïve realism converges with an important topic and an interdependent relationship often escalate into some of the hardest-fought battles that tear apart families, businesses, and countries.

In retrospect, when Ryan and I were dancing, we were experiencing the perfect storm of the factors that are most likely to lead disagreeing counterparts into trouble. Dancing was extremely important to us—we spent every waking minute and every spare dollar taking lessons, practicing, seeking out sponsors, and looking for ways to get better than the other couples around us. In performing all of these activities we were 100 percent interdependent. Every decision, from which competition to enter to whether a particular step was getting us off beat, had to be made jointly. And being human, we could only see ourselves, our dancing, and each other from our own vantage point. Although ballroom dancing is an unusual hobby, it turns out that a similar analysis can be applied to most parenting fights, professional disagreements, and policy battles. Decisions that literally deal with life and death (abortion, gun rights, environmental policy, vaccine mandates) that affect everyone in the population, and where both parties believe they have the winning argument because either science or a fundamental moral consideration is on their side, regularly leave people frustrated, angry, and baffled at the folly of their fellow humans.

WHAT CAN WE DO ABOUT ALL OF THIS?

Although naïve realism is impossible to eliminate (how would you get through life if you stopped believing your own judgment?), there are ways to minimize its negative impact.

The first step is trying to cultivate some minimal awareness of the bias. I am not advocating questioning all of your beliefs all the time—that would leave you paralyzed with indecision. Indeed, most decisions people make in their daily lives are actually just fine and enjoy broad support from fellow humans. However, questioning the evidence behind your own beliefs *when you encounter disagreement* is a much more manageable task. Think of it as a conditioned response: When somebody disagrees with you and you think they are being ridiculous, it may be time to stop and think. The awareness of disagreement and your own (often automatic) judgment about the other person's flaws of logic or character should be like a warning bell in your head to make you consider why their point might have some merit. Could there be information you are overlooking? Do they have different priorities or preferences? Notice that I am not suggesting that you strive to be "more objective": Most of us feel pretty objective already. Instead, I am suggesting that you consider why a smart, reasonable, kind person would hold the opinion your counterpart is advocating for.

The second clear piece of advice that arises from the naïve realism analysis is to stop trying to persuade people that you are right and they are wrong. This is a hard habit to break since the arguments we make in our own heads sound so incredibly compelling. People who disagree on topics that matter to them are usually ready to meet any argument you make with an argument of their own. And unlike in a televised courtroom drama, you are unlikely to get all the way to the end of the speech that sounded great in your mind before you get interrupted. It turns out that thanks to naïve realism, everyone feels that their argument is the one that will clinch the win for their team. Because of this dynamic, most people who attempt to change others' minds end up frustrated and disappointed.

Experiences like these, at home, at work, and in our civic spaces, make many people avoid disagreement altogether, convinced that discussing the opposing perspective will never lead to anything good and will often end in bitter conflict. But of course, we pay a cost for retreating to the sidelines and staying out of the fray. Even if you don't voice your disagreement with the nonsense advocated by your family members or your colleagues, the disagreement can still live rent-free in your mind. And no matter how much you might tell yourself that "it doesn't matter" and "he's just being ridiculous," your unvoiced opposition continues to cause you hours of frustration, annoyance, and disappointment. However, twenty years into my research career, I am convinced that there is a better way to disagree. In the next chapter, we will discuss people who are naturally better at engaging with opposing views and what makes them different. We will then shift to examining the behaviors that all of us can enact to help us function in a world full of naïve realists without compromising our values or losing our minds.

CHAPTER SUMMARY

- Most people believe that their views of the world around them are accurate and objective. They rarely stop to consider how their environment or their history distorts their perceptions or conclusions. This is called "naïve realism."

- Because of naïve realism, people often explain disagreement by assuming that there is something wrong with those who disagree with them. They thus conveniently attribute disagreement to the other side's lack of information or lack of intelligence. When "informing" the counterpart fails, they often come to believe that the disagreement is caused by bias or bad intentions on the side of their counterpart.

- This analysis suggests that trying to persuade people that they are wrong is a losing battle because they will simply conclude that "you don't get it." Instead, consider what information you might be missing and why a smart, reasonable, kind person might see the world differently.

2

DISCOVERING THE RECEPTIVE MINDSET

MY GRADUATE SCHOOL YEARS WERE STEEPED IN NAÏVE REALISM research. At the time, Stanford had been ranked as the top social psychology PhD program in the world for over fifty years running. My adviser, Lee Ross, was nearing retirement and was revered as one of the greatest psychologists alive. When I walked through the halls of the department and saw the names of the famous researchers whose work I had studied in college, I felt like I had somehow snuck my way backstage at the Oscars. Yes, I was a nerd, but that was just fine with me.

Naïve realism made intuitive sense to me and readily explained an entire litany of interpersonal errors and biases. Every argument I had had with a friend, a family member, or a colleague made more sense in light of this theory. Nevertheless, early into my PhD career, I started feeling frustrated by the attention that behavioral science devoted to the problems of the human mind, with almost no effort devoted to the development of solutions. Academic psychologists like to focus on "basic" science—understanding behavior and mental processes for the sheer scientific joy that understanding brings. However, even as a starting graduate student, I was convinced that the real point of understanding was to make things better. Naïve realism offered a compelling explanation for how relationships went bad. I wanted to find the antidote.

I remember the first time I met Frances Chen. She was one year behind me in the program, pursuing her interest in developmental psychology. Developmental psychologists study how behaviors, thoughts, and emotions change throughout a person's lifetime, with a lot of focus on early childhood when tiny humans acquire a mind-boggling array of skills at a rate unmatched by any other species. Even though she belonged to a different area of the psychology department, Frances came to Lee's lab meeting because all of us were supposed to interact with multiple faculty members to "broaden our horizons."

After listening while all the regular lab members loudly debated the merits of someone's new research idea, Frances made an observation that changed the rest of my career. "You know," she said, "I find it strange that American students approach all information offered to them critically. As if their task is to find flaws in any argument. Asian students start by trying to fully understand the argument, and then they decide whether to be critical or not. I wonder where that comes from. I wonder if it would be worth studying in elementary schoolers?"

Now here is the difference between Frances and me: She posed a broad inquiry about a new idea and whether it was worth pursuing. I immediately formed an opinion about it, asserted my opinion as if it were the obvious truth, and set us in motion: "Forget elementary schoolers! That's a hugely important idea! That's the opposite of naïve realism! We should study it in the context of conflict. What should we call it?"

The idea excited me because it offered a completely different model for how people might approach disagreement. Rather than starting from a place of certainty, could people approach opposing views with curiosity and openness? Is it even possible to reserve judgment until all the facts have been considered? Does anyone do that in real life? What would be the consequences of approaching the world with this mindset? Is this something that you are born with, or can it be taught? Is it even true that Asians do this more often than Americans? How could one measure this thing if it exists?

Frances and I got to work.

WHAT IS RECEPTIVENESS?

The psychological tendency that Frances casually hypothesized to be a common trait of Asian schoolchildren, and that I immediately latched onto as the solution to world conflict, eventually came to be called "receptiveness to opposing views." Over two decades and dozens of studies, we came to define receptiveness as a person's *willingness to access, consider, and evaluate supporting and opposing views in an impartial manner.*

We eventually created and validated a personality scale to measure a person's habitual level of receptiveness. You can take the survey here and learn about how receptively you engage with opposing views on issues that matter to you:

disagreeingbetter.com/survey

The way we came to define receptiveness was a source of much debate among Frances, myself, and every person who made the mistake of asking me what I was working on during those graduate school years. In the beginning, we thought of receptiveness as a person's willingness to listen to or read about ideas they disagree with. In other words, we thought that people who are more receptive would be more willing to watch TV shows representing the opposing ideology; or not change the topic when somebody started arguing for a parenting approach they did not endorse; or not leave the room when hearing about the merits of a nutritional supplement that they considered useless. This definition was appealing because it was "behavioral"—one could easily observe and measure what channel a person was watching, what publication they were reading, and how long they were willing to stay in a particular conversation before stomping off.

However, we quickly realized that we were missing something when we defined receptiveness strictly in terms of observable behavior. How many times have you been in a disagreement and noticed your counterpart mentally checking out of the conversation? You see their eyes glaze over. They get quiet. Although they nod occasionally and say, "Uh-huh," you get the distinct feeling that their mind is far, far away. I know I'm guilty of it. When I was a teenager, my stepfather used to have "family meetings" where he would lecture my stepsiblings and me about our messy rooms and our sloppily done chores. I quickly developed an uncanny ability to sit in the physical presence of the lecture while my mind roamed free. As I grew older, I realized I was not unique—most parents of teenagers have seen this technique executed masterfully. Just because a person is in the physical presence of ideas they disagree with does not mean they are really being receptive to them.

Eventually Frances and I realized that to be truly receptive to an argument, you had to not only allow it to enter your brain through your ears or your eyeballs but also be willing to "noodle on it." In other words, being receptive requires spending some time thinking about an idea and turning it over in your mind, something people do naturally and willingly with arguments that support their beliefs. This part of the definition ended up giving Frances and me a lot of trouble. It turns out that it is difficult to measure the extent to which a person is turning something over in their mind versus spacing out, making their grocery list, or remembering the words to their favorite song. However, in the end, the measure we settled on was attention. In order for a person to get credit for being receptive, we reasoned, we had to be able to show that they were actually paying attention to the information in front of them.

But still there was a problem. The problem was lawyers. Anyone who has consumed as many courtroom dramas as I have knows that TV lawyers always listen very carefully to the other side and deeply attend to the information they are receiving. But are they being receptive? No! They are listening to opposing witnesses attentively with the sole purpose of finding holes in those witnesses' testimony. Not for a second do these TV lawyers stop to consider the possibility that the other side might have a point and that maybe they should just quit arguing before they embarrass themselves any further.* Of course, TV lawyers aren't the only ones who do this: Listening attentively in order to construct the strongest counterargument is as common at the dinner table and in a corporate boardroom as it is in court, real or fictional.

Thinking about the idea that listening carefully is not sufficient evidence of receptiveness—because you might simply be working on your rebuttal—meant that there had to be a third component: fair, unbiased evaluation of arguments on both sides. In other words, to be considered receptive, a person had to not only listen to an opposing argument and pay attention to it, but they also had to evaluate it using the same "yardstick" as arguments supporting their own position. Basically, your brain had to offer equal treatment to information irrespective of where it was coming from or what conclusion it supported.

---

* Talking to real trial lawyers confirms that the TV version is accurate in at least this respect.

After years of arguing with each other, with our classmates, and with our faculty mentors, Frances and I finally settled on a definition of receptiveness. People who were more receptive were:

- more likely to put themselves in the physical presence of ideas they disagreed with;

- more willing to pay attention to the arguments for those ideas when they did hear them; and

- subjected those arguments to the same level of critical scrutiny as arguments for their own side.

The obvious next question was whether it was possible to make people better at this kind of thinking.

RECEPTIVENESS IS NOT PERSUASION

Unfortunately, as Frances and I began designing experiments testing various ways to increase receptiveness, we met with an unexpected source of resistance—a large number of our colleagues who thought that the question we set out for ourselves had already been answered and was therefore uninteresting. The logic of this argument went as follows: Decades of psychological research had been devoted to understanding how people can better change each other's minds. In fact, it was largely due to the flourishing of this research area that psychologists began getting jobs in marketing departments at business schools and exerting significant influence on how both businesses and governments shaped the behavior of consumers and voters. While Frances and I were struggling to define receptiveness, psychologists studying attitude-change and persuasion were coming up with a litany of interventions to sell consumer products, accelerate the adoption of green technologies, and increase people's propensity to save for retirement. This research was having a heyday and already comprised thousands of papers and dozens of books. Every time we brought up receptiveness, somebody would gently suggest that persuasion researchers had already figured it all out and we should probably just go over to the business school and ask the marketing faculty to give us some tips.

Lee, however, immediately appreciated the importance of our idea and the distinction between trying to make people more receptive and actually persuading them to change their mind or modify their behavior. Having worked with Israelis and Palestinians as well as Irish Catholics and Protestants, he understood that the world was full of conflicts where persuasion was simply not on the menu. When people's deep-seated beliefs, identities, and rights to exist were on the line, they were never going to change their mind. Ever. No clever psychological trick, no work of soaring rhetoric, no piece of compelling research would make them abandon the beliefs they would sooner die for. Yet it was those situations that most desperately required a new approach, one that could help people actually coexist peacefully.

Maybe receptiveness could help. Instead of trying to come up with more ways to change each other's minds—an exercise that inevitably resulted in a winner and a loser—receptiveness had the potential to shift the goals of any given interaction. When people went into a conversation intending to listen to, think about, and fairly evaluate arguments on both sides, success no longer required beating one's counterpart into the ground with better arguments. In a conversation where receptiveness was the primary goal, both counterparts could walk away feeling that they gained new information and that the other side had understood them in turn. Persuasion, which was mostly impossible in the first place, would become irrelevant.

Thus persuasion, or lack thereof, became the fourth and final component of the receptiveness definition—a component that was most notable due to its absence. The initial resistance from our colleagues made Frances and me realize that becoming more receptive was very specifically *not* about changing one's own mind or changing anyone else's. Instead, the goal of receptiveness is to approach the world from a perspective of scientific curiosity, being willing to consider and evaluate all arguments with no attachment to a conclusion.

Is it possible that at the end of such an examination a person might change their mind? Maybe. It certainly stands to reason that people who make a habit out of considering a variety of perspectives on every issue are likely to occasionally come across new arguments that make sense to them. But although this might be true on average, there is no reason that in any single interaction listening to somebody's views and considering them deeply and objectively has to shift a person's beliefs. Approaching a conversation with a receptive mindset should not obligate a person to change their mind; it should simply leave them better informed so they can decide whether they ought to or not.

WHAT IS DIFFERENT ABOUT HIGHLY RECEPTIVE PEOPLE

The survey you took at the beginning of the chapter was the culmination of our work to understand what exactly receptiveness is and how to measure it. Having administered the survey to thousands of people under a variety of different conditions, we now know some things that set more receptive people apart from their less receptive peers.

First, extensive research shows that people in general are less willing to access information that opposes their perspectives than information that supports those perspectives. This is called "selective exposure" or the "congeniality bias." In other words, we selectively expose ourselves to information that is congenial to our prior beliefs. This is one reason that American liberals are more likely to watch MSNBC than Fox News, and American conservatives are more likely to do the opposite. People who are concerned about pesticides on their produce are more likely to click on the latest social media posts about how the "dirty dozen" will kill us all. And people who already think that women regularly experience workplace discrimination are more likely to read the latest research supporting this conclusion. Pesticide-related health risks and gender-based discrimination are both undoubtedly bad things, but the human brain seems to get a strange satisfaction from encountering evidence that supports existing beliefs, even if objectively we'd be better off being wrong. However, if you recognize that diverse information helps people make better decisions by offering them a more accurate view of the world, you might also recognize that selective exposure is harmful. By seeking out more and more information that supports our prior beliefs, we are wasting time and energy learning what we already know.

Nevertheless, selective exposure, especially on hotly contested topics like politics, is an incredibly powerful bias. In one of our studies we told liberals and conservatives that they would have to read the websites of famous politicians but that they could choose which websites to read. Indeed, we found that people on average chose 70 percent of webpages belonging to politicians from their own party. However, people who scored highly on the receptiveness scale showed a lower amount of selective exposure, choosing significantly more information from the other side. And this pattern is not unique to politics. In another study we asked baseball fans to list their favorite Major League Baseball team and the team they considered to be their favorite team's greatest rival. We then asked them how willing they would be to have a conversation with a fan of the rival team. Again, people showed an overwhelming bias against talking to a fan of a rival team, but those who were more receptive were more willing to do so. These studies provided evidence that people who are more receptive do indeed expose themselves to more varied information across topics that matter to them.

Second, and in line with our theorizing, people who are more receptive do seem to pay better attention to arguments they disagree with. In a study evaluating this tendency, we recruited people who strongly supported or opposed the Affordable Care Act (i.e., "Obamacare") and asked them to watch two senators make speeches about the law, with one senator praising it and the other calling for its repeal. The participants had to watch the entire long and boring speech to get paid, so they were stuck, just like the teenage me was stuck in our family meetings. But one thing was different: Four times during each speech the video paused so that we could ask participants whether they were truly paying attention. Interestingly, people had no trouble admitting that they were spacing out roughly a third of the time—research participants are generally quick to tell you when they are bored. Importantly, they also reported that they spaced out *more* listening to the senator whose argument they disagreed with.

But not the receptive people. They also spaced out, but they spaced out more evenly when watching the senator they agreed with and the one they disagreed with. In other words, receptive participants didn't somehow have greater control of their attention and they weren't generally better at listening to congressional debate. They were better at giving equal treatment to both sides and letting both sets of ideas permeate their consciousness to a more equal extent.

The final question we were interested in was whether people who were more receptive were better at being fair-minded when they saw arguments they agreed with versus arguments they disagreed with. Most of us think that arguments for the positions we hold are more true, more reasonable, and more relevant to the question at hand than the arguments for the opposition. That's not completely unreasonable: If I thought that the other side's arguments were better, I should have changed my mind. But when two people on opposite sides of an argument both think that their side is more reasonable, more honest, and fairer than the other, one of them has to be wrong!

It turns out that just like everyone else, people who are more receptive evaluate the arguments for their own side more positively. However, in their case, the gap is not as dramatic. They see some merit in opposing positions, and they see some flaws in their own. They don't lionize their own perspective and villainize the other. Instead, they are more willing to acknowledge the nuance and trade-offs that are inherently present in any complex debate.

Future studies yielded additional insights about receptiveness. To see if receptiveness affects the way that people actually behave when left to their own devices, we conducted a study where we recorded the "social networks" of students from master's degree programs at several different universities. A person's social network is simply the people they interact with regularly—friends, colleagues, and family members. Social networks are important, especially in graduate school, because people get information, social support, and access to opportunities from the members of their network. The more people you are friendly with in school, the more likely you are to hear about new internships, popular seminars, ski trips, or free furniture. However, it is also the case that most people are overwhelmingly likely to be friends with those who share similar characteristics—women are more likely to be friends with other women, people of color are more likely to be friends with other people of color, math majors are more likely to be friends with other math majors, etc. Some of this has to do with the opportunities you have to make friends—math majors share a lot more classes with each other than they do with anthropology majors—but some of it has to do with preference. Being around people who are like us is comforting in a way that constantly navigating difference is not.

However, our research shows that people who are more receptive are different in this regard. Across the universities we studied (with both liberal-leaning and conservative-leaning student bodies), master's degree students who were more receptive had more ideologically diverse friendship networks. In other words, in their lives outside of a controlled experiment, they were better at forming close relationships with people they strongly disagreed with than their less receptive peers. As a result, they were able to benefit from more regular in-depth conversations across a variety of controversial topics and sat at the intersection of multiple diverse peer groups, being able to glean ideas and insights from all sides.

UNDERSTANDING YOUR OWN RECEPTIVENESS SCORE

When you took the receptiveness survey at the beginning of this chapter, you received a score sheet with five numbers: your overall receptiveness score and your scores on the four individual components of receptiveness, which psychologists call "factors." Factors are made up of questions that are statistically correlated with each other—people who answer high on one question in a factor also tend to answer high on the other questions in the same factor. All four factors of receptiveness are also correlated—after all, they are all part of the same trait—but the correlations between factors are not as high as the correlations between the questions within any one factor.

All the scores (the overall score and the factor scores) run from 1 to 7, with 1 being the least receptive and 7 being the most receptive. But what does any given number mean?

In your report, you will see your score graphed on a diagram like the one below. The height of the bars on the diagram represents the percentage of people in our database that received a particular score. Your own score is highlighted in a darker shade. The shaded area to the left of your highlighted score represents the share of people who received scores that are lower than yours and the shaded area to the right represents the share of people who received scores that are higher. You can also see your score relative to men, women, Democrats, Republicans, or people at different ages or levels of education.

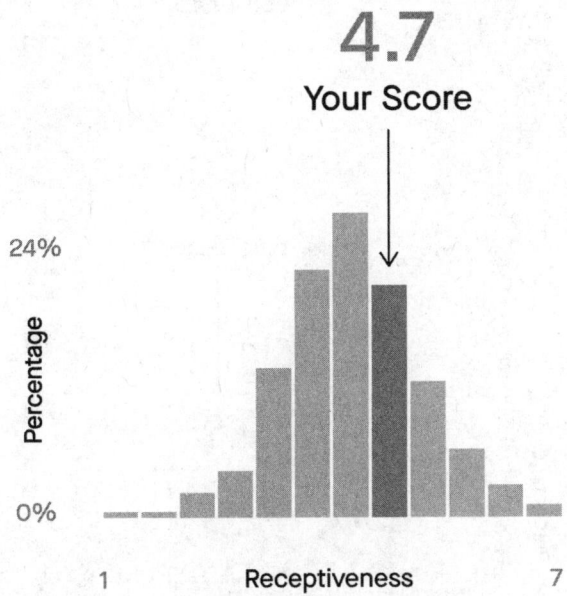

Additionally, you can see your scores for the four separate receptiveness factors presented in the same way. On the next page, you can see my scores from a recent time I took the survey on two of the factors: Emotional Equanimity and Tolerance of Taboo Issues.

As you read this section, keep your own scores handy and

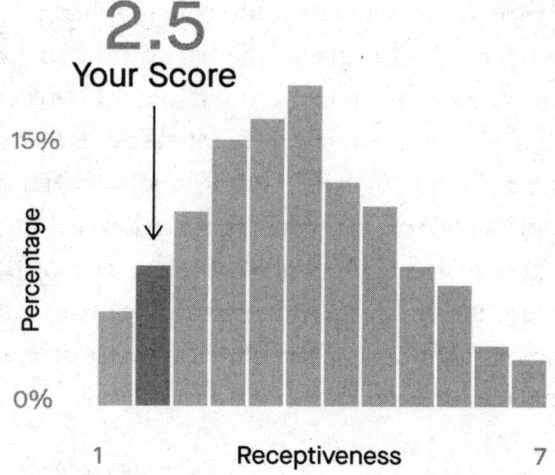

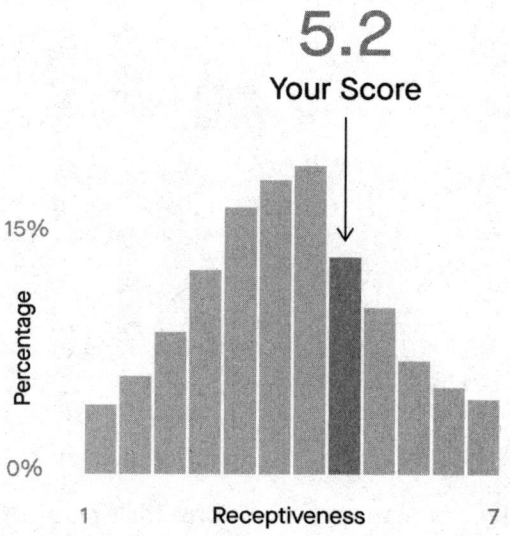

consider why your scores on some factors are higher than your scores on the others. Comparing which facets of receptiveness are easier versus more difficult for you is a good way to start thinking about how you might go about strengthening this tendency in yourself.

Factor 1: Emotional Equanimity

Most people experience a flood of negative emotions when confronted with arguments for opposing views. However, people who are high on the Emotional Equanimity factor have an easier time staying calm, cool, and collected even in conversations that make other people's blood boil. The four items listed below make up the Emotional Equanimity factor. For the purposes of calculating your score, they are "reverse coded"—meaning that checking a higher answer on these questions leads to a lower score, and vice versa.

1. Listening to people with views that strongly oppose mine tends to **make me angry**.

2. I feel **disgusted** by some of the things that people with views that oppose mine say.

3. I often feel **frustrated** when I listen to people with social and political views that oppose mine.

4. I often get **annoyed** during discussions with people whose views are very different from mine.

I find a couple of aspects of the Emotional Equanimity factor particularly interesting. First of all, the very presence of this factor highlights the important role of emotions in our ability to engage with opposing views. Although that might seem obvious to many readers, prior efforts at identifying who is good at considering both sides of an issue, and why, focused largely on cognitive considerations. Personality scales like Need for Cognition, Actively Open-Minded Thinking, and Intellectual Humility focus on people's capacity for logical reasoning and their willingness to juggle arguments for multiple opposing perspectives in their head. For some reason, prior research never considered that people avoid listening to those they disagree with not only because they are not smart enough or unwilling to put in the mental effort but also because it simply ticks them off.

For example, you may have noticed that my Emotional Equanimity score is pretty low. I am a smart person, and I like to think on things—that's why I became an academic. But certain ideas just make me angry. And when I hear those ideas from people I respect, I feel my frustration in a physical way. My heart beats faster, my breathing accelerates, and I even get tension headaches. Knowing how my body responds, I think twice before I expose myself to conversations on certain topics with people I expect to strongly disagree with me. Life is hard enough without asking for more negative emotions, thank you very much!

The second aspect of Emotional Equanimity that I find interesting is *which* emotions seem to come into play when we engage with opposing views. Part of the art of developing a personality scale is coming up with questions that predict the behavior you are interested in. However, you also have to be willing to discard questions that don't end up predicting much of anything. As a scientist, it's bad practice to be too enamored with your theories. When Frances and I were first coming up with the Emotional Equanimity questions, we were influenced by the common belief that people avoid opposing views because they find them to be too threatening. However, questions about threat, anxiety, and discomfort did not correlate highly with the other questions in the scale and ultimately did not predict people's behavior. Instead, in line with the work on naïve realism, the emotions that appeared to matter the most were the ones that would emerge if people were deeply convinced of the validity of their beliefs—that is, anger, disgust, annoyance, and frustration.

Factor 2: Intellectual Curiosity

The second key component of receptiveness is the extent to which people feel curious about the origins of others' beliefs. We designed the following five items to measure the Intellectual Curiosity factor. This subscale is pretty straightforward and lines up with what most people think of as receptiveness. To the extent that people are curious about why others believe what they believe, they are more willing to seek out the information that would help them answer their questions.

1. I am **willing** to have conversations with individuals who hold strong views opposite to my own.

2. I **like** reading **well-thought-out information and arguments** supporting viewpoints opposite to mine.

3. I find **listening** to opposing views **informative**.

4. I **value interactions** with people who hold strong views opposite to mine.

5. I am generally **curious** to find out why other people have different opinions than I do.

One way to think of the curiosity factor is as the "engine" that drives receptiveness. Most people have a natural curiosity about how others view the world. Yet, it is the other three factors that generally stand in the way. The question is, are you curious enough so that the engine can drive you toward having interesting conversations and learning new ideas, even in the face of the psychological resistance produced by the other factors?

The Intellectual Curiosity factor is also conceptually and statistically related to the popular construct of Intellectual Humility. The main difference, however, is that many measures of Intellectual Humility ask questions that hint at a person's lack of confidence in their views or their willingness to change their mind. Since we were trying to be clear about the distinction between receptiveness and persuadability, we made sure that our questions were focused exclusively on curiosity, without any references to one's own certainty or lack thereof.

Factor 3: Respect Toward Opponents

The third factor in the receptiveness scale measures the attitudes people have regarding those they disagree with. Respect Toward Opponents is measured using the following five items:

1. People who have opinions that are opposite to mine often have views that are too **extreme to be taken seriously**.

2. People who have views that oppose mine **rarely present compelling arguments**.

3. Information from people who have strong opinions that oppose mine is often **designed to mislead less-informed listeners**.

4. People who have views that oppose mine are often **biased** by what would be best for them and their group.

5. People who have views that oppose mine often base their arguments on **emotion rather than logic**.

As in the case of the Emotional Equanimity items, the Respect Toward Opponents items are reverse coded such that responding with a higher value results in an overall lower receptiveness score.

Notice that the items in this factor closely track the negative attributions that people make with respect to disagreeing with others as discussed in Chapter 1 on naïve realism. If this factor is the one that results in your lowest score, it is likely that a key barrier that prevents you from engaging with opposing perspectives is that you do not hold the people who disagree with you in particularly high regard.

Factor 4: Tolerance of Taboo Issues

The final factor in the receptiveness scale is Tolerance of Taboo Issues. This factor is made up of the four items below:

1. Some points of view are **too offensive** to be equally represented in the media.

2. Some issues are just **not up for debate**.

3. Some ideas are simply **too dangerous** to be part of public discourse.

4. I consider my views on some issues to be **sacred**.

Of course, every person in the world has some topics that they feel uncomfortable discussing, especially with somebody who sees the world differently. However, for most people most topics are okay. For example, I might be 100 percent sure that I am never going to change my mind about the need for gun regulation, but I am perfectly happy to discuss the various trade-offs between safety and freedom that legislators might, in theory, consider. Other topics—the rights and roles of immigrants, for example—are much more difficult for me to discuss. As an immigrant, this topic cuts close to home and feels somehow "inappropriate" to intellectually dissect, especially with a person who I assume not to have had the same experiences that I had.

How many topics fall into this "taboo" category—not to be discussed or debated out of a concern that the very act of engaging in such a discussion might somehow cause harm—varies from person to person. Some people find themselves less receptive overall because, for them, a large number of topics are simply beyond the pale of discussion.

NOW THAT WE have gone over the factors of the receptiveness scale, you should take a minute to consider your overall profile. Which subscale produced your highest score? Which produced your lowest? Thinking about which aspects of receptiveness come the most naturally to you and which ones pose a challenge should make you ask yourself, "Why?" The goal is not to diagnose yourself but rather to use the scale to generate some insights about why you react to disagreement the way that you do. For example, if Tolerance for Taboo Issues is your lowest factor, what are you concerned would happen if you do discuss an issue you consider off the table with somebody you disagree with? If Respect for Opponents is your lowest score, who in your life were you thinking about when you answered those questions? Once you have an idea of what is driving your factor scores, you'll know what areas you might want to work on if your goal were to increase your overall receptiveness.

INCREASING YOUR RECEPTIVENESS

Although it is useful knowing how receptive you are and which factors are the most challenging for you, to really get going on increasing your receptiveness it is helpful to think about what influences receptiveness in the first place. This is a fundamental question that underpins a lot of psychological research: What exactly drives human behavior? Is it nature? Is it nurture? Is it training? Habit? Parenting? Karma? Fortunately, about seventy years ago, psychologists came up with an elegant framework to think about this question that is still highly relevant today and can help us understand the sources of receptiveness. The idea is deceptively simple:

Some drivers of behavior reside inside a person and are mostly fixed. Your personality, your biology, your gender, your height, your ethnicity are all things that are largely immutable features of who you are. Psychologists will often call these "dispositional factors." However, other drivers of behavior reside in the ever-changing world that surrounds us, what psychologists call "situational factors." Whether the people you are with celebrate or judge a particular behavior, whether you will get paid or punished for performing it, and whether the context makes it hard or easy to execute are all factors that will determine whether you do or do not do a particular thing. These features have little to do with you as an individual and everything to do with the situation you are in.

Any time a person performs a behavior, they do so under the influence of their natural, dispositional inclinations *and* under the influence of situational factors. Some behaviors are more dispositional, some are more situational, but all are at least a little bit responsive to both. This framework is so powerful because it implies that we have a choice about every behavior we want to see more of. We can either look for people who are naturally good at this behavior and try to avoid everyone else, or we can shape the situation to bring out more of the desired behavior in anyone, irrespective of their natural tendencies. And if you are running a family, a company, or a school, or just trying to work on yourself, you might be happy to learn that decades of psychology have shown that situations are far easier to change than personalities.

Imagine you have a nine-year-old who you wish could learn long division. One's ability to learn math is pretty dispositional—some kids just get the hang of it faster than others. But beyond that, kids also vary in their life situations. Some kids go to good schools and have older siblings, engaged parents, and an army of tutors. Other kids have none of those resources. If you take a kid who is naturally good at math and a kid who is naturally bad at math and give them both weekly tutoring, they will both get better. It is possible that the kid who was a math whiz to start will continue to outperform the future theater major, but in the end, they will both have benefited from the extra help. A few months later, their math skills will reflect their natural talents *and* the situation you put them in.

Just like math, receptiveness comes easier to some people than it does to others. We know that receptiveness is statistically related to some well-studied personality traits that have a genetic component, including extraversion, agreeableness, and emotional reactivity. Because receptiveness has an emotional regulation component, something that psychologists have long known to be partly determined by your biology, some people will, on average, have an easier time engaging with opposing perspectives. But just like with any other behavior, while we are stuck with the dispositional part, the situational aspect is under our control.

The main problem with putting yourself into situations that help you cultivate receptiveness is that engaging with opposing views on important issues is fundamentally unpleasant. Listening to people who disagree with you is likely going to annoy you, anger you, and leave you occasionally disappointed with humanity as a whole. Remember the study where we found that talking to somebody you strongly disagree with is worse than going to the dentist? Just like beginning a new exercise program, becoming more receptive involves forcing yourself to do things that don't feel good in the moment, hoping that they will make your life better in the long run. So how do you shape the situation to make practicing receptiveness easier? Take a look at your four factor scores. Inevitably, they will not all be the same. By considering your highest and lowest scores, you can gain insight into which sorts of situations make it easier or harder for you to be receptive and why.

For example, if your lowest score is on the Emotional Equanimity factor, it is worth considering the conditions that give you more or less control over your emotions. Emotional self-control is more difficult when you are tired, are hungry, are stressed, or have consumed alcohol. Considered from this perspective, it is not surprising that the epic family conflicts—the ones we remember for decades and rip relationships apart—seem to always happen over a holiday meal or at a wedding. Who isn't ready to scream by the time they have cooked, cleaned, and hosted for hours, and both Mom and Uncle Joe are a couple of cocktails in? If maintaining emotional equanimity in the face of disagreement is a struggle, you should be especially thoughtful about your physical and emotional resources when you consider engaging with an opposing point of view.

If your biggest barrier to receptiveness is insufficient curiosity, consider some of the benefits of being more knowledgeable about the opposing view and ask yourself about why you are not that curious. Most of the time, you lack curiosity either because 1) you have consumed some poor-quality information that has convinced you that the other side has nothing worthwhile to say, and/or 2) you are conflating being receptive with being persuadable. People who believe they know everything there is to know about a topic (especially if they believe the topic is a matter of objective scientific fact) often have little interest in hearing arguments from people who disagree. But remember, there are many good reasons to thoughtfully examine a point of view, even if you have absolutely no intention of changing your mind. No matter how right you think you are, learning about the arguments and experiences underpinning others' views might lead you to new insights and help you find a way to coexist more comfortably with people who disagree. At the very least, it will make you a more interesting and pleasant conversationalist. To increase your curiosity about others' perspectives, first look for high-quality information sources (and don't use the excuse that everyone on the other side is a fool and thus high-quality information sources don't exist). Second, remember that the point of learning is just to learn—not to have your mind changed.

If your lowest score is on the Respect for Opponents factor, try to make a habit of considering why a thoughtful, reasonable, kind person might hold the view you disagree with. Ironically, that might mean examining points of disagreement with people who you are the closest with—assuming that the people you are close with are ones you consider to be thoughtful, reasonable, and kind. For example, my best friend from high school has always disagreed with me politically. But she is a smart woman who tries hard to be clear and respectful in articulating her views, especially when she knows we are treading on thin ice. I also know that she is a kind person who shares many of my moral values. When she holds a particular view, it makes me have more tolerance toward that view in general. My brain takes an attributional shortcut: "If Amy agrees with this view, there might be something to it."

More broadly, in trying to come up with benevolent explanations for opposing views, challenge yourself to generate ones that you could say to your counterpart's face and that they would agree with. In other words, you can't just say "because they are an idiot" and be done with it. Saying that "she is just too insecure" also doesn't cut it. If your explanation paints your counterpart as somehow intellectually or morally deficient, you need to try a little harder. Over time, learning to think of generous, benevolent explanations for the beliefs of others might restore your faith in your fellow humans. Isn't it nicer to go through the world thinking that other people have had experiences you haven't had and know things you don't know, rather than thinking that everyone around you is nuts?

Lastly, if considering information on a specific topic makes you feel like your head will explode, think hard about why a subject is "taboo" for you. Often, people have an intuition that engaging with particular perspectives is simply not acceptable because it will amplify false or dangerous views or cause harm to vulnerable bystanders. However, a thoughtful evaluation of this reasoning again suggests an approach to having difficult conversations that hinges on changing the context you are in. Any conversation around an important source of disagreement can (and probably should) be held in private, out of hearing range of anyone who could be adversely affected or who can use what they hear to amplify the conflict. If you are working on increasing your receptiveness, you should probably not start your practice with live dialogue on a taboo topic. Instead start with a bit of reading or a podcast—something you can consume in private, in small amounts, and when you feel ready. Broadening the scope of ideas you can consider and turn over in your mind does not need to be done in one bold leap—you can and should start with baby steps.

CHAPTER SUMMARY

- "Receptiveness to opposing views" is a person's willingness to access, consider, and evaluate supporting and opposing information in a relatively impartial manner. Your receptiveness score predicts how you engage with and process information across disagreement and can be measured here: disagreeingbetter.com/survey

- Receptiveness is made up of four components or "factors":
    1. Emotional Equanimity
    2. Intellectual Curiosity
    3. Respect Toward Opponents
    4. Tolerance of Taboo Issues

- Being a more receptive person makes life easier. You are more informed about arguments on both sides. You feel less negative emotions when you interact with people who disagree. You have more diverse and interesting relationships because people who see the world differently are willing to engage with you as well.

- Importantly, receptiveness is not about compromising or changing your mind. However, a key benefit of receptiveness is being able to understand and fairly evaluate opposing views, so that you can make a well-informed decision about whether to change your mind or not.

- To begin increasing your receptiveness, consider which factors are the easiest versus the most difficult for you. Think about the features of your interactions and information consumption habits that can be tweaked to make increasing your receptiveness a bit easier. Like any other skill, your receptiveness can be increased by making small, consistent changes to how you engage with information.

3

IT'S NOT THE THOUGHT THAT COUNTS

WHEN I WAS TWENTY-SIX, DURING MY SECOND YEAR OF GRADUate school, my mom was diagnosed with Stage 4 lung cancer. She was fit as a fiddle, a nonsmoking forty-six-year-old tennis player, a scrappy immigrant who managed to get a PhD in Russia despite the anti-Semitism that was rampant there at the time. She then learned English, brought me to the United States after marrying my American stepfather, and became the primary breadwinner of our family. We were all convinced that a little thing like cancer wouldn't stop her.

But the drugs for lung cancer aren't great. When advances are celebrated, it is because a new therapy extends life by a few weeks or a few months. Her cancer turned out to be not only in her lungs but also in her spine, and, worst of all, in her brain. After surgery, radiation, and months of chemo, we were starting to get desperate. That's when I learned about a new drug called Avastin—a drug that was approved by the FDA for kidney cancer but was working miracles for lung cancer patients whose doctors prescribed it "off label." Avastin worked by choking off the blood supply to tumors. Tumors need a lot of blood to grow, and

Avastin targeted blood vessels in the body that seemed to be growing faster than they had any right to. No blood supply—no tumor.

My mom was being treated at Stanford Hospital by Dr. Charlotte Jacobs, a small woman nearing retirement, who was a world-class expert in lung cancer. I remember hearing the heels of the brown pumps that Dr. Jacobs often wore tapping down the hall as she would approach the exam room for our biweekly checkups. You knew it was her because the heel taps sounded like she was nearing a run. I remember thinking, "If I were her age, and had her job, would I still have the energy to run toward each exam room? Toward every cancer patient and their family?"

At a visit I remember well, full of new hope after discovering Avastin, I pitched the idea to Dr. Jacobs. She said no. Because the cancer had gone to the brain, a drug that destroyed the cancer's blood supply might cause a brain bleed that would kill my mother faster than the cancer, or else leave her severely disabled. I argued that the cancer in the brain was gone, killed off by weeks of radiation therapy. The CT scans of the brain had not shown any new masses in months. Dr. Jacobs argued that there could still be bits of cancer in the brain too small for the CT scan to catch, and that is why the drug was not indicated for patients with any history of brain tumors. I pushed back that it was not indicated for lung cancer patients at all, but the internet was full of stories of doctors who prescribed it with great success. I quickly went from arguing to begging. Dr. Jacobs refused more firmly and pointed out that not only was there risk to my mother, but she might lose her medical license and go to jail for malpractice if she did something so obviously foolish. My family and I went home disappointed.

Several weeks later, Dr. Jacobs surprised me by raising the topic of Avastin again. Apparently, oncologists go to monthly meetings cheerfully called "tumor boards," where specialists from different medical centers in the region discuss particularly thorny cases. The Northern California tumor board included lung specialists from Stanford, Berkeley, UCSF, UC Davis, and others. Dr. Jacobs presented my mother's case and my Avastin idea to her colleagues. After some discussion, they agreed that it was in fact a terrible idea. She was very sorry she didn't have better news.

Only a few weeks later my mom's brain swelled up from a large number of new tumors that had been too small to detect on earlier CT scans but finally decided to go wild. It turned out that Dr. Jacobs was right about Avastin—it would have probably killed my mother slightly faster than the cancer ultimately did.

Yet, having lost my mom nineteen years ago, I still remember the day when Dr. Jacobs told me that she took my idea, an idea that she thought was so terrible it could land her in jail, and presented it to colleagues from several universities. Just in case it had a shred of merit. Just to give it a chance. Maybe just to make me feel that she tried. She did not change her mind, and the cancer still took my mother, but I have rarely felt a more profound sense of another person's receptiveness than I did in that conversation.

I did not know it at the time, but this experience eventually helped me realize that receptiveness is not about thoughts and feelings (I have no idea what Dr. Jacobs was thinking or feeling at the time) but about how you behave toward others. Behaving receptively means offering people unambiguous evidence that you truly heard what they had to say and understood why it matters to them. It took another dozen years of research to figure out exactly how people can learn to do what Dr. Jacobs did naturally. Understanding the fundamentals of this skill set is what can turn some of our bitterest arguments into respectful, caring, and ultimately productive exchanges of ideas.

FROM THOUGHTS TO BEHAVIOR

Anyone who has put a child through college and marveled at the massive tuition, housing, and meal bills might be excused for thinking that American universities are awash in money. But the reality is that tuition can't even keep the lights on, let alone pay for the research equipment, athletic facilities, art spaces, and massive amounts of scholarships and fellowships that top schools provide. Universities, Harvard included, have to keep coming up with new, creative ways to try to make ends meet. A classic and highly successful approach to this problem is "Executive Education"—programs that can bring in revenue in exchange for giving advanced professionals the opportunity to study at a fancy university for a couple of weeks and leave with a certificate attesting to a new skill set.

For a faculty member, Exec Ed courses are fun to teach. You get to interact with incredibly accomplished people from all over the world—doctors, judges, human rights activists, generals and admirals, CEOs, and even some minor royalty.* The students are there to learn academic content, but also to network, eat out at area restaurants, and buy Harvard swag for their kids. Importantly, teaching in these courses is also a great research opportunity. If you can persuade Executive Education students to participate in your studies, you get access to a hugely diverse group of people coming from different backgrounds, holding strong opinions, and possessing a variety of interesting life experiences.

The study that made the research program on receptiveness take an unexpected turn was conducted during a program for officials in American state and local government—a room full of

---

* It's better not to know these things in advance. There is nothing more anxiety provoking than knowing that there is a Bush or a Kennedy or a Nobel Peace Prize winner in your classroom.

fire chiefs, police chiefs, city council members, mayors of small towns, and state legislators.

The experiment itself was simple. Students in the Executive Education program came to a computer lab on the first day of class and sat individually in private cubicles. Prior to the exercise, they had all completed the receptiveness scale and reported their opinions on a series of controversial topics—marijuana legalization, police brutality, the death penalty—topics that most people would be very hesitant to discuss with new colleagues, especially colleagues with whom they might disagree.

After answering these opinion questions, each person was assigned a topic and a conversation partner. We selected partners so that each pair disagreed on their assigned topic, but otherwise the assignment of partners was random. And because the topics were so sensitive and it's generally not a good idea to tick off students that are paying for a very expensive educational experience, we also arranged for the conversations to be conducted via an anonymous online chat that took about twenty minutes to complete.

Having earlier asked all participants how receptive they typically were and how receptive they felt they had been in this particular conversation, at the end of the chat, we also asked each person about their perceptions of their partner. Did they think that person was receptive? Did they want to work with them later in the program? Executive Education courses are full of team exercises and projects, and students always appreciate getting to know more people and expanding their professional networks. Asking participants if they were interested in working with their conversation counterpart was a good way to find out if that person had made a positive impression.

The original point of the experiment was so straightforward that I worried that the results would be too obvious to be publishable—I simply wanted to demonstrate that the people who reported being more receptive prior to the conversation would be seen as more receptive by their counterparts afterward. To me, this hypothesis seemed self-evidently true: Thousands of participants who had taken the receptiveness scale had demonstrated that they were more willing to read information from the other side, that they had thought about it more deeply and evaluated it more fairly. We also knew that they got less upset engaging with opposing views and had fewer negative perceptions of those they disagree with. Surely these psychological tendencies would come through during actual interaction. Although the main hypothesis seemed pretty boring to me, the study still seemed worth conducting because the data would allow us to investigate a series of other questions. What *exactly* do receptive people do differently in conflict? How do they navigate difficult conversations and win the trust of their counterparts? What wisdom can they impart to the rest of us?

The data turned out to be equal parts disappointing and frustrating. People who reported being more receptive in their daily life did not come across as any more or less receptive to their disagreeing counterparts. They were not seen as more attractive collaborators or more thoughtful advisers. We turned the data this way and that, and no matter which analytical approach we tried (and we tried many!), we could detect no reliable relationship between self-reported receptiveness and counterpart evaluations.

Yet, people did rate some partners as definitely more receptive than others. The evaluations of receptiveness among our 238 pairs of government officials spanned the entire length of the 1 to 7 receptiveness scale. And importantly, the people who were rated as having been highly receptive during the conversation were also rated as much more desirable collaborators for future tasks and exercises during the program. Our participants clearly valued receptiveness (or whatever they thought receptiveness looked like). They wanted to build future working relationships with disagreeing colleagues whom they believed to be more open to and interested in their perspectives. What we couldn't figure out for the life of us, however, was what made people *think* that their counterpart was or was not receptive and why this did not match up with people's self-reported perceptions of their tendencies.

There was another oddity in our data. Remember that in every pair, both people rated each other's receptiveness at the conclusion of the conversation. Strangely, those ratings were correlated. In other words, people who rated their partners as being more receptive were also rated as being more receptive by their partners. In planning the study, we formed the pairs largely randomly, only caring that the two people in any given pair disagree on their assigned topic. Since the participants had no idea who their partner was, there was no way that they could have colluded on the scores they gave each other. So why was there a correlation in perceptions of receptiveness at the end of the conversation?

In summary, here is what we had:

1. People who said they were receptive in life were not seen as very receptive by their disagreeing conversation partners.

2. People who were seen as more receptive by their conversation partners were also more trusted, were seen as having better judgment, and were considered to be more desirable future collaborators.

3. Over the course of the conversation, partners came to hold correlated perceptions of each other's communication style.

The first observation, that people's self-reported receptiveness was not correlated with partner perceptions of receptiveness, initially scared me. My paranoid brain imagined that something was wrong with the receptiveness scale that I had spent years developing. However, I took a deep breath and remembered that across many experiments, the scale had predicted the way people process information: what they choose to read, how much attention they paid, and how they evaluated the information they took in. The scale wasn't broken—it consistently predicted information processing and even who people chose to be friends with. The issue was that these internal mental efforts and preferences were not apparent to conversation counterparts, probably for the simple reason that they took place inside participants' heads. It seems that our participants didn't know how to *express* their receptiveness.

The second point was more comforting, but still confusing when considered in combination with the first. Our participants liked and valued more receptive counterparts, or at least counterparts who they, by whatever criterion, had judged to be more receptive. The problem was that since what people saw as signaling receptiveness in their counterparts seemed to have no correlation with what that person had said about themselves, we had no idea what people seemed to be enjoying so much.

To rule out one totally obvious explanation, we checked participants' attitudes on the issue they had discussed. Maybe people simply liked counterparts who changed their mind, and this is what came across as being receptive. But no, the data showed that almost nobody changed their mind about anything. Our participants were seasoned government employees. As such, they stuck to their convictions on hot-button policy issues and were not at all swayed by a twenty-minute-long conversation with a relative stranger. Although we were relieved that perceptions of receptiveness were not explained by a person's willingness to change their mind, the mystery of what exactly was seen as being more receptive persisted.

The third observation was the most intriguing. Whatever the quality was that people seemed to call receptiveness was also "contagious." However much of this quality participants had, by the end of the conversation their counterpart seemed to end up with a similar amount. Now, we just needed to figure out what this quality was.

To find out, we analyzed the actual text of the online conversations that the pairs of participants had engaged in. Remember that our participants sat in separate cubicles and couldn't see each other. The only mode of communication available to them was the words they typed. This meant that whatever made people feel that their partner was being receptive had to be hidden in those words. What we had to do was stop trying to understand how the words of receptive and unreceptive people differed and instead try to understand how the words of people *perceived* to be receptive or unreceptive differed.

Language is behavior. Every word and phrase we utter is a choice we make from among tens of thousands of words and phrases we could have uttered instead. Language is also observable. What we say or write is perceived by other people who then form opinions about us, our intentions, our thought processes, and our personalities. Our study participants made linguistic choices. Those choices were observed by their counterparts in the form of words, which in turn shaped counterpart perceptions. The level of receptiveness that was happening in participants' minds was helpful to them personally because it led them to get more out of the conversation, but it was irrelevant to their counterparts because it could not be perceived. Contrary to the old adage, it is not in fact the thought that counts. What counts is how you behave, and in conversation, that largely means the words you choose.

Participants who had scored highly on the scale and were putting in the mental effort to engage with their counterparts' arguments did not know the right words to say to convince their counterparts that this was in fact what they were doing. And because the people they were talking to couldn't see what was happening in their heads, they didn't get credit for the mental work they were putting in. Just like I had no idea how seriously Dr. Jacobs was considering my crazy Avastin idea during our initial argument, people in general have a very hard time judging if somebody is being receptive or not. After months of debating the results, the study with our state and local government executives made my colleagues and me realize that to improve conversations, we had to change people's behavior, not their thoughts and feelings about disagreement.

THE RECOGNITION THAT internal mental processes are less predictive of conflict outcomes than overt observable behavior caused a dramatic shift in my research program and my thinking about how to teach people to disagree more effectively. It also made me realize why most other approaches fall short.

How many times have you been told to be more empathetic, open-minded, take the other person's perspective, exercise intellectual humility, or be a better listener? It's all good advice, and you should try to follow it as often as you can. However, most of this advice has a limited impact on your conversations for three specific reasons.

First, most people have no idea how exactly to execute many of these approaches. How do you become more empathetic? Where is the "empathy dial" in your brain? In general, most people don't know what concrete actions to take to shift their mental processes. As with any habit, changing mental habits requires planning, practice, and an understanding of what exactly is getting in the way. Telling a person to be more empathetic is like telling them to be a safe driver. You kind of know what it means, and you can do it in perfect weather on an empty street. But when driving at night through a thunderstorm, you need more precise instructions than "drive carefully." You need someone to tell you, "Place your hands at ten and two o'clock on the steering wheel, keep your speed below forty miles per hour, and never brake and turn at the same time." Because of this lack of precision, in the heat of a disagreement, when emotions run hot and you can hear the decibels rising, most of us can't execute the advice to "put yourself in the other person's shoes."

The second problem is that most people already think they are doing an excellent job being empathetic and considering the other person's perspective—or at least are doing as good a job as that other perspective deserves. Because we think we are right and the other person is wrong, we feel somewhat put upon when somebody helpfully suggests that we should engage more deeply and thoughtfully with the other person's wrongness. Having made up a story in our own heads about why the other person disagrees with us, we assume we already understand their perspective as much as is reasonable to do. When told to question our assumptions, we search our minds, review the reasons why our position is correct, and congratulate ourselves on a job well done. And because all of these processes happen in our heads, they cannot be evaluated for thoroughness or objectivity by anyone on the outside.

But the biggest reason that the advice to change what you think and how you feel often fails to improve the manner in which disagreement unfolds is that your counterpart can't see you doing any of these things. The only way to get credit for all your hard work, to actually make your counterpart feel heard, or to elicit from them a reciprocal willingness to thoughtfully engage with your own perspective is to signal mental processes through actions. Nobody can read your mind. Only through observable behavior can we convince a person on the other side of the conference room table or on the other side of the bed that we are truly engaging with their point of view. Rather than thinking receptively we need to behave receptively. And the best way to do that is through language.

LANGUAGE IS CONTAGIOUS

When we realized that participants in our experiments were rating each other's receptiveness based on the language communicated through the chat and not based on what was happening in their counterparts' heads, we also realized why participants' ratings of each other converged over time. Language is contagious. In other words, when one person says something, it increases the probability of their partner saying something similar. Obviously, we don't mimic every word other people say exactly, but certain characteristics of language do make counterparts behave in a linguistically similar manner. For example, a warm, friendly tone is more likely to be met with warmth and friendliness. By contrast, a cold, condescending tone will result in the same.

In fact, linguistic mimicry is so deeply engrained and has been demonstrated so widely that it is probably related to behaviors that humans engaged in before language had fully evolved. Primates and other animals also imitate each other's utterances and nonverbal behavior. Monkey see, monkey do. The most familiar example of this among humans is "laugh tracks" in sitcoms. It is very hard to keep a straight face when you hear a bunch of other people laughing. Even if you think the joke is dumb, you still smile, if only to avoid being perceived as the only grumpy weirdo in the room. Humans are social animals, and we effortlessly and thoughtlessly follow the example provided by those around us.

The fact that the partners in our study rated each other's receptiveness similarly had only one reasonable explanation: Just like other characteristics of language, receptiveness was being mimicked. And this in turn opened a really exciting possibility—if people naturally and effortlessly mimic receptiveness in disagreement, then a simple way to make somebody more receptive to you is to express receptiveness to them! The Golden Rule—treat others the way you want to be treated—could be the solution to making people in conflict thoughtfully engage with your own perspective. Using language that signals receptiveness could prompt the other person to do the same toward you, resulting in more positive interactions even as people continue to see the world differently.

Personally, I find the fact that receptive language is contagious equal parts ironic and empowering: ironic because it turns out that the best way to fix the people around us is to fix ourselves first, and empowering because I love the idea that I can shape the conflicts around me by modeling the kind of behavior I want from others. I don't have to blindly hope that someone will decide to make the effort to hear my point of view. I can assert control over the situation by treating them the way I want to be treated and know that more likely than not, they will follow suit. Finally, it seemed like I had discovered a way to make people listen to me the way I wanted to be listened to!

WORDS VERSUS BODY LANGUAGE

Hold on, you might say. Language is not the only way we have of communicating. What about nonverbal behavior, or what people refer to as "body language"? To keep our discussion focused, I will not dissect claims about nonverbal signals of deception, dominance, or sexual attraction. Our goal is to figure out the most effective way to communicate receptiveness. Let's consider whether body language can accomplish this specific task well.

Nonverbal behavior has the benefit of being actual behavior—it is something you perform that is visible to others rather than something that exists entirely on the inside of your head, such as thoughts and feelings. Like language, nonverbal behavior is also effortlessly imitated. People easily mimic each other's postures and facial expressions, for example. The problem with body language (as compared to language language), however, is the huge amount of ambiguity that is introduced by both the communicator and the receiver in the course of any nonverbal information exchange.

A few years ago, I was at a conference geared toward figuring out how to restore trust in journalism. Part of the program involved breaking into small groups and sharing approaches that participants (mostly experienced journalists) knew for increasing trust among interview subjects and readers. Inevitably, in my group the topic of body language came up, with one journalist sharing the insights from a workshop she had attended earlier. In the workshop, she learned to keep an open posture so that her interview subjects felt that she was listening to them—an idea that she found both intriguing and powerful. When asked to explain more specifically what an open posture meant, she shared that one trick was to carry a notebook that was as small as possible (like the ones that would fit into a breast pocket), so that it would not form a physical barrier between the journalist and her interviewee.

The other members of my group were genuinely excited about this trust-building hack and started asking questions to learn more. What is the biggest size of notebook you can have? Does this mean you can't use a laptop? What if I put my notebook down flat on the table? Might a very small notebook also signal that I am not very interested in the conversation? The questions quickly made it clear that while there was a lot of enthusiasm about using body language to communicate engagement with one's counterpart, how to actually do it in practice remained a mystery because any nonverbal signal can be interpreted in multiple ways.

An additional challenge to communicating engaged listening with body language comes from the fact that many people have gotten highly skilled at faking it. Even if you have never been to therapy or read a self-help book, you still know that good listeners are supposed to nod, smile, say "uh-huh" at regular intervals, lean forward, and maintain good eye contact. Unfortunately, it turns out that all of these behaviors are remarkably easy to perform while doing exactly zero thinking about what your counterpart is trying to convey.

In a study we conducted a few years ago, we wanted to know how good people were at discerning whether someone was actually listening. For this study, we asked pairs of strangers to get to know each other during a face-to-face conversation conducted in a small room. The room had one odd feature: During the conversation, a television screen hung behind one of the participants playing a series of muted commercials. The participant who had their back to the screen was told to simply ignore the commercials when they walked in. Their counterpart, however—who sat in full view of the screen mounted behind their partner's head—received secret instructions. In one experimental condition, the counterpart was told to pay close attention to the speaker and ignore the commercials. These participants were promised a bonus payment if their partner evaluated them as being a good listener. In the other experimental condition, the counterpart was told to memorize the products that were appearing on the screen while *faking* good listening. These participants were also promised a bonus payment for being seen as listening well but could receive an additional bonus depending on how well they recalled the commercials.

It turns out that people are remarkably good at this task. The participants in the second group remembered a large number of commercials—confirming that they followed the instructions and paid attention to the screen. But across both groups, the majority of participants were rated as excellent listeners by their counterparts. We'd told them to make their counterpart feel heard, and they'd done it, regardless of whether they were actually listening. However, the speakers could not tell the difference in the quality of listening between the two groups. This study and others like it strongly suggest that nonverbal signals of listening can't tell you whether your counterpart *really* heard and understood you.

The second challenge to using body language for communicating receptiveness comes from the dynamics of disagreement on the receiving side of the equation. Whereas in casual conversation (like those in our study with the distracting commercials) listeners are very good at sending fake signals of listening, it turns out that in disagreement, receivers tend to make the opposite error. Specifically, communicators interpret disagreement as a sign of poor listening, irrespective of whether they are actually being heard or not. When confronting a person who seems to be disagreeing with us and deciding on whether they are a good listener, we conclude that the answer must be no because if they were listening, they would have agreed with us by now! This pattern, which is directly in line with the theory of naïve realism, was recently demonstrated in a series of experiments by Bella Ren and Becky Schaumberg, researchers at the University of Pennsylvania. In their studies, participants interacted with people who disagreed with them and then rated their listening quality. Of course, there was a twist—all the disagreeing counterparts were actually fake. This enabled researchers to perfectly control the text of the responses that the counterparts sent to the real experimental participants, which varied only in whether at the end they expressed agreement or disagreement with the participant's argument. And although all participants received exactly the same signals of listening (because the fake counterparts always responded in exactly the same way), the counterparts who in the end continued to disagree with the speaker were rated as being worse listeners and being less engaged.

What is the moral of the story? Interpreting whether a person is truly engaged with our perspective, i.e., is being receptive, is an error-ridden process. First, nobody can read anybody's mind, so whatever is happening in your head has little influence on your counterpart's opinion. Additional errors are introduced by the fact that on the one hand, listening is easy to fake with a little effort, and on the other hand, in cases of disagreement, people don't believe even genuine signals of listening. This leaves us with a question: What is an accurate (or at least more-difficult-to-fake) signal of receptiveness that people will recognize as such and give you credit for?

The answer is: words.

Words have several advantages over body language for communicating receptiveness. First, words are *the* defining feature of conversation. You can have a conversation by text or on Slack without any body language at all. But unless you are a trained ballerina, you cannot have a conversation based strictly on body language. This means that improving how you communicate receptiveness with words will help you in every conversation—in person, on Zoom, by text, or even if you put quill to parchment and send the result by owl.

Second, as much as we misunderstand each other's words, we misunderstand body language much more. A huge experimental literature is dedicated to the fact that the same nonverbal signals are often interpreted differently by different people. The way we interpret words is far more consistent from person to person and situation to situation.

Imagine I am looking you intently in the eyes. Am I challenging you to a fight? Am I signaling romantic attraction? Do I think you might have an eye infection? Am I being secretly held hostage and hoping that my intense eye contact will prompt you to call 911? In that moment, saying "I am really angry at you" or "You are really hot" or "What's that on your eye?" gets the point across with far less room for error. Certainly, the words can also be confusing. You might start rubbing the wrong eye or think that I am joking and not actually coming on to you, but on average, the verbal message is far more likely to be interpreted accurately.

One final concern I often hear when discussing the relationship between words and body language is the potential weirdness that might arise if your body language and your words say two opposite things—like if I said "You are so hot" while leaning away from you and making a disgusted expression with my face. Fortunately, this problem is extremely rare. Human words and faces and bodies all tend to work together. If you make your words sound receptive, your body is likely to follow your words, at least to a certain degree. In fact, it would take a lot of work to make the two send clearly opposite signals.* If you focus on your words, the body will come along.

CHAPTER SUMMARY

- Being perceived as receptive has important interpersonal and professional benefits. Across studies, we have seen that even in the most severe disagreements people who are seen as receptive get more help when they struggle, are likely to be invited into more work teams

---

* Doing one thing with your body while saying the opposite with your words is a common comedic device. A familiar version of it is sarcasm, and many people are quite bad at it.

and projects, and are seen as more desirable future communication partners.

- Perceptions of receptiveness are most clearly correlated with linguistic behavior, i.e., the words you say, which is great news because choosing your words carefully is far easier than changing the way your mind works or subtly tuning your body language.

- Acting receptively makes others do the same for you. This implies that each of us has control over the conversational environment around us. If you can manage your own words, you can subtly influence your counterpart to treat you the way you want to be treated. The fact that receptiveness is contagious makes it a powerful tool for improving all of your interactions.

4

THE AWESOME POWER OF SIGNALING LEARNING GOALS

IF YOU HAVE RAISED TEENAGERS, YOU KNOW THAT TO THE EXtent that they talk to you at all, it tends to be at weird times determined by them alone. My middle daughter likes to lay unsolvable problems at my feet at around eleven at night. There is no anticipating it, except that it must be a school night, ideally toward the end of the week when everyone is tired. Having worked a full day, taken care of my ninety-four-year-old grandmother, made family dinner, worked on some homework with each kid, put the seven-year-old to bed, given the dog his allergy medicine, and made a very large pot of coffee for the morning, I am usually half-asleep when I come to kiss her good night. At a moment like that, Izabella likes to surprise me with a curveball: "Mom, my back still hurts, and I don't think the PT is helping, and what makes you think our doctor is any good?!"

In the back of my mind, I hear the rumble of distant thunder, the change in the air that signals that the teenager is stressed, tired, and should be approached with utmost caution. But in the front of my mind, the part that's still explicitly controlling my mouth, the only thing I can think about is my own warm bed that is only a few feet away in the next room.

Like the practical woman that I am, I start by trying to solve the problem: "I am sorry, baby. Do you want an Advil?"

Izabella: "No, I've been taking Advil, and it doesn't help. My back is still completely BROKEN, and nothing makes any difference, and I just don't understand why they didn't read the MRI right the first time, and Tara said I should go get acupuncture, and I was looking at acupuncture on TikTok, but it doesn't make sense to me because why would little needles . . ."

As she begins to spiral, I try my best to soothe her: "Baby, your back is not broken. It's healing, it's just going to take a whi—"

But of course, she won't be soothed: "No, Mom, it IS broken, and I don't care what you call it because it hurts and I can't do anything and I am going to go to college in a couple of years and I will never have any fun again, and I can't do back handsprings in college, and they said it would heal but it doesn't, and . . ."

Losing patience, I try to correct her on the facts: "Lovey, you don't need to do back handsprings in college, but you can if you want to. The doctor said that it takes different amounts of time for different people. You are young and healthy, you are out of the brace, you are doing your PT, it's just . . ."

But as tears start rolling down Izabella's face, it becomes clear that she is not interested in my medical knowledge: "MOOOOM!!! Quit interrupting me! The PT is not working, and you are not listening to me. You never listen to me and you are not even trying to help!"

At this point, I grow both frustrated and a little hurt thinking about all the faraway volleyball tournaments I have driven to, all the high school essays I edited late at night, and all the sisterly squabbles I have mediated over the years. *I* never listen? *I* am not trying to help? Deciding that there's no reasoning with her, I try to put an end to the discussion: "Izabella, its eleven p.m., there is nothing we can do about it right now. I've had a long day, and I want to support you, but you are driving me crazy. Let's get some sleep and talk about it in the morning."

Now I'm the one in trouble: "All you ever want to do is to go to sleep. You never make time for me. I feel like this all the time, not just at eleven p.m., but you are never around, and you never talk to me!" Sobbing, turning away from me, she is fumbling around for a box of tissues without making eye contact. That gibe hits home because I do work a lot and she does sound truly upset. So I give up on sleep, settle on her bed, and, having realized that there is no easy fix, begin seriously considering the situation as I should have done from the start.

EVERY PARENT HAS been there. In fact, every human has at some point been faced with a surprise eruption from an emotional, hormonal, exhausted friend, family member, or colleague. The first natural response when someone complains is to solve the apparent problem: "Do you want some Advil?" When that attempt is not met with the level of appreciation you are hoping for, you try to correct their seeming confusion about the state of the world. Like the naïve realist that you are, you assume that once they understand the facts, everything will be better: "Your back is not broken, it's healing," or "Yes, the dog *has* been fed," or "You know, he is *your* client. This deadline should be on *your* calendar." At some point, you realize that despite your best efforts at helpfulness and your commitment to setting the record straight, you are the one in trouble for being a bad parent/spouse/friend/child/colleague. At that point, you become less interested in helping the other person and more interested in telling them what a jerk they are being. Not surprisingly, that doesn't go over well, either.

One realization, however, has recently dramatically changed my approach to these conversations. The realization was inspired by my colleagues Mike Yeomans, Alison Wood Brooks, and Maurice Schweitzer and their research on conversational goals. Like many profound insights, this one is again quite simple: In any conversation, both people are pursuing a multitude of goals. People not only want to exchange information (which is what we all *think* we are doing in conversation) but also might want to make a social connection, find or give comfort, make a joke, get away with a lie, avoid blame, or simply pass the time. Yet we rarely stop to figure out what our goals actually are, let alone what they should be or what's the best way to pursue them. We almost never consider our counterpart's goals.

Similarly, talking to someone who disagrees with you—a unique kind of conversation—also could serve a variety of goals. However, until a few years ago, nobody thought to ask what people's goals in disagreement are, how well they do at achieving them, or whether the choice of what goals one is pursuing makes any difference.

Take my fight with Izabella. My explicit, clearly stated goal was going to sleep. That goal was temporarily overshadowed by the fact that my kid seemed to be in pain and I wanted to help her. The helping goal, however, was directly at odds with the sleeping goal, so any help I offered had to be quick (hence the Advil).

My other goal was to convince her that things are progressing as they should be. Izabella is prone to anxiety and a part of me was convinced that she was blowing things out of proportion. If I could convince her that her doctors actually do know what they are doing and normal teenage bones eventually heal, she would get some sleep and everything would be better in the morning.

(Hence me interrupting her to tell her that she is misjudging her own experience.)

But that's just scratching the surface of the goals that a person might have in this conversation. What are some others?

One goal might be to more thoroughly understand what is actually going on with Izabella's back. How much pain is she in? Does it hurt sitting, standing, lying? How consistently is she doing her PT? What does the physical therapist say about it? Has she used ice or heat? How much Advil has she been taking already?

Another goal might be to understand what is going on with Izabella psychologically. Has she been getting enough sleep? Is she worried about her back because the volleyball season is starting soon? Is being constantly sore making her cranky and annoyed more generally? Has having her first real medical issue surfaced a broader set of concerns about the frailty of the human body?

Yet another goal might be to see this conversation as an opportunity to continue building a trusting relationship with my kid. I have a teenager that will actually talk to me about her problems. Maybe I should be jumping for joy and using this conversation to show her that confiding in me is the right thing to do. Maybe if I had more patience, this conversation would be a bridge to the next conversation about dating, or school, or drugs—the type of discussion that most teens need to be carefully coaxed into.

Finally, I could pursue the goal of making Izabella feel heard—to let her rant and cry and complain about the incompetence of doctors and the unfairness of life, the stupidity of teachers and volleyball coaches, and all the real and imaginary offenses committed by her two sisters. Rather than correcting her overgeneralizations and negativity, I could have given her the space to express what she feels with care and patience, and without judgment. I could have sat there and let her emotions wash over me, knowing that as a grown woman, I have more capacity to deal with them than she does.

Too bad that last plan doesn't occur to me at the beginning. Instead, it occurs to me fifteen minutes in, when she is sobbing, and I have finally stopped trying to argue her into seeing things from my adult perspective. Not arguing gives me a chance to pat her on the back (which she grudgingly allows) and gather my thoughts. A little sheepishly, I remember that I study conflict for a living and think about how I really ought to be better at this by now. Then I take a breath and say, "Okay, lovey, what do you think is going on here?" Then I shut up and listen.

CONVERSATIONAL GOALS IN DISAGREEMENT

Many experts on conflict have advised that what one ought to do in disagreement is to take on a "learning orientation" or an "inquiry mindset." The logic behind this advice seems sound. Disagreement should proceed more smoothly if we approach it like scientists seeking to understand our counterpart rather than lawyers trying to persuade them. When I first came across this advice, it sounded like an excellent idea. It also sounded very much in line with my research team's thinking about the benefits of receptiveness. However, digging through the research literature, my students and I came to realize that, like much advice on conflict, these seemingly sensible suggestions had no experimental evidence to support them. Not only did we have little idea about whether a particular set of goals was actually better or worse to pursue in practice, we didn't even know what goals people actually pursued or if anyone explicitly thought about their goals in the first place.

My student Hanne Collins (now a faculty member at UCLA) decided to figure it out. We started with a simple series of studies asking research participants to imagine talking with someone they disagree with on a variety of topics and to list the goals they anticipated having during that conversation. What are people actually trying to accomplish when they disagree?

Analyzing the goals that participants listed supported what the experts before us had implicitly claimed: People in disagreement were concerned with two broad categories of pursuits—learning and persuasion. In other words, in considering what they hoped to achieve when talking to someone they disagreed with, people listed things like "understanding their point of view," "learning about their perspective," and "figuring out why they believe what they believe." We called these responses "learning goals." They also listed things like "convincing them I am right," "proving that their argument makes no sense," and "pointing out their biases"—responses we came to call "persuasion goals." Learning and persuasion goals made up roughly 80 percent of all the goals listed in our first study, suggesting that these were indeed the dominant objectives people had in disagreement. Importantly, people listed roughly as many learning goals as persuasion goals—42 percent and 38 percent, respectively.

In the same study, however, in addition to asking people about their own goals, we also asked them to offer their best guess about the goals embraced by their counterparts. This is where things got interesting. Whereas people believed that they themselves were roughly equally interested in both learning and persuasion, they believed that their counterparts were *five times* more interested in persuading them than learning about their point of view. In other words, in listing their counterparts' goals, 71 percent of the time participants listed goals having to do with persuasion and only 16 percent of the time goals that had to do with learning. It was clear that in imagining disagreements, people inferred very different objectives for themselves versus others.

Having replicated this result several times and found it to be consistent, our next step was to test whether approaching a disagreement with a learning goal rather than a persuasion goal would improve outcomes, as prior advice had claimed. Given that thus far our findings pretty much conformed with the insights of everyone who came before us, we thought the answer would be a definitive yes. In several subsequent studies we instructed people to approach their disagreements with the goal of learning about their counterpart, understanding their point of view, figuring out why they hold the beliefs that they do, and gaining insight into the other's reasoning. We then compared the conflict outcomes of these participants to the outcomes of others who were left to approach their disagreements however they naturally would.

The results were stunning. Instructing people to take on a learning orientation made not a bit of difference. The transcripts of conversations showed that participants in both conditions behaved in exactly the same way, and as a result they were evaluated identically by their counterparts, which ultimately led to similar overall conversational experiences. Thinking that the fault was ours for not instructing participants correctly, we tried again, and then again. We gave them clearer instructions, bolded and underlined the important bits, and made sure that they read carefully. Yet, the results were the same: Telling people to be more curious, to try to understand, and to be willing to learn made no difference.

Eventually, we went back to the drawing board. What if, we wondered, instead of telling people to embrace learning goals, we convinced them that their counterparts were the ones who wanted to learn from *them*? What if what really mattered was not people's internal goals for the conversation but what they believed their counterparts' goals to be? In other words, instead of changing people's own orientation toward the conflict, maybe we should be changing their beliefs about the other side.

In a new set of studies, we did exactly that. Participants prepared to have an online chat with someone they strongly disagreed with. Before the chat, they filled out a questionnaire asking them about their goals for the conversation. The questionnaire itself was irrelevant, except that it gave us the excuse to show the participants a fake questionnaire purportedly filled out by the person they would be interacting with. This fake questionnaire was constructed such that in all cases the conversation partner had a moderate level of interest in convincing the real participant of their point of view (i.e., they held moderate persuasion goals). What differed, however, was the learning goals that these counterparts supposedly embraced. In half of the cases, the partner with moderate persuasion goals was also extremely interested in understanding the participants' perspective (the "high learning goals" treatment). In the other half, the partner was not at all interested in learning the participants' perspective (the "low learning goals" treatment). The participants then received a message from their partner making an argument on an issue they disagreed on and were asked to evaluate this individual and their message.

We ran multiple studies using this basic setup. In one version, American participants first expressed their opinion regarding creating favorable conditions for hiring women in science, technology, engineering, and math (STEM) fields. Then they received a message from a conversation partner who held the opposing view on this controversial issue. In another version of the study, we recruited Israeli participants and asked them how they felt about offering an unfettered "right of return" for Palestinians to live in Israel. We then showed them a message from a Palestinian counterpart who argued in support of such a policy and stated that it was a requirement of any future peace deal.

In both cases, showing participants a fake questionnaire suggesting that their partner was interested in learning about the participant's own point of view had dramatic results. Participants saw this individual (who disagreed with them on one of the most controversial issues we could think of) as more moral, more reasonable, more trustworthy, more likable, and more intelligent than the counterpart who made the same argument but claimed to be uninterested in understanding the participants' own perspective. The participants in the "high learning goals" condition also saw the arguments as more persuasive, relevant, true, and evenhanded than the *same exact argument* presented by someone not showing an interest in learning!

In yet another demonstration of this basic idea, we paired Biden and Trump supporters in the run-up to the 2020 presidential election in an online chatroom and asked them to debate who would be the better president. After the discussion, participants evaluated their counterparts and the quality of the conversation. They also reported their own goals during the interaction and their beliefs about their counterpart's goals. As in the prior studies, participants' evaluations of their partner and their experience were overwhelmingly driven by whether they believed that their counterpart wanted to learn about their perspective. More than the participants' own desire to learn, more than their beliefs about their partner's persuadability, or how much the two actually disagreed, it was their sense that the other side wanted to understand them that made bitter political opponents conclude that they just had a pleasant conversation with a reasonable, intelligent, moral, trustworthy human.

What is it about believing that another person wants to understand our point of view that so dramatically changes the dynamics of disagreement and prevents it from turning into conflict? And why did telling people to be more curious about their partner and try to learn about them fail? The answer goes back to naïve realism. Remember that in the course of explaining to ourselves why we disagree, we tend to stereotype our opponents. The main features of this stereotype are: 1) that people who disagree with us are not too bright—that's why they "don't get it"; and 2) that they have selfish, malevolent motives—that's why they "don't want to get it." Showing a desire to learn about someone else's perspective powerfully violates both components of this stereotype.

First, seeking to understand an issue from multiple perspectives demands intelligence. It's hard to write a person off as dumb when they are eager to engage in the complicated mental gymnastics that are required to balance the evidence for both sides of an issue and evaluate it fairly. Second, extensive research shows that feeling heard and understood generates positive emotions. When a person anticipates feeling heard, it feels like receiving a lovely gift. When someone tells you that they want to truly understand you, it's difficult to continue thinking of them as a selfish jerk.

By contrast, telling people to try to enter the conversation with curiosity and a desire to learn didn't work because most people think that they are already doing the right amount of learning. Remember that most people believe themselves to be roughly equally committed to persuading their counterpart and to understanding their point of view. Given that most of them also think that they are right and that their counterpart is wrong, holding these two types of goals in equal measure seems quite generous. By contrast, in considering their counterpart, they think that this other person (the one with the crazy, wrongheaded beliefs) is mostly out to persuade them. So, from the standpoint of any given party, it is the other person who needs fixing, not themselves. Conflict outcomes improved when we convinced our participants that their counterpart, the wrongheaded jerk, was interested in understanding them and learning about their perspective.

HOW TO EXPRESS LEARNING GOALS

In our studies, participants received bogus questionnaires telling them that their counterpart wanted to learn about their point of view. The obvious question this approach raises is: How would you clearly show your willingness to learn in the real world, outside of the experimental setting? One might be tempted to fall back on traditional advice: Listen attentively, don't interrupt, use warm body language. But remember that in the previous chapter we learned that people regularly struggle to accurately interpret the contents of others' minds or subtle nonverbal signals. Instead, the approach that seemed to us most likely to work was using words to directly tell our counterparts that we want to learn from their perspective and understand their point of view. Before broadcasting our recommendation out into the world, however, we decided to run some experiments to make sure that our ideas were actually correct and stood up to research scrutiny.

Once again, we asked participants to write a message to someone who disagrees with them about affirmative action policies for women in STEM fields. Each participant wrote three to five sentences explaining their perspective and submitted them to us. We then took their arguments and implemented our own advice: Without changing a word of what the participant had written, we added two sentences at the beginning and one sentence at the end. The sentences at the beginning were one of the following three options:

- This is an important topic. I'm curious to hear what people who disagree with me think about this issue. From my perspective . . .

- This is an important topic. I'd really like to learn more about the different points of view on this topic. From my perspective . . .

- This is an important topic. I want to understand what other people who disagree with me think about this issue. From my perspective . . .

The sentence at the end was one of these options:

- That's how I think about the issue, but I'd love to understand other points of view.

- That's how I think about the issue, but I'm curious to hear what people who disagree with me think about this.

- That's how I think about the issue, but I'd like to learn about other perspectives on this topic.

As you can see, all of these sentences use different words to make the same point: I have an opinion, but I also want to understand where you are coming from. The reason we wrote six versions was twofold. First, we wanted to say it twice—at the beginning and at the end of the participant's real argument—just to make sure people noticed. Second, we wanted to try a variety of combinations to make sure that there was nothing magical about the specific words we used, but instead that it was the overall message that did the work. We then took the original arguments and the arguments modified by us and sent them to different groups of participants, all of whom reported having the opposite stance about gender-based affirmative action in STEM fields than the stance articulated in the message they ultimately received.

What we found was that adding two simple sentences at the beginning and at the end dramatically improved how the arguments landed. Using the same measures as in the prior study, we saw that our little three-sentence intervention made the supporters of opposing policies see each other as more intelligent, moral, trustworthy, and objective. Even though the person being evaluated still made exactly the same argument, they were seen more positively for showing a bit of curiosity in a way that was clear and recognizable.

Notice that this approach does not require anyone to agree, compromise, or soften their stance. The original text included between our added expressions of learning goals were the words that the participants themselves had written. But those simple phrases led recipients to see the arguments in a different light. Without conceding any ground at all, this approach allows you to change the impression you make on your disagreeing counterpart with just a sentence or two. Expressing your desire to learn decreases the odds of conflict escalation and makes it more likely that the conversation will flow into a productive direction.

WHY EXPRESSING LEARNING GOALS IS HARD

Having read about this research, you might naturally assume that it was conducted *after* the nighttime fight I described with my daughter because, had I been armed with these insights at the time, I would not have made the mistakes that I did. Unfortunately, however, just knowing what to do is only half the battle. You still have to make yourself do it. It turns out that even when people know in principle that expressing a desire to learn is the right move, they need to do it verbally, and even when we tell them exactly the right words to say, many of them (including me) ignore this good advice.

Consistently expressing your desire to learn about and understand your counterpart is difficult, especially in the moment of an escalating disagreement. Understanding where the difficulties stem from, however, can help us overcome them. At a high level, three things stand in the way: impatience, overconfidence, and pride.

Impatience

Remember that my argument with Izabella was late at night. I wanted to solve the problem fast. I didn't want to listen to a breathless teenage rant about all the ills of the world. I just wanted to give her Advil and tuck her in. Most of us live harried lives, and most disagreements creep up when we are trying to accomplish something else that also needs doing in a hurry. Going to bed, running out the door, finishing up a meeting, sending out a deliverable, making a decision about a product launch, or picking a cellphone plan all take longer when somebody disagrees with you. Further extending the process by then asking them to help you understand their thinking and engaging in thoughtful inquiry about their assumptions and values feels like a frustrating waste of time.

But that desire to save time is a trap. And the belief that you will get there faster without trying to understand the other person's perspective is an illusion. Have you ever bought a bookcase that needs to be assembled, looked at the novel-length instruction manual, and thought that you can figure it out faster on your own? In the name of saving time, you skip the instructions and plunge in. But just when you thought you were done, you find some extra screws that were supposed to hold the whole thing together. Taking the bookcase apart and starting from scratch, you wish you had followed the damn manual.

Trying to barrel through a disagreement to save time has a similar dynamic. It seems tempting in the beginning, and sometimes it works fine (I own plenty of furniture that got assembled sans manual). However, when it fails, it fails quite spectacularly. In the effort of saving yourself ten minutes of listening to somebody's reasoning or feelings, you have set yourself up for a much longer fight with that person who is now demanding to be heard. Even if the fight does not erupt immediately, you might have unwittingly reinforced a relationship dynamic where a person who you value (a friend, a family member, an employee) has received additional confirmation that you don't care about their views. And although they might not say anything explicit about it in the moment, the cost usually becomes apparent in the long run. The bookcase without the supporting screws will eventually fall over, likely at the worst possible time.

Overconfidence

The temptation to just tell the person they are wrong without taking the time to express your curiosity is magnified by our overconfidence in our ability to ultimately win the argument. "Confidence" is something that is generally considered a good thing in modern Western culture. "Overconfidence," by contrast, is defined as being more confident than you have any right to be given the objective evidence at hand. For example, if I don't study for a test because I expect to get an A based on my current knowledge, and then I get a B-, that's overconfidence. I made a prediction about my performance and my actual performance fell short of that prediction.

People are overconfident about all sorts of things (and underconfident about a few). Part of the reason that this bias persists is that we rarely gather performance data on ourselves and our forecasts, so that our predictions go untested. A few years ago, Jennifer Logg, a professor at Georgetown University, and I decided to find out if people are overconfident in their ability to persuade disagreeing counterparts. We ran a series of studies where we simply asked people about a topic and told them that we would pair them with somebody who disagrees with them for an online debate. We then asked them whether they thought they would win the debate. It turns out that people are wildly overconfident about their persuasion skills. Across several studies, three times more participants claimed that they would persuade their counterpart than the number who allowed for the possibility that they would be persuaded. Of course, because for every person who wins an argument there has to be a person who loses, our results mean that on average our participants were not being realistic about their chances. In other words, they were being overconfident.

The way overconfidence thwarts our willingness to express learning goals is by leading us to believe that we can just explain our point of view to our counterpart and be done with the disagreement. Remember, as a naïve realist you think you are right. And as an overconfident naïve realist you also believe that you can convince other people of your rightness. I was very confident that Izabella's back was doing exactly what backs do after a sports injury and that the solution was patience, physical therapy, Advil, and sleep. I thought that as an articulate person with a PhD who has dealt with many injuries in my dancing days, I could convince a fifteen-year-old that everything would be fine if she just listened to her doctors and her parents. Since I was so confident about both my views and my ability to impart them to my child, I thought there was no point in asking her about her experiences and her feelings because in the end we would end up in the same place anyway. Big mistake.

Pride

The final enemy of expressing learning goals in disagreement is pride. People expect disagreements to have winners and losers. We defend our positions, attack each other's arguments, disarm our opponents, and take a firm stand. The very words we use when we talk about disagreement make it clear that we generally think of these interactions as battles of both wits and wills. When people find themselves in this militaristic mindset, expressing learning goals feels like weakness. After all, you are telling your partner that there is something you don't know or don't understand. You are asking them to help you learn something new because your current grasp of the situation is incomplete. Expressing learning goals feels like admitting out loud that your partner (who, remember, you think is wrong) has something valuable to teach you. This is difficult for a lot of people, especially in ongoing conflicts, when they are concerned with their status relative to their counterpart, and when others are watching.

The role of pride leads to a weird pattern wherein our beliefs don't line up with our behavior. Most people recognize that expressing learning goals is the right thing to do. They just don't want to do it. For example, in a couple of studies we have shown people two different arguments—one with an expression of learning goals and one without. We then asked participants to choose which one they would send to a person that they disagree with. We found that the vast majority of people (over 80 percent) picked the argument that expressed learning goals—people seem to understand that this approach has benefits.

However, when we give people the chance to write their own argument and ask them to make sure that they include an expression of learning goals, they struggle. Part of the problem is that they can't come up with the right words. But even when we give them sample phrases, many participants do a cursory job at best.

Instead of clearly and repeatedly stating that they are interested in their counterpart's perspective, they write a forceful argument and then include a half-hearted (and often snarky), acknowledgment that the other person might possibly have something interesting to contribute. By going into the interaction guns blazing, they preserve their pride and sense of verbal dominance at the expense of having a productive conversation. As a result, they lose precious opportunities to improve relationships and to pick up on some new ideas, instead making futile efforts to convince their counterparts that they are wrong.

SO, THERE IS good news and bad news. The good news is that expressing your willingness to learn has large and robust effects on conversation outcomes. It's also pretty easy to do. You don't have to fundamentally change the way you think or feel; you just need to use words to make your counterpart aware of the fact that you are trying to understand their perspective and learn about their views. You don't have to be poetic; you can simply use the phrase suggestions we used in our studies and that I listed earlier in the chapter.

The bad news is twofold. One, when people encounter disagreement, they go in with the assumption that their counterparts are not interested in learning about their perspectives. So, if you are the person who is trying to express a desire to learn, you are fighting an uphill battle. This means that if you want to make sure your efforts are recognized, it's best to be extremely clear and a little repetitive. The second problem is our own reluctance to use these tools. Because we are often impatient, overconfident, and worried about seeming weak or uncertain, we don't express learning goals even if theoretically we know it's the right thing to do.

But there is one more piece of good news. Like any behavior, expressing a learning goal becomes natural with practice. The implication is that you should not wait until you are in the middle of Thanksgiving dinner to try using this technique for the first time. Instead try it now. Think of someone who you strongly disagree with and write them a short message about why you disagree. Then slap on some learning goals. Remember, just a couple of sentences at the beginning and the end will do. Now reread your message. Don't you sound like a more reasonable person already? With a little practice, expressing your desire to learn can become the first powerful tool in your constructive disagreement toolbox, making each encounter with a disagreeing human less frustrating and more informative.

CHAPTER SUMMARY

- Although most people report that they are interested in both learning and persuasion during disagreement, they assume that their counterparts are primarily out to change their minds and have no interest in learning. This pattern is related to naïve realism—we assume that people who disagree with us are just not sufficiently intelligent or caring enough to make the effort to understand us.

- Overcoming this assumption is important, however, because people think much more highly of disagreement counterparts who also want to learn about their perspectives.

- To effectively signal your desire to learn, use clear, repetitive language instead of relying on more subtle signals—remember that your counterparts will need some convincing!

- Don't let your biases stand in the way. It's better to ask a silly-sounding question and feel a little sheepish than launch into an argument because you made some incorrect assumptions about your counterpart, their beliefs, and their intentions.

5

ASKING THE RIGHT QUESTIONS

WHEN MY HUSBAND COMES HOME FROM WORK, HE OFTEN WALKS into chaos. Something is on the stove, someone is on the phone, the dog is barking, a kid is coming in from sports practice, another is going out to a tutoring session, and a pile of unopened Amazon packages graces the kitchen counter. I am normally still dressed in my work clothes, with a kitchen towel slung over one shoulder, the phone pressed to the other, chopping, microwaving, and directing traffic. As I said, chaos.

Having wrestled down the dog and added the latest pile of mail to the Amazon packages, he sometimes jumps into question-asking mode: Has anyone taken out the trash? Why is the dog's food bowl empty? When will dinner be ready?

As you know if you have ever been confronted with a barrage of questions in the middle of a stressful situation, this often does not go well. His questions feel like an interrogation, as if the general has just arrived for a surprise visit and the troops must line up to be inspected. While he is firing questions, I am thinking, "Why the hell is it my job to know if the trash got taken out? And if the dog's food bowl is empty, then fill it. Don't ask me about it!"

Of course, as in every marital spat, there are two sides. Ryan's side is that when he walks in, he doesn't know what's going on in his own home. He'd like to contribute and needs some basic information to be able to do so. The question about the trash is not an accusation but an offer to ask a listless teenager to take care of it. Asking why the dog bowl is empty is his way of finding out whether the dog ever got fed or if he just finished eating. And wondering about the timing of dinner is just an inquiry from a hungry person who wants to know if he should have a snack or wait. Ryan's mistake isn't asking questions. It's that he isn't asking the right kinds of questions.

ALMOST ALL NEGOTIATION and conflict management books tout the benefits of question-asking. The logic this advice is commonly based on is that in any dispute between two people, there is information that you simply do not know and would be useful to you if you did. Rather than making assumptions, you should simply ask the other person to tell you what you need to know. This approach, the argument goes, can prevent us from making costly mistakes that stem from acting on inaccurate information or faulty assumptions about your counterpart. It can also help find new solutions to whatever problems you and the other person are facing that would not have occurred to you when you didn't know what you know now.

However, there is a second and possibly equally important function to question-asking. Just like every other utterance in conversation, questions serve to communicate information about the question asker to the question recipient (and whoever else might be looking on). In other words, when a question is asked, it is not only the case that the respondent ends up sharing information for the benefit of the asker. It is also the case that the very act of asking the question (as well as what exactly the question is and how it was asked) conveys information about the asker to the respondent. The information exchange is a two-way street.

So what kinds of information might questions convey? It turns out that questions speak volumes. For example, extremely detailed, technical questions can convey that the asker is very knowledgeable about a particular domain. A car buyer who asks about how this brand of tire versus that brand of tire performs on wet pavement clearly has more experience driving sports cars than a car buyer who asks why a Ford has a horse logo on it. A coworker who asks why you are always being so condescending to them probably does not really want to know *why* you are being condescending. Rather, they are telling you that they've noticed and they want you to stop.

In conflict in particular, what matters is not the grammatical form of an utterance (whether it has a question mark at the end) but instead whether the words convey curiosity and engagement. However, because most people don't think about what their questions are communicating to their counterparts, lots of questions fail miserably, instead conveying accusation or judgment, or merely making an argument in question form. For example, asking, "What kind of idiot would possibly think that's a good idea?" technically counts as asking a question, but is pretty unlikely to de-escalate conflict. This "question" communicates condescension, bafflement, and frustration—not curiosity or a desire to learn. By contrast, "I'd like to understand what led you to believe that" is *technically* not a question but conveys curiosity much more effectively. As always, overlooking the details gets us into trouble: Asking questions seems good at a high level, but only some questions are helpful while others can actually make things worse.

My graduate school coauthor, Frances Chen, and I learned this lesson the hard way when we first began working on receptiveness. To us, it seemed self-evident that people who asked more questions would be seen more positively by their counterparts (we had absorbed the same pop psychology as everyone else). What we wanted to test instead was whether instructing people to ask more questions in disagreement would make those people themselves become more receptive. Our theory was that when people observed themselves asking thoughtful questions, they might forget that they were doing so because the experimenters instructed them and would attribute their behavior to their own genuine receptiveness to the other side. This is called "self-perception" and is one of the most important ideas in social psychology. When people aren't sure how they feel about a particular thing, they try to infer their feelings by observing their own behavior. We thought that by making people's behavior appear more receptive to themselves, we could actually make people more receptive.

To test this hypothesis, we conducted an experiment where participants who we preselected for strongly holding a particular opinion viewed a video expressing the opposing point of view. At the end of the video, we instructed these participants to either ask three questions of the speaker or write three sentences expressing their reactions to the speech. The study was conducted on the Stanford campus and our video featured a leader of a student organization advocating for universal veganism. The speaker's claim was that animal farming was a fundamentally cruel and unethical practice and that the only way to live an ethical life was to completely stop consuming animal products. Even among the liberal Stanford student body, the idea of giving up the milk in their lattes and the cheese on their pizza was not a welcome message. We thought this type of disagreement, a disagreement that went at the participants' fundamental views of their own virtue and put that virtue in direct tension with their lifestyle, was a strong setting for testing the power of question-asking.

Unfortunately, after spending weeks walking participants through the experiment one at a time, we had to throw out most of the data. Reading through the questions our participants wrote made it clear that they were struggling to comply with our instructions. Most questions were of the form, "What kind of idiot . . ." or "How could you possibly believe . . ." Some were clearly arguments in the grammatical form of a question—"What would you say to a farmer who loses his livelihood because of your concern for cows?" or "Where did you get your data that humans don't need meat to survive?"

We tried again. Instead of simply telling participants to ask questions, we gave them specific instructions on what kinds of questions to ask: open-ended questions for the speaker that would help the question asker better understand why the speaker feels the way they do. We further instructed participants to set aside their own agreement or disagreement with the speaker and focus on questions that communicate their desire to understand. Finally, we warned them against offering counterarguments in question form. We called this style of question-asking "elaboration questions"—questions that invite the speaker to "please elaborate."

Our instructions helped matters somewhat, but the results were far from perfect. We still had to eliminate data from participants who asked aggressive, argumentative questions, which is generally frowned upon as a research practice. The dataset that remained showed some of the predicted patterns: participants who asked elaboration questions of the preachy vegan reported being more willing to talk to this person if given a chance in the future, and saw proponents of veganism as a group less negatively than the control group who had been instructed to just write down three comments. They also evaluated the speaker's message as being more valid. The study was published in a short paper and generally made little impact on the world. However, for Frances and me, it did lead to some interesting insights.

The first thing it made us realize is that simply telling people to ask questions during disagreement is not good enough. In fact, left to their own devices, people ask exactly the wrong kinds of questions, propelling themselves further and further into a conflict spiral while at the same time patting themselves on the back for having asked a question. Our participants struggled to demonstrate anything that looked like curiosity and only did better (but far from well) once we gave them very specific instructions. Keep in mind that our participants were highly competent Stanford students getting paid for performing a specific task in an experiment. We can safely assume that people embroiled in real conflict (for example, the real parents of a student who comes home from college demanding that his family become vegan) are likely to struggle even more. Good questions don't come naturally and require thought and planning.

Having realized how difficult it is to get people to ask good questions, but still being curious about what would happen if they would, we decided to write the questions for the next study ourselves. In this setup, participants came to the computer lab expecting to discuss a proposed campus policy with another student. They were told that Stanford was considering instituting a new graduation requirement—a set of comprehensive exams covering the core curriculum—and that the fictitious Office of Undergraduate Affairs was seeking student feedback regarding this proposed policy. In reality, all the student participants, who, as a rule, understandably opposed an additional set of exams at the end of their senior year, discussed the policy with me.

Here is how the study unfolded. After learning about the topic, the participants received a chat message from their counterpart (me) with a full-throated argument in support of comprehensive exams. For several paragraphs, the fictitious nerdy student went on about the added prestige a Stanford education would gain if every student passed this difficult set of tests and the unfairness of easy majors that diluted the Stanford brand.

The key manipulation came at the end of the message, when half of the participants received a single expression of curiosity asking them to elaborate on their disagreeing opinion. We were wondering if this single question tacked on to the end of a lengthy argument would make any difference.

After I sent the message, I sat around waiting for the real participants to type their responses. Taking on the role of the experimenter, I then messaged the real participants that they were out of time and the study was about to conclude. Finally, I sent them a parting message as their fake counterpart: "Well, I still think equal exams for everybody would be best, but I guess we are out of time. Bye." In this way, all participants knew that their counterpart, whether they had asked a question or not, had not changed their mind.

At the end of the study, participants filled out questionnaires about their counterpart and their overall impression of the conversation. It turned out that a single elaboration question, even at the end of a lengthy ramble about the glories of comprehensive exams, led the students to see their counterpart in a more positive light. They also saw them as more open-minded.

However, that wasn't the most interesting part. After the study, we assembled all the messages that the real participants wrote. We then showed these messages to three independent raters who had no knowledge of the study hypothesis. These three people found the messages written by the participants who had received the elaboration question to be more receptive and open-minded than the messages written in response to the same pro-exam argument that did not finish with a question. In other words, an elaboration question at the end of an argument encouraged receptive behavior in our participants, even when faced with a disagreeing conversation partner and a topic that might have dramatic consequences for their own future. Similarly to the study I described in Chapter 3 that showed that receptive language was contagious, it seemed that asking an elaboration question elicited a more receptive response from disagreeing counterparts.

What makes elaboration questions work? The previous chapter gives us a good clue: Elaboration questions express curiosity and the desire to learn from a counterpart's perspective. But they are not the only approach. Let me tell you about another.

THERE'S NO SUCH THING AS TOO MANY QUESTIONS

Years ago, my colleague Alison Wood Brooks and I got into an argument. Alison studies conversation and firmly believed that asking more questions is a better approach than asking fewer questions. I disagreed. I recalled the barrage of questions I often face from Ryan and thought that too many questions would be annoying. Alison thought that I was a mediocre conversationalist, not sufficiently concerned with making my counterpart feel heard. I thought she was casually applying a general rule of thumb that just happens to work for her to everyone in the world. Instead of continuing to argue about it, we decided to collect some data.

For these studies, we paired up participants and asked them to "get to know each other." We then left them in the incredibly awkward position of having to chat to a perfect stranger for fifteen minutes. In each pair of participants, one person received no additional instructions and had no idea that anything strange was afoot. However, the second person was told to either ask "at least nine questions"—an amount we knew was theoretically possible but quite high for a fifteen-minute conversation, or to ask "no more than four questions"—a comparatively low amount. We wanted to know which experience the participants who had not received special instructions would like better. So at the end of each conversation, we asked them.

As expected, people who were told to ask nine questions asked more than those who received no instructions, who in turn, asked more than those who were instructed to ask no more than four. Importantly, when we asked the participants how much they liked their partner, the high question-askers were liked *far* more than the low question-askers. Alison was right and I was wrong!

Despite the fact that nine seems like a huge number of questions to ask in a fifteen-minute conversation, people seemed to appreciate it instead of being annoyed by it. In fact, the only part of these results that made me feel better about my own faulty psychological intuition was that, just like me, participants didn't expect this to be the case. When we asked a different group to predict the outcome of the study, they did not think that asking a high number of questions would lead to more positive conversation outcomes than asking a low number of questions. So, participants were as clueless as I was and benefited from our guidance. If we didn't tell them to ask more questions, on their own they wouldn't have thought it was a good idea.

But there was an interesting twist. When we submitted the paper for publication, our reviewers wanted to know *why* question-asking leads to better liking. Like me, they were skeptical and wanted to understand why people weren't annoyed by being asked a ton of questions in one sitting. In order to answer that question, we went back to the transcripts of all those conversations.

We figured out that in the thousands of questions our participants generated, there were several distinct question types. Some were basic introductory questions—"Where do you live?"—and some were the now familiar rhetorical questions, like "Why would you do that?" But the questions that actually increased liking were what we came to call "follow-up" questions—questions that directly referenced what the speaker had just shared while asking about a related topic.

Here is an example of a short conversation:

Participant A: *"What do you like to do for fun?"*

Participant B: *"I love to read biographies."*

Now Participant A has a choice of what to say next:

Option 1: *"I really like sci-fi novels!"*

Option 2: *"Do you have any pets?"*

Option 3: *"Aren't biographies depressing?"*

Option 4: *"What's the best one you've ever read?"*

Option 1 is not a question at all. This is an attempt to make a connection based on shared love of reading—a mistake I myself would have made before seeing our data. Option 2 is a "full switch" question. This person is asking for more information, but it is not connected to what Participant B had just shared. When a person volunteers that they love reading, what they are also saying is that they want to talk about books. Switching the topic shows that you missed part of the point. Option 3 is a rhetorical question. Participant A thinks biographies are depressing (after all, the protagonist normally dies at the end) and wants Participant B to know how they feel. It's a fake question.

The winner is Option 4. This is a real question (it's asking for information), but it also demonstrates that Participant A heard what Participant B wants to talk about. This question demonstrates what psychologists call "responsiveness"—the sense that the person you are interacting with is paying attention to you and caring about your conversational experience (a word that sounds confusingly like "receptiveness" but is actually a different psychological construct). It turned out that in our study the follow-up questions were doing all the work to increase participants' liking of their counterparts. The people who asked their partners questions that directly referenced the last thing that person had said and showed that they cared enough to pursue their partner's topic of interest were rated as more responsive, and it was this responsiveness that made them more likable.

These later results also explain why Alison and I had such different intuitions about what lots of questions do to the dynamics of conversation. Just as I anticipated, based on my kitchen encounters with my husband, a barrage of unrelated questions did not help matters; what worked well was instead asking questions that pursued the topic of conversation set by one's counterpart, thereby demonstrating that you heard what they had shared earlier and were willing to indulge their desire to talk about it. In other words, what matters is not just asking a lot of questions but asking the right kinds of question.

THE DANGERS OF BOOMERASKING

Beyond knowing the right kinds of questions to ask, it's also helpful to know the kinds of questions not to ask. We have already talked about not pelting your partner with a bunch of unrelated questions and trying to sneak in your own argument by hiding it inside a snarky question. Even worse is a crime that my colleague Mike Yeomans calls "boomerasking"—a question that a person asks only because they want to answer it themselves, waiting for the question they sent toward their partner to come back to them like a boomerang. Here is an example:

Participant A: *"How was your summer?"*

Participant B: *"It was good. We went to visit my parents in Colorado, although getting there was kind of a nightmare."*

Participant A: *"Our summer was great too! We went on a beach vacation in Florida, and Suzy and her new boyfriend came with us, and you know, he is a really nice guy. I really like him. He is thinking about going to law school and I hope that they make it work, because I think he would be really good for her. I mean you know how she's been . . . But the beach was so nice, and we discovered this great little place in Pensacola and I am thinking that maybe we should get a condo down there, you know, in case Suzy marries this guy, and wouldn't it be great to be able to vacation all together?"*

If you are Participant B in this scenario, you have just received a clear message that Participant A did not really want to hear about your summer, or your aging parents, or how much you currently hate one particular airline. Instead, they boomerasked the question, knowing that you would ask the same question back to them out of politeness. They then used this opportunity to talk about their fabulous vacation, the fact that Suzy finally has a new boyfriend who is going to law school, and even managed to throw in the fact that they will soon be proud owners of a condo in Pensacola.

Boomerasking feels tempting when people want to share information with their counterpart but don't know how to introduce it into the conversation. Instead of simply saying what we want to say, we pretend to care about our counterpart's perspective just long enough to have an excuse to say what we've wanted to all along. In a series of experiments Mike Yeomans and his colleagues conducted on this topic, people consistently underestimated the negative consequences of this approach. Instead of conveying curiosity, as questions are intended to, boomerasks convey a lack of sincerity. The recipient knows that the question was simply an entry point for the question asker to start talking about themselves and, not surprisingly, they don't appreciate being taken advantage of.

Although boomerasking has primarily been studied in nonconflictual conversations, you can easily imagine how it might seem like a good idea but ultimately backfire in the case of a simmering conflict. Think of a person who does not know how to bring up the fact that they are frustrated or unhappy with a particular situation. They might decide that asking their counterpart a question will then give them the license to answer that question themselves, which will allow them a smooth entry into sharing their own feelings.

For example, picture walking into your manager's office for your weekly project check-in and his asking you, "So, Stephen, how do you think the project is going right now?" Not realizing that you are about to step on a land mine, you say, "I think it's going pretty well. We've all been working long hours because a lot of the projections Sherry had done last quarter needed to be redone, given the results of the launch. But the team doesn't mind because we all realize how important this work is. Thank you for asking."

Instead of praising you for your commitment, asking about how the projections are changing, or offering additional resources, your manager says instead, "Well, let me tell you how I think it's going . . . I have been hearing a lot of negative feedback from the team about the lack of effective project management that has been leading to ridiculously long hours. In fact, HR is starting to get wind of this, and frankly the project budget can't support all this overtime. Plus, Sherry feels like her reputation has been undercut because the launch seemed to falsify the assumptions in her projections, and you know that she is really tight with the client team. On top of that, other clients are wondering why their needs are not being addressed. I mean, I really don't know what's going on over there. Why didn't you tell me there were problems?"

Consider what the manager just communicated with this classic boomerask: *When I ask you questions, it is not because I am curious about the answer but because I am too uncomfortable to offer negative feedback directly. I will pretend to be curious but offer no support or responsiveness if you disclose something vulnerable or negative. Next time I ask a question, don't bother answering because I am not really looking for information.* The recipient of such a boomerask now likely feels that they have been "tricked" into thinking that this was a conversation about them and their needs, and probably feels more resentful than if their manager had begun the conversation by stating that they had heard negative feedback and wished to discuss it.

Boomerasking stems not only from people's inherent discomfort with directness. Ironically, it is likely an unfortunate byproduct of our well-intentioned idea that simply asking more questions will improve the outcome of most disagreements. The manager in the above example might have been following such advice by beginning the conversation about the struggling project with a question. The problem, however, is that people are not that easily fooled. You can't ask a single question, barely listen to a short answer, and then launch into your own version of the events. Remember, the point of asking questions is to demonstrate one's curiosity and caring. And in conflict, where your counterpart is likely to be skeptical about those very things, you have to try a little harder. Boomeraskers remind me of the old scene in *Winnie-the-Pooh* when Pooh tries to steal honey from a beehive by grabbing on to a blue helium balloon and pretending that he is a little rain cloud. But the bees are not that dumb and sting the silly old bear all over his cute velvet nose. Like bees, people are not that dumb. If you want to show caring and curiosity through question-asking, you have to make more than a minimal effort. Otherwise, you get stung on the nose.

ASKING INAPPROPRIATE QUESTIONS

Yet another common question-asking error that is particularly relevant to disagreement comes from research by my friend Einav Hart, a professor at George Mason University. Whenever I talk to Einav, she has a mischievous gleam in her eye and a sardonic tone to her voice. It somehow seems fitting that one of the things she does is make people ask each other inappropriate questions to see how their conversation counterparts react.

Different people and certainly different cultures consider different lines of questioning "inappropriate." However, there are some common topics, including asking about money, religion, and sexual practices, that most people agree are off the table in casual conversation. In her research, Einav and her coauthors defined sensitive questions as questions that are 1) about topics that are uncomfortable to discuss, 2) inappropriate for the social context, or 3) about information respondents would rather keep private. Yet one can imagine how avoiding any topic that fits these parameters puts important constraints on our ability to navigate conflict. Oftentimes the answer to why someone is upset, avoidant, or angry has to do with money, politics, sex, or some other delicate topic that might be considered inappropriate in whatever culture or context you are in.

The good news is that Einav's research finds that people dramatically overestimate the discomfort caused by such questions. In other words, question askers think that they will make their counterpart uncomfortable by "going there," but their counterparts actually appreciate having the ability to talk about something that they rarely get to discuss. In order to conduct these studies, the researchers came up with a long list of questions and had people rate them in terms of awkwardness, invasiveness, and inappropriateness. The "winners" in the awkwardness category included such gems as "Have you ever had an affair?" "How much is your salary?" and "What are your views on abortion?" By contrast, questions that were not considered particularly sensitive included pretty vanilla topics, such as "What are you views about the weather?" "What are your current job responsibilities?" and "Are you a morning person?"

Having generated lists of sensitive and nonsensitive questions, researchers then went on to arrange conversations where, in each pair, one participant received special instructions and the other did not. In half of the pairs, these special instructions required the participant to ask their counterpart questions from the sensitive list. In the other half of the pairs, the special instructions only contained questions from the vanilla, nonsensitive list. As in the other studies I described earlier, the counterparts of the participants that received the special instructions did not know that anything was amiss—they were just in a chat with a person who was asking them a bunch of questions, either a little risqué or totally boring.

At the end of the study, all participants had to report how they thought the conversation went and how much their partner enjoyed it. Perhaps not surprisingly, the participants who were assigned to ask perfect strangers about their history of sexual infidelity, their illegal drug use, and their views on abortion expected their counterparts to have been uncomfortable and to form somewhat less favorable impressions of them. However, it turns out that they were wrong. The participants on the receiving ends of the questions were equally comfortable with both question types. In other words, in the same conversation, the question askers and their counterparts had different ideas about how the same behavior would be experienced and interpreted. The questions that people normally avoid asking for fear of making somebody uncomfortable turned out to be pretty benign. But what does this have to do with conflict?

We often fail to inquire about our counterpart's beliefs, reactions, or experiences specifically to avoid generating discomfort. But it turns out that people love talking about themselves! Humans have a powerful need for self-expression and to be seen by others as they see themselves. Being asked questions that might feel uncomfortable for the asker presents the respondent with an opportunity to discuss something that might weigh heavily on them and that they have had few opportunities to talk about. Asking a seemingly inappropriate question in a way that demonstrates care and genuine desire to understand your counterpart's perspective can, in fact, be seen as the asker going out on a limb for the respondent's benefit.

Safely deploying sensitive questions in the real world might take a bit of finesse, but that does not mean you should simply avoid them for the sake of etiquette. For example, you might precede a sensitive question with a bit of a trigger warning: "Hey, I've been meaning to ask you something for a long time, and I didn't know how to go about it in case it makes you uncomfortable. Is it okay if I ask you something about your relationship with Michelle?" This "soft ask" allows the other person to mentally prepare themselves or to reply by saying that this is not a good time. It also communicates that you are putting work into trying to be thoughtful and sensitive, not just leaping into a difficult topic out of reflexive nosiness. Of course, when asking a sensitive question, you should settle in, prepare to listen to the answer, and potentially ask several follow-up questions. For example, if the answer to the above is "Michelle lost all of our money to her gambling addiction and I am about to file for divorce," you can't just switch to a discussion of the latest season of *The Bear* and duck out of the conversation in thirty seconds. Showing curiosity and responsiveness is still required, even if, and especially if, the conversation turns out to be incredibly uncomfortable for everyone.

CHAPTER SUMMARY

- Although question-asking is an important part of navigating disagreement effectively, not all questions are created equal, and people make consistent mistakes in their question-asking behavior. One of the worst is giving ourselves way too much credit for snarky, gotcha questions. A good mental rule of thumb is that if asking a question in a disagreement made you feel superior relative to your counterpart, you probably should not have asked it.

- Keep an eye out for "boomerasking"—asking a question to fake curiosity so that you can slip your own point of view into the next conversational turn. Remember that people are smart, and we all have decades of conversational practice to draw on. Recipients recognize that a boomerask is a fake question, which often makes this move backfire.

- Two kinds of questions work well because they also show at least some awareness of your partner's perspective and behaviorally demonstrate good listening:
    1. Elaboration questions, which ask your partner to elaborate on their views, tacitly recognizing that those views are likely different from your own.
    2. Follow-up questions, which require a person to have listened carefully to the answer to the previous question and ask something related.

- In disagreement, these two question types can work sequentially. An effective approach is to start with an elaboration question, listen to the response, and then continue with a series of follow-up questions, each one gathering more information about your counterpart's perspective and further demonstrating that you have heard and processed their response.

- Don't be scared of sensitive questions. If you are prepared to buckle down and show curiosity and concern for as long as it takes the other person to talk themselves out, they will likely appreciate your broaching of the topic.

6

LISTENING WITH YOUR WORDS

THE PREVIOUS TWO CHAPTERS HAVE OUTLINED TWO KEY ELE-ments of receptive behavior: 1) signaling that your goal is to learn about and understand your counterpart's perspective; and 2) asking additional questions to get more information and show that you are really listening via the questions you ask. But how many questions are you supposed to ask? When do you know that you are done? How can you be confident that you have truly understood your counterpart's point of view and have enough information to sensibly address their (clearly misguided) beliefs? It turns out that actually understanding someone else in a way that convinces them they have been understood is trickier than most people believe.

The psychological research literature boasts hundreds of studies on the phenomenon of "perspective-taking"—the ability to see things from another person's point of view. Psychologists are fascinated with perspective-taking because it's a uniquely human experience, infinitely more sophisticated than what our closest animal relatives can accomplish with their brains. Most other animals have no idea that they have a mind, let alone that their peers do as well. Being able to infer what is going on in someone else's head would seem like magic to a dog, if dogs understood the concept of magic.

In addition to the feeling of evolutionary superiority, perspective-taking is fun to contemplate because it is a great feeling. The sense that you "get it" and are "on the same wavelength" fosters a profound feeling of connectedness with others. It's as if all of us can do a little bit of mind reading. The problem is that the feeling is mostly illusory.

Recently, an international group of psychologists published a paper containing twenty-five different experiments involving thousands of participants to test whether people could accurately take on the perspective of another individual. It's one thing to claim that you are good at seeing the world from another's point of view. It's quite another to show experimentally that the person who is trying hard to take another's perspective is any more accurate about that person's preferences, needs, or beliefs than a different person just guessing about those things based on the contents of their own brain.

It turns out that people are terrible perspective takers. In one experiment after another, people trying to take on another's perspective failed to make accurate inferences about the person whose mind they were contemplating. People thought that they knew what the other person believed, but when tested, they turned out to be wrong. In fact, they were wrong so often that the journal reviewers were initially skeptical of the results. The authors of the article kept collecting more data to make an even stronger case. Across many tasks, in the Middle East and in the United States, strangers, friends, and spouses all failed to accurately see the world from another's point of view. An even bigger problem, however, was people's convictions about how accurate they were. When asked how sure they were that a particular guess was correct, people were vastly overconfident in their inferences regarding others' beliefs and preferences relative to how accurate they actually were according to objective measures.

Both our perspective-taking failures and our blindness to them are bad news for conflict outcomes. Remember that in conflict settings, a few things are already stacking up to make having a productive conversation more difficult. First, we tend to make negative assumptions about the other side's motives. Second, we are not particularly excited about exploring and testing those assumptions because conversations about disagreement are unpleasant. On top of that, we feel strongly that we already understand the other person because we tried hard to take their perspective and came to some sensible-sounding conclusions. The likely result is that we will never actually stop arguing long enough to seriously interrogate our own beliefs. Indeed, now that I've told you that perspective-taking mostly doesn't work, it's not clear how one would even go about it.

Should we just make peace with the fact that like in the case of our animal cousins, our minds are inaccessible to each other, or is there a better way? Of course there is—it's language! In fact, in the twenty-fifth experiment of the paper, the authors offered the participants a simple intervention. They instructed romantic couples to have a five-minute conversation. Having a short time to simply use words to ask for and receive information on the relevant topics made the aspiring perspective-takers dramatically more accurate at predicting how their counterparts felt. The authors termed this technique "perspective-getting."

On one hand, this finding feels obvious: Of course talking gets you more information! But on the other hand, it also illustrates the massive levels of misunderstanding that exist even in the closest relationships. People who think that they know each other intimately still learned about each other after talking for *five minutes*!

The part of these experimental results that disturbs me the

most, however, is the level of overconfidence people reported with regard to their perspective-taking. We have already talked about the idea that overconfidence can be a very costly bias. Just as people are overconfident in their ability to win arguments, people are also overconfident in their understanding of the world around them, including the contents of others' minds. Overconfidence in our perspective-taking abilities leads us to assume that we understand where our counterpart is coming from long before we actually do. Even when we signal our desire to learn and ask our partner to explain their perspective, we often fill in the gaps in their (usually poor) storytelling with our own assumptions and biases. As a result of thinking that we understand what they have to say long before we really do, we launch into our rebuttals prematurely. Because listening to someone we strongly disagree with is not very fun, we are motivated to assume that we've learned all there is to learn long before we truly have. This combination of overconfidence in our perspective-taking skills and aversion to letting the other side talk often leads people into trouble even when they go into the conversation with the best of intentions. So how do we know that we have really done enough listening and it's our turn to talk? How do we know we fully understand the other person's point of view? The answer is simple—when *they tell us so* with words.

WHAT MEDIATORS KNOW ABOUT LISTENING

If you want to see question-asking and expressions of curiosity performed masterfully, watch a professional mediator practice their craft. Mediators have hard jobs. Daily, they walk into conflicts that have reached such a fevered pitch as to require professional help because the parties simply can't deal with each other any longer. They will intervene in a divorce complete with a custody battle, a contract renegotiation between factory workers and a large corporation, and the latest flare-up in a generations-long ethnic conflict. The mediator is often received with hostility because both sides expect them to be biased in favor of the other. They must build trust, figure out the underlying facts of the dispute, and cool down people's emotions—all before the parties run out of patience and storm out of the room again. Some mediators work alone, hanging up a solo practitioner shingle like your neighborhood mechanic; some work for large firms; and some work for national and international agencies whose mission is to stop people from sinking more time, money, and lives into unwinnable conflicts.

As a researcher, I find the mediation profession fascinating—for me, it is the path not taken, the one that got away; the grittier, more practical, more *real* version of my own professional life. Of course, as soon as I had a chance, I dragged some real mediators into my classroom so that I could mine their expertise for new ideas. This is how I met Hawk and Moira.

Unlike what the names suggest, Hawk and Moira are not undercover agents with secret identities. Hawk is actually Kevin Hawkins, a six-foot-five Black man with graying hair and the warmest smile you've seen on anyone besides Santa Claus. To his friends he is "Hawk," and since I've never seen anyone not become his friend within seconds, I've never actually seen anyone call him Kevin. Moira is Moira Caruso, a petite Irish American woman from North Carolina who in four-inch heels barely reaches Hawk's shoulder but makes up for her size with an unrivaled mixture of conviction and sass. Mediators often work in pairs, and these two have worked together enough that she knows all his food quirks and cocktail preferences and he calls her "Sis."

When I met them, Hawk and Moira worked for the Federal Mediation and Conciliation Service (FMCS), a small agency of the United States federal government, and one I suspect most of you have never heard of. FMCS was created in 1947 by an act of Congress with the mandate to minimize the impact of labor-management conflicts on the flow of U.S. commerce. As the labor movement gained both popular and legal support in the United States, the federal government decided that it might be a very good idea to employ a team of conflict management professionals to make sure that every dispute between a union and a corporation did not end in a strike, and every strike did not last as long as it would take overconfident humans to come to their senses. Ever since then, a few dozen federal mediators have been crisscrossing the country, shuttling from conflict to conflict, conference room to conference room, keeping our trucks running, our phones working, and our nurses and meatpackers only using sharp instruments for their intended purpose.

In fulfillment of that mission, at the height of the COVID-19 pandemic, Moira found herself mediating a resource management dispute between the leadership of a U.S. state and several indigenous tribes. Although the details below have been altered slightly to protect the confidentiality of the parties and simplified to focus on the key events, the story is an important illustration of the process that must unfold for conflict counterparts to ultimately come to feel understood.

The parties in the conflict (state representatives and tribal leaders) were negotiating regulations around the management of a species of elk that was growing scarcer by the year and was extremely important to everyone involved—for sport, tourism, subsistence, and cultural value. A multiyear resource management plan previously agreed to by the state and the tribes had collapsed, and parties were negotiating yearly—which is to say that as soon as a deal for any given year was reached, it was time to start negotiating again. Over two dozen tribes had some stake in the management of the elk population, so not only was the state constantly negotiating, but it was doing so with each tribe separately, investing ridiculous amounts of time and resources and often pitting the tribes against one another.

At the initial assessment conducted by the mediation team and involving all the parties, it seemed that all anyone wanted to do was blame and accuse. But one key issue of contention became central. The state and the tribes could not agree on whether to apply the latest version of a widely accepted assessment model (we'll call it "the MV3") to predict how a host of environmental factors would affect future elk population levels. The state thought this was a no-brainer. Why not update to the latest model to get the most accurate data? When the tribes hesitated, the state assumed that they were holding out due to sheer stubborn spite, to intentionally prevent an agreement from emerging, and in this way to show their power over the process. By contrast, the tribal managers saw the MV3 as the latest way for the state to ram new and damaging policies down their throats. They saw absolutely no reason to agree to it.

In meetings with the individual parties, Moira noticed that all parties kept bringing up the same term—"best available science"—but using it in different contexts. On the one hand, the refrain of the state was "They won't even agree that MV3 is the best available science!" By contrast, the tribes would claim, "They use MV3 in the name of 'best available science' to cover all manner of sin!"

When Moira asked what they mean by "best available science," the parties looked at her as if she had just asked whether grass was green. It seemed that the only thing that parties *could* agree on was that this was a ridiculous question! Of course, everyone knew what "best available science" meant! But Moira suspected that perhaps there was more to it, since the term came up so often and seemed charged with meaning and emotion. The mediation team organized a facilitated discussion to understand how the parties really understood the term.

When session participants wrote down anonymous definitions of "best available science," it became clear that the seemingly harmless phrase brought up different and powerful associations for different people. Here are some of the responses that were offered:

1. "Best Available Science = manipulation to meet a desired outcome."

2. "Why does it matter. There's no political will to follow best available science."

3. "MV3 is simply data. It doesn't have a will or an agenda. The facts are facts. How can you argue with fact??????"

4. "It has to be agreed to by the co-managers."

Having examined the various reactions, Moira asked for more clarification around number 4.

"For the person who offered this, or anyone who feels similarly: Do you mean that you feel the tribal co-managers have to *agree* with the science if it is ever to be used?" On one hand, this seemed like another goofy question. How could anyone agree or disagree with science? Wasn't the point of science that it was objective and for everyone?

But discussing the question prompted the sharing of several stories about how communication of research findings has failed in the past. Specifically, the tribes found prior briefings overly technical and lacking useful insights. They also felt that the reports from the state contained bias, featuring additional conclusions that were not supported by the data.

A tribal rep spoke up: "This comment with all the question marks . . . the one about arguing with facts. What do you have to say about the fact that personal beliefs and information that's not supported by the MV3 report winds up in your damn policies? How is that 'best available science'?"

Not surprisingly, that comment led to a lot of back-and-forth, until Moira asked another innocent-seeming question: "I wonder if the state could talk a little bit about the decision-making and communications that accompany the data when it is given over to the tribes?"

As the state representatives went about explaining their process for turning raw data into reports and policies, one of them voiced a realization: "We are conflating science with data. MV3 is just data. Science is a process of inquiry; of synthesizing and analyzing data—that's science. That process could improve, and it could be more clear, inclusive, and transparent."

Another state rep added: "The data will never be perfect, and we'll always be revisiting what we know, but we need to act on something in the meantime."

With this, the mediation team had some items to test with the group. (In mediation-speak, "test" means ask another question to see whether a particular person's articulation of where things stand fits other people's impressions.)

Moira: *"It sounds like we're getting a better sense of what's been bothering our co-managers. Could we check for some understanding?"*

A spokesman from the state responded first: "We hear (and frankly agree with) the sentiment that how we talk about some of the data is overly technical at times and probably should tell more of a story. It could also contain some disclaimers about assumptions made."

Moira: *"Does that sound right?"*

A few people nodded thoughtfully.

Moira: *"Okay, how about something from the tribes?"*

A spokesman from one of the tribes responded: "I think we can obviously agree that MV3 is the best of the data that exists. And yeah, a lot of . . . maybe all of our frustration comes from the rest of what is actually being called 'science,' the process and the decisions that are made before and after the data comes out. If we can make some headway there, I think we've done something."

At the end of the meeting, the parties agreed to MV3 as the basis for modeling in what, mere months later, would become a ten-year overarching resource management plan between the state and tribal co-managers. More than 120 people reached agreement over a series of Zoom calls—a feat that many thought was impossible—because persistent and thoughtful question-asking uncovered the root of the disagreement, even though everyone *thought* they already knew what the root was.

THE LISTENING TRIANGLE

Moira's story is an example of leveraging the Listening Triangle, a technique used by many mediators that closely dovetails the research-backed approaches in the previous chapters and offers an excellent framework for putting the pieces together. Although this approach was first systematically described by Moshe Cohen (another Boston-based mediator) as a tool to be used by conflict management professionals, different variations are frequently used under other names and mere mortals can also take advantage of it as long as we put in some patient practice.

Step 1 in the Listening Triangle is expressing one's desire to learn. Because a mediator is not party to the conflict and has not seen it unfold, they might say something like: "I would like to understand your point of view. Why don't you tell me what happened?" By contrast, if the conflict is your own, you might use one of the phrases from the earlier chapter: "I understand that you and I disagree on this. I'd like to hear your perspective." Or "It seems you are upset with me now. Can you tell me how you are thinking about this situation?" Another humorous but profound formulation of Step 1 can be found in the work of yet another excellent mediator, Adar Cohen, who likes to frequently remind himself and everyone around him of a grounding fact: "You don't know anything." If a person doesn't know anything, it suddenly becomes okay for that person to ask questions. Indeed, it might be okay to even ask those questions to which a different person *thinks* they ought to know the answer, like "What is 'best available science'?" As you might imagine, Step 1 requires overcoming some amount of pride and overconfidence. Even if you think you know, just assume for a second that you don't, and ask.

Step 2 is listening to the answer. Step 2 might sound easy, but it's not. Listening is hard for several reasons: The reason you are having this conversation in the first place is because there is disagreement. It is likely that the first thing your counterpart says will be something you think is inaccurate or even offensive and that you wish to "correct." Because you are also likely to believe that "you get it," you might decide that you don't need to hear any more (remember, most people are overconfident in their perspective-taking abilities). In order to execute Step 2 well, you must resist the powerful temptation to interrupt.

That temptation is increased by the fact that your counterpart, who is probably also not thrilled to be in this conversation and may be a little nervous as a result, is likely to be rambling and disorganized in their explanation of whatever is happening from their point of view. When I try to execute the Listening Triangle, I often find myself irritated that the person speaking keeps bringing up multiple seemingly disconnected points, repeating themselves, circling back, contradicting their own earlier statements, and generally confirming my earlier belief that they are being emotional and unreasonable. When will I get to talk and tell them why they are soooo wrong about everything? The key to executing the Listening Triangle correctly, though, is to take a deep breath and keep your mouth shut.

In Moira's case, which occurred on Zoom with over a hundred people representing the state and a dozen native tribes, listening took not minutes but hours. For a mediator or a diplomat this is not uncommon—part of the task is letting parties recall old grievances, share concerns, vent, find connections between different events, or talk about their kids. All of this investment of time and emotional self-control serves to gather information and show your commitment to the process of understanding and your willingness to do whatever it takes. Next time you struggle to listen for ten minutes without interrupting, just thank your lucky stars that you are not a professional mediator!

Step 3 begins when the speaker comes up for air. Mediators and therapists call it "reflection." Reflection is simply using words to behaviorally demonstrate to your counterpart that you have indeed been listening. For example, you might say: "So let me see if I've got this right . . ." And then you try to earnestly and to the best of your recollection repeat what you just heard.

There are several features that are important to performing reflection effectively. First, your reflection can't be a caricature of the speaker's perspective. For example, you can't say, "So you are saying that I am a terrible manager, and everything wrong with our performance this quarter is my fault, and you are just a genius

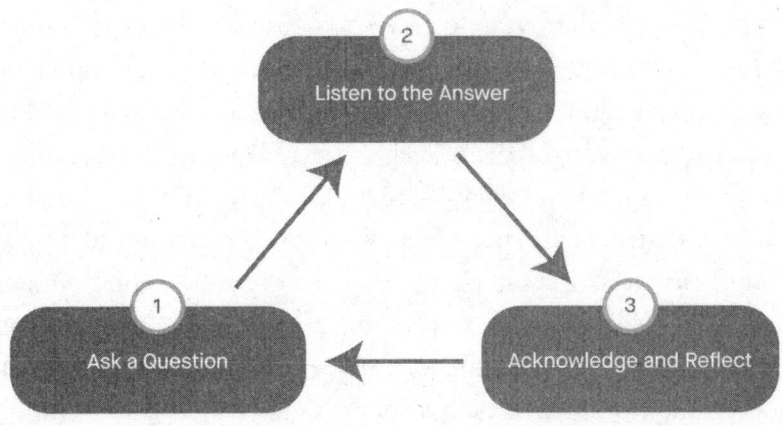

because you saw it all coming!" That might have been exactly what they were saying, but once again, snark is not going to help you. Second, you can't use this time to subtly begin counterarguing, "You seem to think that I have been neglectful of my managerial responsibilities (which, by the way, I kind of disagree with), and also, with regard to our performance this quarter . . ." Finally, reflection is not an IQ test. The goal is not to demonstrate to your partner that you have incredible working memory and can repeat what they said verbatim (which can also sound like a caricature). Rather, the goal is to show that you are trying your hardest to understand them, which can be best achieved by paraphrasing, even if you get some things wrong.

The key to a successful execution of the Listening Triangle is to finish the reflection step with another question: "Did I get that right? Is there anything I missed?" This is the "testing for understanding" that Moira referred to in her story. What most people find surprising is that even if the mediator (or you) did an excellent job listening and reflecting, the speaker is likely to then say something like, "Well, that's kind of it, but there are a couple of things that I guess I didn't mention. I think this is also connected to that situation last year. Remember when Irene quit, and she said . . ."—and then your counterpart just keeps talking. They might restate some of what they said before, they might add new details, they might contradict themselves and confuse you, but again, the key is to let them keep going. When they seem done, you again reflect what they shared: "Okay, so I am now understanding that part of the reason you are so upset about this is because this feels like a continuation of the Irene situation and when I didn't respond to your email it sounds like it made you think . . ." And after you are done reflecting, guess what? You ask another question: "So does that sound right? Am I understanding correctly?"

The Listening Triangle is a cycle. Every round of question > listening > reflection leads to another question that sets the whole thing in motion again. On each round, more details emerge, more clarity is achieved, and the listener has a chance to prove with their behavior (through verbal reflection) that they are really hearing the speaker and are interested in getting it right.

Students in conflict management courses are often surprised by how many rounds of the Listening Triangle happen before a speaker is fully "talked out." Yet the investment of time is well worth it. At the end of the exercise the listener can be confident that they truly understand the speaker because the speaker has verbally confirmed that the listener finally got it right. The speaker, on the other hand, has felt truly heard because over and over the listener verbally demonstrated that they have in fact been listening. The power of the Listening Triangle is that it makes it so humans don't need to be mind readers: We can use language, the most sophisticated cultural accomplishment of our civilization, to prove to each other that we are listening and to know for sure the moment when we have successfully grasped the contents of someone's mind.

A common conclusion of this process is for the speaker to turn to the listener and say, "Well, that's what I think. But I am curious how you feel about this." That's when you finally know you've got it.

MASTERING THE LISTENING TRIANGLE

Like most ideas in this book, the Listening Triangle is deceptively simple. Memorizing three steps is easy, but consistently executing them when you are angry, confused, or exhausted is very difficult. The key is to master the technique to such an extent that it becomes your default when you suddenly find yourself in need of it. Here is a simple approach for getting some practice rounds in.

Find a friend, family member, or a coworker and ask them about their day or what they did the previous weekend. The key is to find a topic that you don't know about so that you can ask genuine questions, but also one that is pretty harmless so that this first practice conversation does not arouse any strong emotions. Plan to practice the Listening Triangle for at least fifteen minutes—unless your counterpart is very chatty, you will find that fifteen minutes feels like an eternity!

Begin with Step 1 to get the conversation going: "Hey, how was your day? What happened at work?" or, alternatively, "How'd last weekend go? You had some big plans, right?"

Pre-commit yourself to listening attentively for Step 2. If your counterpart gets talking, don't interrupt, don't jump in to tell them about how your boss is *also* a jerk, or how you also loved the new Chinese restaurant. If your counterpart keeps going and going, try not to space out. Let them talk while showering them with nonverbal and paralinguistic signals of attention—nodding, saying things like "uh-huh" and "hmm," smiling if they are telling you something positive and frowning if they are telling you something negative. The point is that Step 2 is all about your counterpart—you are giving them what amounts to a mental back rub, and if you are bored and your hands are sore, too bad.

Step 3 comes in when you sense a pause in their narrative. Here, you have to make sure that you resist the urge to turn the spotlight on yourself. Remember, your goal is to use words to show them that you were paying attention. Try to reflect back to them what you just heard, not by restating the mere events your partner conveyed but rather by paraphrasing what you believe the events made your counterpart feel or think. For example, saying, "It sounds like you went to the new Chinese restaurant and your dad had the Peking duck" would be a pretty weird reflection. However, saying, "So it sounds like you had a surprisingly good time with your dad at dinner. And who knew he liked Peking duck?" makes it sound like you understood the underlying sentiment behind your friend's restaurant story.

Now remember that this is a cycle. Step 3 is supposed to lead back to Step 1—the one that shows that you are interested and would like to hear even more. You might say, "What do you think made this dinner with your dad different? As I remember, it doesn't always go that well, right?" Or "That's interesting what he said about your sister. What do you make of that?" A question like this shows that you are fully engaged in the conversation, are curious to hear more, and are even connecting this conversation to prior times your counterpart shared something about their family relationships. Now that you have set the cycle back in motion, sit back, relax, and try not to interrupt.

During your first few attempts at the Listening Triangle, you might find a few things surprising. First, some people find it difficult to resist making an interpersonal connection by talking about their own similar experiences or reactions. Agreement and validation feel good, and as soon as your partner says something that you can relate to, it's tempting to interrupt and point out that you have also had a similar experience and then launch into your own narrative. Personally, I am perpetually guilty of this conversational error, so I try to keep an eye out for it and correct myself in the moment. The risk is that if you start talking about how you also really liked the new Chinese restaurant, you might take the conversation in a totally different direction. Your counterpart might have wanted to share the intimate details of their family drama but instead find themselves discussing different ways of frying tofu. Yes, it might be an interesting conversation, but not the one they were trying to have.

The second challenge is that some people are chatty and some people are not. When a person gives you a relatively short answer to a question, it often feels difficult to think of a good follow-up question quickly enough. If they continue to give short answers, you might have to ask ten questions in a practice period just to fill the fifteen minutes of the exercise. Observe your own struggle and consider why you can't think of anything to ask. Is it that you don't really care about what they did last weekend? Is it that you are embarrassed to not know certain things? Is it that none of the questions you can come up with seem sufficiently interesting or thought-provoking?

If you struggle with asking questions that seem sufficiently clever, remember that the Listening Triangle is not about you. You are not the star. You are simply using questions to prompt the other person to share *their* story. When I was first married, I had one consistent experience when I would attend work parties with my husband. A group of near-strangers would awkwardly gather around some catered appetizers and try to make conversation. Somebody would say something inoffensive and not particularly interesting and then there would be an awkward lull. My strategy for filling the lull was always to tell a funny, charming (usually too-long) story about something that happened to me. Ryan's strategy was always to ask a follow-up question. The questions he asked were also usually of the mostly inoffensive and (in my mind) not particularly interesting variety. I always tried to be clever and funny and provocative. He asked people how their flight was or what they thought of the cheese plate. The surprising thing was that people loved answering his questions. They quickly went from talking about their flight, to describing their entire trip, including its purpose, its highlights, and how it changed their view about the merits of ecotourism or the American Southwest. Next thing you know, everyone in the group would be swapping travel stories, complaining about luggage fees, and recommending favorite restaurants in distant cities. Rather than listening to one person telling a story, everyone was sharing, engaging, and having a good time.

I used to struggle with asking simple questions because I was trying to come across as smart, funny, and interesting. But that's not the point. The point is to make your counterpart feel as if *they* are smart, funny, and interesting. The questions themselves don't have to be brilliant.

The reflection step can also lead to some surprising experiences. Successfully restating your partner's perspective in a way that feels accurate to them can feel incredibly gratifying to both people. It is really nice to hear somebody say, "Yeah, you are right. That *did* make me feel uncomfortable! What was he thinking inviting himself over to our house? I am glad you also recognize that it's a weird thing to do!" In this interaction, the speaker feels good for having been understood, and the listener feels good for being the kind of person that "gets it." However, a surprising amount of time we get it wrong. "No, that did not make me uncomfortable . . . I mean, we've been friends for a long time, and he stays over all the time. It's just that I was stressed about work, and I didn't really feel like watching TV all weekend." However, moments when reflection doesn't "work" are not the end of the world. You listened to somebody, restated what you thought they were trying to say, but it turns out that's not what they were really trying to say. Maybe there is more to it, or maybe the flavor wasn't exactly right, or maybe you tried to impose your own understanding and interpretation on their story. Don't get weird and offended or (worst mistake ever!) tell the other person that they were supposed to feel the way you thought they felt. Just say, "Oh, that's interesting. So, what happened then?" Remember, the Listening Triangle is a cycle. The cycle just keeps going.

Practicing the Listening Triangle on safe topics like weekend plans and favorite recipes is a good way to build up the microhabits involved in the process and to understand which aspects you struggle with. As you start feeling more and more comfortable with the rhythm of the cycle, try increasing the difficulty of the topic. Don't leap right into reproductive rights or who is right or wrong in the Middle East, but maybe try to understand why your coworker never recycles their soda cans or why your friend insists on buying plants that keep dying on their windowsill. Going from a completely inane topic to one with a potential for mild conflict will help you experience what it's like to ask questions and restate somebody's perspective when it is likely that you have already made a negative attribution about them and the reasons for their behavior. In this case, you must go beyond trying to be curious and exerting the mental effort to come up with a question, to also overriding your own confidence in your negative assumptions so that your questions are true questions. When you become comfortable with the Listening Triangle and can apply it across a variety of different situations, ranging from minor household disagreements to difficult conversations about identity or policy, you will know that you are ready for the next phase of a disagreement—the one you've been dying to get to all along—making your own argument.

CHAPTER SUMMARY

- People have a difficult time gauging whether they really understand others and tend to assume that they do even when they don't.

- To ensure that you have really understood your counterpart and to also make them *feel* understood, you can practice the Listening Triangle:
    1. Ask a question.
    2. Listen to the answer.
    3. Reflect back.
    4. Start from the beginning.

- The Listening Triangle enables you to show that you are listening, using words to demonstrate first your curiosity, then your understanding. In deciding whether you do or don't understand the point your partner is making, wait for them to verbally confirm before you assume that you now get it.

- Practice the Listening Triangle on trivial topics with little potential for conflict before escalating to more challenging settings.

7

THE H.E.A.R. FRAMEWORK—SHOWING RECEPTIVENESS WHILE MAKING YOUR POINT

AT THIS POINT IN OUR DISCUSSION, YOU SHOULD HAVE SOME VERY solid ideas about how to take any conversation and insert a dose of curiosity and responsiveness so that you can come to understand why exactly the person across from you is insisting on whatever crazy thing they are insisting on. These tools can serve you in two ways—they can de-escalate what would otherwise be a yelling match into a sensible conversation where your counterpart comes to feel truly understood and respected; *and* they can end the cycle of silent rumination in your own head because you might finally come appreciate that the other person does in fact have some sensible reasons to believe whatever they believe. All of this is a very good start to having an easier, more peaceful life among other people and improving your ability to work with them on difficult things like parenting or climate policy.

Nevertheless, although using behavior to signal the desire to learn and demonstrating high-quality listening can have powerful effects, everything we've discussed so far has carefully circumvented the proverbial elephant in the room. Namely, we have done nothing to address how *you*—the person who has been patiently expressing curiosity, asking good questions, and reflecting your counterpart's perspective—can also make your point and be heard. With all this listening and question-asking, when do you get to talk?

You want—indeed, you need—to make your case too. In fact, this need may be one of the main reasons why you fail to execute on the well-meaning advice of therapists and conflict coaches to be more empathetic and curious. All that empathy and curiosity take a great deal of work and patience, patience you generally don't have and work you don't really want to do. When you are being honest with yourself, you understandably wonder what's in it for you. Since you are probably not a professional therapist, you might feel that it is not your job to listen patiently while other people vent, especially when you believe you are right. If you think you just need to say your piece and have the other person acknowledge your rightness, you might be forgiven if you feel tempted to skip all the question-asking fluff and get to the point. Indeed, there are many situations where saying what you came to say feels worth it, even if some feathers get ruffled along the way.

However, there is a big difference between ruffling a few feathers and starting World War III. Indeed, in many cases, people don't go into disagreements intending to start a big conflict. It just sort of sneaks up on them. The challenge is figuring out how to say what you want to say while minimizing the risk of a big blowup. Is there any way to make a clear case for your own point without setting the conversation on fire? How can you explain your side while continuing to demonstrate receptiveness? The next two chapters will give you a "starter tool kit" for achieving this objective.

CAPTURING CONVERSATIONAL RECEPTIVENESS

In Chapter 3, I told you about a simple study during which government executives discussed hot-button policy issues and then rated how receptive their counterpart had been during the conversation. You might remember that the study was a disappointment because participants' ratings of their own receptiveness did not match their partners' evaluations of them. Furthermore, how receptive a person thought they had been during the interaction did not predict how much their partner wanted to work with them or trusted their judgment. However, the lack of a correlation between self-reported receptiveness and the impressions people left on their partners notwithstanding, some people were indeed seen as more receptive than others. Despite the fact that they were all instructed to express their own point of view and then paired with a disagreeing stranger to debate their perspectives, and despite the fact that at the end of the study virtually nobody changed their mind about the issues, some people managed to come across as more engaged with their partner's perspective than others. How did they do it?

The interactions between the government executives unfolded over chat while participants sat in cubicles in a computer lab, unable to see one another. This means that whatever signals of receptiveness were transmitted had to be transmitted through text. So, a group of research assistants and I decided to read the messages. Unfortunately, after reading hundreds of messages, and debating the text for hours, we realized that finding patterns in unstructured conversations is actually incredibly difficult. The messages differed on many dimensions, and it was anyone's guess which ones were the most important to perceptions of receptiveness. To solve the mystery of how exactly the people who appeared to be more receptive differed from the ones who didn't, we needed more data and more sophisticated statistical tools. This is how I began to work with Mike Yeomans, the lead researcher on the boomerasking research I told you about in Chapter 5.

Mike got his PhD in management at the University of Chicago, where he learned many of the same research techniques the rest of us employ: how to set up a clean experiment that vividly captures a particular facet of human nature and how to ask participants questions about their experience that allow researchers to quantify subtle psychological processes. But Mike was not satisfied with this approach because it left a lot of data on the proverbial "cutting-room floor." Namely, any psychology experiment that features two people interacting with each other also produces a lot of text—the words that the participants say to each other while interacting. However, the vast majority of researchers do not analyze any of the words the participants say, instead only focusing on the questionnaires they fill out. The reason for this is both practical and cultural. From a practical standpoint, analyzing unstructured language (the way people really talk) requires a lot more computing power and much more sophisticated statistics than analyzing questionnaire responses. From a cultural standpoint, because a couple of decades ago neither the computing power nor the statistics were widely available, psychologists decided not to bother. So, the vast majority of the field simply didn't think of analyzing (or even recording) the hours and hours of conversation that our experiments were generating.

Mike, however, has a rebellious streak. So, after graduating from the University of Chicago with his very normal management PhD, he basically retrained himself in computational linguistics by collaborating with other scholars working on the cutting edge of computer science, psychology, economics, and communications. When we began working together at Harvard, he opened my eyes to the treasure trove of data that unstructured conversation presented. The conversations between our state and local government Executive Education participants that seemed like a black box with no key to most psychologists were exactly what Mike's newly acquired skill set was made to unlock. However, to analyze the data we already had, we needed even more data.

Over the course of several months, we collected writing samples from online research participants who were asked to respond to messages on controversial policy issues. At the beginning of the study, we always asked participants about their opinion on a topic so we could then show them a message that we knew they would disagree with. Thousands of participants (whom we called "Writers") composed responses to opposing views on topics ranging from the Black Lives Matter movement to U.S. efforts to fight terrorism to marijuana legalization. We then showed these messages to thousands of other participants (whom we called "Raters") and asked them to evaluate how receptive the Writers seemed to the perspective articulated in the message they were responding to.

Importantly, prior to doing this task, we asked the Raters to read about receptiveness and how receptive people engage with ideas differently than unreceptive people. They learned about the receptiveness scale from Chapter 2 and thought about how highly receptive versus not very receptive people engage with disagreement. We gave them a practice test to make sure they understood what receptiveness was and how it was measured. Now their goal was to evaluate the writing samples we showed them and rate how receptive each of the Writers seemed.

In the end of this exercise, we had collected thousands of messages on a variety of different controversial topics, with those messages ultimately evaluated by thousands of other people for how receptive they made the author appear. To figure out what the messages rated more receptive versus less receptive had in common, we employed the tools of natural language processing, or NLP. The idea behind NLP is that language is extremely complex and multidimensional, but you can still conduct statistical analyses on it if you can figure out how to turn all the words into numbers. The process begins by breaking text into sections made up of one, two, or a handful of words. To figure out what makes somebody sound receptive, you then figure out which words and phrases most frequently occur in the writing samples rated by humans as most receptive, versus which phrases occur in the writing samples rated as least receptive. How do you do that? You literally count. However, since we are dealing with thousands of messages, each containing hundreds of words, which in turn make up hundreds of thousands of phrase combinations, the counting quickly becomes overwhelming, so you automate the process by writing an algorithm—a mathematical formula—that counts and adds up words that match specific characteristics.

When all was said and done, our algorithm produced a long list of words and phrases that seemed to occur more frequently in the messages rated as most receptive, and a different list that occurred more frequently in the messages that were rated as the least receptive. Carefully reviewing the lists made us realize that the words and phrases fell into specific categories, each with a clearly detectable theme. We came to call these categories "features of receptiveness." Some of these categories include words and phrases you should say more of—the ones that occurred more frequently in receptive-sounding text and what we call "positive features"—while other categories include words you should say less of—the ones that were more frequent in unreceptive-sounding text, the "negative features."

In addition to simply identifying the features, the algorithm also computed how important each feature seemed to be by calculating how much, on average, it impacts human receptiveness ratings, as well as how frequently each feature occurs in people's actual language. If you are going to exert effort to change how you talk, you should use more of the positive features that have a big impact on the receptiveness score while avoiding the highly impactful negative features. Relatedly, if a particular negative feature shows up in language frequently, you should pay a lot of attention to avoiding it. By contrast, if a feature is extremely rare, you can probably just ignore it altogether. Knowing what to say, what not to say, and which parts of the formula matter the most goes a long way toward giving us clear guidance on improving our signaling of receptiveness.

Feature Type	Feature Name	Examples
Positive	Agreement	I agree, You are right
	Acknowledgment	I understand, I get it
	Subjectivity	I think, In my opinion
	Hedges	Sometimes, Maybe
	Positive Emotion	I love, Great, Not bad
Negative	Reasoning	Because, Therefore
	Negative Emotion	Not good, Terrible
	Disagreement	I don't agree
	Adverb Limiters	Just, Only, Simply
	Negations	Did not, Would not, Never

When people use a high number of the positive features identified by our algorithm and a low number of negative features, their speech takes on a particular flavor. This flavor, it turned out, is what the state and local executives in our experiment seemed to value in their partners, even as they continued to disagree about the topic at hand. We came to call it "conversational receptiveness"—a communication style that relies on specific words and phrases to signal one's willingness to engage with the opposing point of view.

Conversational receptiveness is related to but distinct from the "cognitive receptiveness" described in Chapter 2 in that it focuses on the language that people use in the course of disagreement, not how they respond to opposing views intellectually or emotionally. Because conversational receptiveness relies on language, which is clearly observable and algorithmically measurable, we had good reason to believe that it might make more of a difference to conflict outcomes than other, more subtle signals. It also offers us the solution to the key challenge I posed at the beginning of the chapter—conversational receptiveness enables us to state our own point of view while decreasing the risk of conflict escalation!

THE BENEFITS OF CONVERSATIONAL RECEPTIVENESS

Having identified the features that make up conversational receptiveness, we set out to test whether and to what extent the use of this communication style impacts conflict outcomes outside of our lab. An interesting opportunity to test this question presented itself on Wikipedia.

Take a look at any Wikipedia page. At the top left, directly below the title of the article, there is a tab labeled "Talk." The Talk tab is a place where Wikipedia editors can debate any given piece. They can change or add to content, explain their edits, or make a case for why they believe the information was wrong in the first place. As you might imagine, given that Wikipedia contains millions of articles and people all over the world can leave a comment, some of the discussions turn contentious. In fact, some become so contentious that Wikipedia editors (who are human like the rest of us) sometimes stoop to calling each other nasty names. Since all of this is done in writing and publicly, there is a permanent record of who called whom what. Over the years, this problem became prevalent enough that Wikipedia devised a special policy to combat what it politely refers to as "personal attacks." When Mike Yeomans learned about this system, he became curious: Does using more conversational receptiveness in expressing disagreement with a fellow Wikipedia editor protect you from being called a nasty name on the internet?

Luckily for us, a group of computer scientists from Cornell University had recently assembled and published a whole dataset of discussion threads from Wikipedia talk pages. Having sorted through thousands of articles, they created a collection made up of matched thread pairs, with threads in each pair being of approximately the same length and related to the same article. The key feature of the dataset, however, was that in each pair one of the talk threads ended in a personal attack and the other concluded peacefully. We wondered whether the level of conversational receptiveness in the first message of each thread could be used to predict whether, at the end of the thread, people would start calling each other names and lose their Wikipedia credentials, or whether the conversation would end amicably.

Indeed, this is what we found. The level of conversational receptiveness in the beginning of lengthy discussions on Wikipedia was in fact a significant predictor of how likely the thread was to end with a personal attack. Interestingly, when we consider two people in an argument (one who ultimately ends up being the "attacker" and one who ends up being the "attackee"), we could also see *whose* language was more predictive. We found that people who ended up on the receiving end of the attack used substantially less conversational receptiveness in their writing than their matched counterparts who were engaged in debates of similar length and on similar topics. In other words, it's not that some people (the "attackers") routinely flew off the handle because they were jerks. Rather, many of the attacks came after the person on the receiving end was so unreceptive from the beginning of the discussion that it seemed like they brought a personal attack onto themselves.

The Wikipedia results were promising because we saw that conversational receptiveness, enacted by random people on the internet and across a huge variety of topics, seemed to work. Using the words and phrases that our algorithm identified as being associated with perceptions of receptiveness appeared to de-escalate brewing conflict outside of our experimental setting. But notice, the Wikipedia study is not an experiment. We are seeing that people who used more conversational receptiveness were less likely to receive a personal attack in the course of a disagreement, but we don't know that their use of conversational receptiveness *caused* this more benevolent treatment. Maybe some Wikipedia editors are just smarter? They know that seeming receptive to other perspectives is a good idea, but they also happen to make better arguments. Maybe they are avoiding being called names not because they are using conversational receptiveness but because they are universally respected by their peers. Or, maybe, some topics are more inflammatory. You might imagine that two discussion threads, one about whiskey and one about vodka, are both about alcohol, but maybe whiskey experts feel more strongly about their drink of choice, and this topic is bound to lead to conflict no matter what conversational style anyone uses. This is what researchers mean when they declare that "correlation does not mean causation": Just because use of conversational receptiveness is correlated with a lower frequency of personal attacks, it does not mean that it *causes* the decrease in personal attacks. Other things that are happening alongside of conversational receptiveness might be the actual cause. The only way to know for sure is to run a real experiment.

The logic of a basic social science experiment is simple: Researchers recruit participants and randomly assign them to one of two groups. Because participants are assigned randomly, both groups end up being about the same on all relevant characteristics. On average, people in both groups end up equally educated, of a similar average age, similarly articulate, and similarly prone to yelling during disagreement. Then, we take the participants in one group and train them in conversational receptiveness. Now the two groups are the same in every way *but one*. If the trained group has better conversations across disagreements, we will know that it was the receptiveness training and not something else that caused the improvement.*

The trickier part is how exactly do we go about training conversational receptiveness? Remember, the algorithm came out with hundreds of words and phrases that make people sound either more or less receptive that we boiled down into themes that we called "features." The table at the beginning of this chapter presented you with the list of the top 10 most important features that all those words and phrases could be divided into. But one thing behavioral scientists know for a fact is that you have to keep

---

* This is also why large sample sizes matter a lot. If I ran an experiment where I randomly assigned ten people to a treatment or control condition, and one of the people in my control condition had a serious anger management problem, I might decide that my treatment worked because the conflicts in that condition were milder. However, in reality, the result would simply have been a function of one person's scores having a lot of influence over a small dataset. This becomes much less problematic if we have one hundred or one thousand people in our experiment, such that one odd duck can't influence the average performance of the whole group.

things simple and memorable for people to adopt a new behavior. "Leaves of three, let it be" or "Eddie Ate Dynamite, Good-Bye Eddie" has taught thousands of children to stay away from poison ivy and how to match guitar strings to corresponding notes, respectively. We needed something simple and memorable to teach people about receptiveness.

THE H.E.A.R. FRAMEWORK

Remember that the algorithm not only helped us identify which features increased and decreased perceptions of receptiveness but also which features were the most important because they had the greatest impact or could be ignored because they were very rarely used in natural conversation. I am not very creative, but thankfully my students are.* After a bit of brainstorming, they came up with a snappy acronym to help people memorize the most important features of conversational receptiveness. The acronym is H.E.A.R., as in "I HEAR you." H.E.A.R. became a way for us to teach people a "receptiveness recipe"—years of research condensed into a list of four bullet points.

The "H" in H.E.A.R. stands for "Hedging your claims." Hedging makes it clear that no matter how right you think you are, you recognize that there are exceptions to nearly every rule and that most issues are complex and multifaceted. Here are some examples:

"While most doctors believe that COVID-19 vaccines are generally safe and effective, some people have experienced dangerous side effects."

"It seems that most immigrants are law-abiding and well-intentioned people, but many reasonable voters are still likely

---

* The credit for the H.E.A.R. acronym goes to Hanne Collins (now faculty at UCLA) and Charlie Dorison (now faculty at Georgetown).

to believe that borders should be secured and laws should be followed."

Using hedging words such as "sometimes," "perhaps," "possibly," "most," and "some" shows your counterpart that you recognize the complexity and nuance of the world we live in. A point made with a verbal hedge ("I think that most of the time women do just as well in high-stress jobs as men") is more likely to advance the conversation productively than the same point made without the hedge ("Women do just as well in high-stress jobs as men").

The advice to hedge accurate claims can sometimes raise eyebrows among people who are concerned about sounding less certain than how they really feel. But remember, the goal is to show that you are engaged with the other person's point of view, not that you have so completely rejected it as to have zero doubt about your own correctness. To the extent that the issues we debate are multifaceted and complex, hedging shows a person to be more thoughtful and have better judgment than someone who expresses their own views with no room for doubt.

The "E" in H.E.A.R. stands for "Emphasizing agreement." Almost in any argument, two people can find something to agree on. You might be pro-life, and I might be pro-choice, but we both agree that parenting is hard work. You might believe that gun rights should be limited, and I that they are fundamental to individual freedom, but we both agree that a gun in the wrong hands can lead to tragedy. You might think we need to cut staff and I think that we need to add more, but we both agree that client satisfaction is our top priority. Using words such as "we both agree that" or "I also want to" or "I share some of your concerns" allows parties to identify common ground, which is often more extensive than they initially assumed. Highlighting shared areas of understanding makes people feel that they are on the same team, navigating the disagreement together.

Importantly, emphasizing areas of agreement does not mean changing your mind or compromising. Rather, it means recognizing common values and experiences that connect us all and devoting a few words toward making that agreement explicit. In cases of known disagreement (like when we belong to different political parties or different competing departments, or when we've had this argument before), people tend to exaggerate the magnitude of that disagreement and hold negative and often inaccurate beliefs about their counterparts' views.* Emphasizing agreement can mitigate the effects of those stereotypes by highlighting to your counterpart how much you have in common.

The "A" in H.E.A.R. stands for "Acknowledging other perspectives." In most disagreements, people are eager to make their point quickly and repeatedly. They will often interrupt their counterpart to contradict their ideas, as if the opposing argument is an annoying stinging insect that must be swatted out of the air as quickly as possible. Go ahead and ask your spouse to explain their perspective on a long-running disagreement and try not to interrupt them for five minutes—it is incredibly difficult! Acknowledging the opposing perspective is even harder. Acknowledgment means that when it is finally your turn to speak, you must donate some of your own precious airtime to restate the other person's point of view so as to show them with your words that you really heard them. This may be done with phrases such as "I understand that you really care about . . ." or "Thank you for telling me about . . ." or "You are suggesting that . . ." Performing acknowledgment effectively means slowing down the argument to show you're listening even as you are about to launch into your own spiel.

Acknowledgment is certainly not a new idea. Many of you

---

* We will discuss research on such "false polarization" further in Chapter 9.

may have taken a leadership or communication training that advised you to tell counterparts in disagreement that you "hear them." Indeed, this advice has become so common that poor execution of acknowledgment has spawned a variety of popular memes. On Instagram and TikTok, a variety of comedic characters (my favorites are evil-looking cats) say things like "I hear you, but . . ." The stony-faced expression of the cat makes it very clear that it did not in fact "hear." By contrast, effective acknowledgment requires restating the counterpart's point of view in your own words, to behaviorally demonstrate that you did in fact do the listening and understanding that you want to get credit for. For example: "I hear you, but we just don't have the budget" is no good. A better version might be: "I hear you. You are really concerned with how the quality of the cabinet hardware will impact the overall appearance of the new construction. I know that meeting the highest standards of quality is really important to you. I just don't think we have the budget." In this example, the speaker demonstrated that they heard their counterpart and the exact nature of their concerns. They didn't just claim that they understood with no evidence. Notice that in both cases the end is the same—the speaker believes that there is no budget for upgraded hardware—but the fact that they demonstrated listening through acknowledgment makes a big difference in how that conclusion is likely to land.

You might have noticed that the A for Acknowledgment in the H.E.A.R. framework is very similar to the Reflection step in the Listening Triangle. In many ways the two are the same move, but they occur at different times in the conversation for slightly different purposes. Reflection is a step performed when you are gathering information to ensure that the conclusions you are reaching about your partner's perspective are accurate. You reflect what they said so that they can correct you if you are getting it wrong.

Acknowledgment happens when you are making your own point and ensures that when you do so, you do it with the active recognition of your partner's point of view.

The "R" in H.E.A.R. stands for "Reframing to the positive." The R does double duty by reminding you to avoid negation words (such as "can't," "don't," won't," and "no") and negative emotion words ("hate," "terrible"), and adding more positively valanced words ("great," "like," "win"). For example, if I am feeling frustrated in a conversation because my counterpart has interrupted me, I might be tempted to say, "I hate it when people interrupt me. Please don't." But instead, the same message can be delivered by saying, "I can tell it's hard for you to hear me out. I would really appreciate your letting me finish."

Just like the earlier components of H.E.A.R., "Reframing to the positive" is not intended to change the core of the message. The speaker is still conveying their desire to finish their sentences at their own pace. But adding the positive framing creates a perception of warmth and is more likely to avoid escalation.

H	**E**	**A**	**R**
Hedge your claims	Emphasize agreement	Acknowledge other perspectives	Reframe to the positive
"I think it's possible that . . ."	"I think we both want to . . ."	"I understand that . . ."	"I think it's great when . . ."
"This might happen because . . ."	"I agree with some of what you are saying . . ."	"I see your point . . ."	"I really appreciate it when . . ."
"Some people tend to think . . ."	"We are both concerned with . . ."	"What I think you are saying is . . ."	"It would be so wonderful if . . ."

The H.E.A.R. framework captures a lot of the important components of conversational receptiveness, but if you have a bit of extra brain space, I want to highlight two more that are worth keeping an eye on. First, try to avoid reasoning words such as "because," "therefore," and "explain." These words often crop up when you are patiently trying to enlighten your counterpart about the obvious and extremely logical conclusions that anybody with half a brain ought to draw in a particular situation. "And because heat rises, the car will be much warmer if you use the vents by your feet." Heat does rise, and the car will probably be warmer, but the explanatory words make the argument sound condescending. By trying to sound extra smart and logical, you are actually decreasing the chances that your counterpart will take your well-meaning advice.

The other feature to avoid is "adverb limiters." You can be forgiven if you have never heard the term, but adverbs are words that modify other words. Adverb limiters are the little words that make the word coming after them seem smaller, and less consequential. "It's just polite to ask before you borrow somebody's stuff." Or "I am merely suggesting that we consider the consequences of this policy before we roll it out company wide." Words like "just," "simply," "merely," and "only" are often intended to show that what you are asking for or claiming is simple, obvious, and should be easily agreed to. But instead, they serve to minimize the validity of your counterpart's view and again, add a dash of condescension. Try to avoid these little packets of conversational poison.

THE RECEPTIVENESS RECIPE turned out to be easy to learn. In experiment after experiment, we presented the components of the H.E.A.R. framework to research participants and gave them some examples of each feature. It turned out that they could easily incorporate our advice into arguments on a variety of topics. We knew that they were doing it well because both our algorithm and people who disagreed with the trained writers could tell the difference. The participants trained in conversational receptiveness were seen as more trustworthy, more objective, and more desirable as future teammates and collaborators by those with whom they disagreed. Importantly, these effects persisted even when people debated some of the thorniest topics of our day: the necessity of COVID-19 vaccines, affirmative action in hiring, the Black Lives Matter movement, and the American investment in fighting international terrorism. And importantly, because participants were randomly assigned to receive or not receive training in conversational receptiveness, we could conclude that their word choice, and not some other extraneous features, caused these positive outcomes.

One final point is worth highlighting. Although conversational receptiveness was effective, one might wonder whether it was more effective than other interventions we could have suggested to our participants. In a new study, we compared three groups: a group of people who were told to communicate in their own natural style, a group of people who learned the "receptiveness recipe," and a group of people who received advice to think differently about their counterparts. Specifically, we told this final group to be empathetic toward holders of opposing views, to take their counterpart's perspective, to exercise intellectual humility, and to consider arguments for the opposite point of view. In other words, instead of telling them what to say, we told them what to think and how to feel.

Our results showed that both types of interventions helped. However, the participants who received the "receptiveness recipe" wrote messages expressing their points of view that were twice as receptive (according to our algorithm) as those who were told to think and feel differently. On one hand, this is not surprising. The people who were told exactly what to say said what they were supposed to. On the other hand, this finding highlights a profound point: If you want people to act differently, you need to tell them how to execute the behaviors you are asking for. Telling people to be empathetic leaves it up to them to translate those feelings into behavior. Teaching them the H.E.A.R. framework avoids all the errors they might make along the way.

In the end, the recipients of the messages only saw the text of the messages. They could not tell what their counterpart was intending to communicate, only what they effectively communicated. As we predicted, the writers of the messages who received the recipe were evaluated more positively than the writers of the messages who received instructions to shift their mindsets.

In sum, using conversational receptiveness enabled our research participants to express their point of view while being seen as more reasonable, thoughtful, and trustworthy, even when they were discussing some of the most inflammatory topics we could think of. It also led their counterparts to be more willing to have additional conversations on these and other topics, opening the possibility of ongoing dialogue and problem-solving. When participants were not trying to score a quick rhetorical point by being extra clever and dogmatic in their arguments, they were seen as the sorts of people that others want to keep talking to. And isn't that the key to influence?

RECEPTIVENESS BREEDS RECEPTIVENESS

The H.E.A.R. framework can be incredibly effective for helping you engage with opposing perspectives, while at the same time maintaining peace of mind because you know things will not get out of hand. It's a tool kit that finally takes away the uncomfortable choice between avoiding disagreement on the one hand, and risking conflict escalation on the other. By consistently practicing H.E.A.R., you can approach disagreements more confidently in your ability to maintain your relationship with your counterpart while saying what you truly believe. The other big benefit of H.E.A.R. is that it is completely transferrable across different life situations. You can use it with your colleagues, with your spouse, with your teenagers, with your neighbors, and at your union meeting. You can acknowledge others' perspectives about the need to purchase a standing desk, hedge your claims about the risk of GMOs, and find areas of agreement around DEI training. H.E.A.R. is a multi-tool—simple, effective, and portable.

Our ongoing studies revealed two additional big benefits of using H.E.A.R. Many facets of language (and, more generally, interpersonal behavior) are contagious. People naturally take on each other's emotional tone, accents, and facial expressions. However, at the beginning of this research program, the extent to which this basic rule of thumb would apply to receptiveness was not obvious. When we first analyzed the data from our state and local executives, we noticed that partners' ratings of each other's receptiveness converged over time. That was our first hint that something about the words people chose shifted the tenor of the conversation. However, developing an algorithm that precisely measures the amount of conversational receptiveness in any piece of text allowed us to measure the extent to which and the exact way in which one person's language influenced another's.

What we found is that when one person in a conversation receives even minimal training in conversational receptiveness, their counterpart naturally mimics this style. Importantly, they not only mimic the specific words and phrases they just heard but also seem to incorporate other features of receptiveness that were not used by their counterpart. For example, if one person uses a lot of hedging, their counterpart will also begin to hedge. However, they will go one step further and use a bit more acknowledgment and fewer negations. In other words, using conversational receptiveness subtly conveys to your counterpart what kind of conversation this is. It's not a fight, it's a discussion. It doesn't have to be nasty; it can be warm and thoughtful. This tacit recognition of what game we are playing makes people adjust their behavior to fit the rules.

The fact that receptiveness is contagious has several important implications. One is that we don't have to worry that by being receptive we are going to leave ourselves open to being linguistically bulldozed by our counterpart. One might imagine that if I hedge my claims, acknowledge your perspective, and avoid negations, I will open the door to you stomping all over my arguments. However, that does not seem to be the case. Receptiveness breeds more receptiveness in part because of our automatic tendency to mimic each other and in part because nobody actually wants to have a big fight. When you give your counterpart a road map for having a civil conversation, they will gladly follow you away from the ledge.

Second, recognizing that receptiveness is contagious gives you power over all of your conversations. People want to feel powerful in disagreement; they want to win. But remember, when the topic is important to both sides, neither side budges. The desire to win gets us into trouble by creating a stalemate that breeds frustration and resentment. Receptiveness offers a different kind of power. It allows us to set the tone for the conversation and take the aggression and negativity out of our partner's words. Rather than restoring a feeling of equality by rising to our counterpart's level of argumentativeness, we can model receptiveness and watch our counterpart come down. We can have control over our conversations and exert leadership over others' behavior without directly confronting them or demanding that they use a different tone. This is the closest I've ever come to learning a scientifically validated Jedi mind trick.

Finally, it seems that using the H.E.A.R. framework makes the initial user (you) a bit more receptive as well. In a series of recent experiments, we took people who felt strongly supportive of the COVID-19 vaccine effort and trained them in conversational receptiveness. We then paired them up with vaccine-hesitant counterparts and observed the now familiar result: Our vaccine-hesitant participants thought that the vaccine advocates trained in conversational receptiveness were more trustworthy and reasonable than advocates who used their own improvised best efforts to make a compelling case for vaccination. Importantly (especially since consequential heath attitudes are generally not shifted in one quick conversation), the vaccine-hesitant participants were also far more willing to have ongoing conversations with counterparts trained in conversational receptiveness. The surprising part, however, was that the pro-vaccine advocates who had been trained in conversational receptiveness also found their counterparts to be more trustworthy and reasonable. They did not adopt their skepticism toward the vaccine, but expressing themselves in a receptive manner seems to have opened their eyes to some reasons for exercising greater tolerance toward the opposing view. I think this last finding is particularly important for people who not only want to change their conversation partners but also want to feel differently in conversations across disagreement themselves. Finding reasons to continue respecting and appreciating people who disagree with us, even on the most heated and consequential topics, is definitely worth the time it takes to memorize a four-letter acronym.

CHAPTER SUMMARY

- Analyzing text across hundreds of disagreements on hot-button topics can tell us which specific words and phrases help signal receptiveness while making your own point and thus prevent conflict escalation. This communication style is called "conversational receptiveness."

- A good way to start using this approach is by practicing the H.E.A.R. framework:

1. Hedge
2. Emphasize Agreement
3. Acknowledge Other Perspectives
4. Reframe to the Positive

- H.E.A.R. is relatively easy to learn and dramatically improves how people who disagree with you react to your ideas. Most importantly, it opens the door to ongoing dialogue, making long-term influence possible.

- An important and surprising benefit of this approach is that receptiveness is imitated in disagreement—one person who uses receptiveness has the power to improve the overall tone of the interaction by modeling the style they want their counterpart to take on.

8

WHAT'S YOUR STORY?

CONSIDER THESE TWO ARGUMENTS ABOUT GUN VIOLENCE AND gun regulation. As you're reading, think about how each argument makes you feel. Do you feel persuaded? Do you feel annoyed? Do you believe the claim the speaker is making? Do you think the speaker is an objective person who has reached reasonable conclusions based on their experiences in the world? Do you trust their evidence? Which argument would you make if given the opportunity?

Dr. Sakran (Version 1):

Every day, 327 people in the United States are shot with guns and 117 are wounded. The U.S. gun homicide rate is twenty-five times higher than that of other high-income countries. One in five Americans says that they have a family member who has been fatally shot. The United States makes up 35 percent of global firearm suicides while accounting for just 4 percent of the world's population. These statistics inspired me to go into medicine and to become a trauma surgeon so I could give people a second chance. But what I realized is that despite how excellent I may think I am as a surgeon, if someone comes in that's been shot in the head, there's very little that I can do to save that person's life. And that's why the best medical treatment is prevention.

Dr. Sakran (Version 2):

When I was seventeen, I never realized that I was mortal. But then one autumn afternoon, I went from being this healthy high school senior to collateral damage in a shooting. A fight broke out after a high school football game, and a stray .38 caliber bullet tore through my throat and trachea, damaging my carotid artery. And that moment, when I was nearly killed, inspired me to go into medicine and become a trauma surgeon, so I could give other people the same second chance that I was given. But what I realized is that despite how excellent I may think I am as a surgeon, if someone comes in that's been shot in the head, there's very little that I can do to save that person's life. And that's why the best medical treatment is prevention.

Okay, time to choose. Which do you think is the better argument? If you support more restrictions on gun ownership you might find the statistics in Version 1 compelling and the story in Version 2 terrifying. You might shake your head in dismay and wonder why gun violence persists in the United States despite the obvious reasons to do something about it. But guess what? Although you think that you chose whatever you chose based on merits, the reality is that your overall reaction to these two arguments is largely predetermined by your original opinion on the issue. Furthermore, if you are a person who already believes in greater gun regulation, your opinion as to which argument is stronger doesn't really matter. These arguments are not for you because preaching to the converted is a waste of breath. The more interesting question is, which argument is more palatable to people who are not convinced, the people who disagree with the perspective offered by the speaker, the people who are skeptical about both the merits and the logistical feasibility of greater firearm regulation?

To answer that question sensibly, we now need to define what we mean by "prefer." As I've told you from the beginning, if your goal is immediate persuasion and the topic is one that is important and ideologically laden, you are probably not going to achieve your goal and might even do some damage while trying. Remember, however, that a conversation can have many goals beyond persuasion. One common goal is simply for both parties to be able to register their disagreement and explain why they feel the way they feel. In many conversations (especially ones around ongoing points of contention), people know that the other side will never change their mind. But they still feel compelled to say something. The risk of saying something, however, is that the conversation may escalate into an argument. If your goal is to say something, but the kind of something that won't ruin the rest of the evening/weekend/vacation, which version would you pick?

Expressing your views without blowing up your relationship is a fine goal, but you might be feeling slightly more ambitious. You might want the other side not only to know that you disagree but also to understand why. You might want them to accept that a reasonable, well-intentioned, thoughtful person can walk around in the world holding your particular set of views for very good reasons. In other words, beyond simply saying that you believe that there should be fewer guns in civilian hands, you want the other person to respect and understand your reasons for holding this belief. Which argument would you choose then?

I have heard both of the arguments delivered by Dr. Joseph Sakran, executive vice chair of surgery at Johns Hopkins Medical

Center, one of the best hospitals in the United States and home to one of the busiest level 1 trauma centers. When Dr. Sakran took one of my courses, I had no idea he was a fancy trauma surgeon. He was one of several hundred students I taught that year, but one who happened to be particularly excited about becoming a better negotiator and thus raised his hand all the time. Every class has a couple of overachievers, people who stand out in their level of commitment to learning even when compared to other Harvard classmates. But unlike most who leave my classroom never to be heard from again, Joe stayed in touch. Eventually, I googled his name to find out why he was so interested in my work. Here is what I learned.

HOW JOE LEARNED THE POWER OF STORYTELLING

Joe is only a year older than I am, and also a child of immigrants. Because of that, it is easy for me to picture his upbringing in Falls Church, Virginia, a nice, safe suburb of Washington, D.C. But of course, every suburb is safe until it isn't. As much as Joe's parents devoted themselves to their kids, obsessed over their education, and opened their home to all of their friends in the hopes of knowing what was going on in their kids' lives, they could not protect their son from everything. When he was seventeen years old, while hanging out after a high school football game, Joe was struck and almost killed by a .38 caliber bullet that was fired during a fight in a nearby park, a fight that had absolutely nothing to do with him.

Joe survived his injuries due to the skill of a trauma surgeon at Inova Fairfax Hospital. But the surgery was just the beginning of a grueling recovery. He spent a month in the hospital, then six more months recovering at home, where he had to relearn how to swallow. Though a promising student, he had to go to college locally so his parents could continue to care for him. Even today, he has a rasp to his voice, courtesy of his surgically reconstructed voice box.

Surviving the shooting was only the first remarkable thing that Joe did. The second was becoming a trauma surgeon himself. Instead of turning away from tragedy, pain, and the endless litany of preventable idiocies that rob humans of life, he dove right in. Now, he is one of the top specialists in the country, serving in one of the deadliest cities in the United States, working twenty-four-hour shifts patching up victims of car accidents, stabbings, trampoline accidents, and many, many, shootings.

Given his personal experience and his profession, you would think that Joe has strong opinions about guns. And he does. But he also knows his goal—and the goal is not to win casual arguments over dinner. The goal is to have fewer bullet-riddled bodies on his operating table. And achieving that goal requires many conversations with people who dramatically disagree with him about the appropriate role of firearms in our society. Joe also knows that any one conversation will not lead to policy change. As a result, he has to communicate in a way that leads to the next conversation, and the next, and the next. In the service of that goal, Joe tells his personal story. He knows all of the statistics and the research facts, he could give you nightmares for weeks talking about what exactly a bullet does to a human body, and, yes, he could win every single dinnertime argument. But to create change, you have to build consensus, not make people feel stupid or scared. Storytelling became a skill that Joe honed like a new surgical technique—a skill that has already likely saved lives through initiatives and policies that Joe's advocacy work made possible.

THE SCIENCE OF STORYTELLING

Storytelling is not a new idea as a tool for persuasion and behavior change. From ancient parables to modern marketing campaigns, influencers have long wielded storytelling to subtly shift people's views of a situation. People intuitively recognize (and research supports) the idea that when you watch a commercial for cough medicine where a pretty mother tells you that the medicine worked for her child, you will be more likely to buy the cough medicine than if the commercial featured the same woman in a business suit reading the clinical trial results off a PowerPoint slide. However, for a set of reasons that we will discuss in Chapter 9, when in disagreement, most of us automatically default to the PowerPoint version, supporting our arguments with facts, figures, and a generous sprinkling of condescension instead of sharing the human story of how we came to hold our beliefs. But since arguments with facts and figures have failed to resolve human conflict so spectacularly, several years ago, multiple researchers, including myself, began to wonder whether sharing a personal narrative would be more effective than hoping that superior erudition will rule the day.

The first really compelling paper that I came across on this topic was written by Josh Kalla and David Broockman, political scientists at Yale and UC Berkeley, respectively. These researchers conducted several impressively ambitious experiments in collaboration with a canvassing company—an organization that sends employees door-to-door to talk to voters about different issues. Many of you have probably had at least one or two experiences with canvassers—you are sitting at home, minding your own business, making dinner or yelling at your kids, when somebody knocks on the door. What usually follows is an awkward conversation in which the person on your doorstep tries to educate you about some local proposition you've never heard of, while you try to close the door with minimum fuss and get back to your cooking or your yelling. The task of closing the door is infinitely easier if that person is advocating for something you strongly disagree with. In those cases, you can simply slam it in the canvasser's face because how dare they try to change your mind on something you have already decided!

Knowing that the standard canvassing approach does not usually change hearts and minds, Josh and David decided to try something different. For one of their experiments, they created three different versions of a "canvassing script," the spiel that the canvasser says after you have made the mistake of answering the door. The goal was to soften respondents' attitudes toward undocumented immigrants, a topic that is frequently in the news, highly politicized, and one to which people have very strong, emotional responses. In one version of the script, the canvassers simply knocked on the door, introduced themselves to the voter, and then had a short conversation on a topic completely unrelated to immigration. This was the control condition. In the second version of the script, the canvasser asked the voter about their views about illegal immigrants and then proceeded to correct their misconceptions and provide accurate information about various immigration-related issues. This was most akin to a traditional canvassing script where a person shows up at your house and tries to change your mind with information you may already know but probably don't trust or don't want to believe.

The really interesting script was the third one, centered around an approach that the researchers called a "nonjudgment exchange of personal narratives." In this version, the canvasser was supposed to ask the voter for their views on immigration but to be very careful not to express any judgment about their response. The canvasser would then ask if the voter knew anyone who is an immigrant and continue with follow-up questions about that person and their relationship to the voter, ultimately asking the voter what they think being an immigrant feels like. Irrespective of the voter's response, the canvasser would then tell an immigration story either about themselves, a friend, or a family member and ask the voter about whether they can relate to any part of the story.

The next segment of the conversation focused specifically on encouraging compassion toward immigrants. The canvasser would ask the voter to share a story where someone showed them compassion. They would also share their own story of compassion, which (not surprisingly!) was related to their earlier story about the immigration experience. Finally, the canvasser circled the conversation back to the voter's original stated opinion about undocumented immigrants and tried to correct their misperceptions and provide information, just like in the second version of the script that did not involve all of the nonjudgmental narrative-sharing.

These conversations were not particularly long. For example, the conversations in the condition where personal narratives were exchanged and compassion was discussed took about ten minutes to implement. The conversations in the other conditions were even shorter. However, the results were impressive. In surveys sent out weeks after the conversations took place, voters who engaged in the nonjudgmental exchange of personal narratives had more positive attitudes toward undocumented immigrants and were less supportive of legislation that would limit their rights than voters who experienced the script that did not involve an exchange of narratives or voters who did not talk about immigration at all. The survey did not in any way reference the earlier conversations and covered many different political topics. Thus, it is safe to assume that in answering the survey, the voters reported their genuine views and were not simply acquiescing to psychological pressure to respond in a particular way. Two other experiments in the same paper produced similar results on a different topic and using different procedures. The clear takeaway that impressed the research community was that a nonjudgmental exchange of personal narratives can help discussions on some of the most contentious issues of our time proceed more productively and actually result in attitude shifts.

Since the first time I read Josh and David's paper, I was impressed with the findings and the ambitious method: Recruiting and training hundreds of canvassers in different parts of the country to talk to thousands of voters face-to-face is not an easy feat! However, the study left me with many questions. On the one hand, the treatment was clearly successful. It is not easy to change people's attitudes on any politicized topic, and it is truly impressive when this attitude change persists several months after the experiment. On the other hand, however, the "nonjudgmental exchange of personal narratives" is a classic example of what social scientists call a "kitchen sink intervention"—an approach where, in the service of an ambitious goal, researchers throw in everything but the kitchen sink to try to shift a hard-to-change human behavior. The problem with this approach is that in the end, you know *something* worked, but it's hard to tell what, exactly.

To consider a simpler example, imagine that you wanted to decrease the amount of petty crime on a college campus. You might start by hosting sessions during freshman orientation about the importance of locking one's bike and one's dorm room. You might create a group of volunteer student escorts to help people travel safely at night. You might hand out loud whistles so students can call for help if they feel threatened. You might hang up posters that encourage bystanders to report suspicious behavior. If in a few months you observe less crime than before the measures went into effect, you will be quite pleased with yourself because your hard work paid off. However, if you wanted to answer the question of exactly which measure was effective (for example, to save money on implementing the initiative the following year), you would have no way of knowing. Was it the orientation sessions? Was it the whistles? Was it the posters?

Remember that in the canvassing experiment, the winning intervention began with people stating their perspective and having the canvasser listen to their opinion in a nonjudgmental way. We know that being listened to feels good and makes us think more positively of the listener. We also know that being asked follow-up questions is a delightful experience. Could that have been the magic sauce? Maybe the voters reported more positive views about immigrants because they simply liked the canvassers (many of whom were immigrants themselves). The narrative part comes next. The voter tells the story of an immigrant they know and imagines what it would be like to be an immigrant. The voter then hears a similar story from the canvasser. Is it telling a story about an immigrant and imagining the immigration experience that softens their stance, or is it hearing the story from the person standing on your front porch that does the work? Then on top of that, there is a whole discussion about compassion, both the experience of receiving it and how it relates to immigration. Maybe that's the key?

When you conduct a huge, ambitious field experiment, throwing in everything you've got is the right approach. Separating all the individual bits and testing them one at a time is prohibitively expensive and time consuming. However, after you hit on a successful approach, it's time to go into the lab and separate the ingredients. Although the intervention was called a "nonjudgmental exchange of personal narratives," did sharing the narrative really have anything to do with the results? And if it did, was it the telling or the listening that made it work?

To more precisely understand the effects of personal narratives on conversation about opposing views, I teamed up with David Hagmann, a professor at the Hong Kong University of Science and Technology, and Catherine Tinsley, my coauthor from the first receptiveness scale paper and a professor at Georgetown University. We were particularly interested in the effects of telling your own story and how this approach might compare to making a similar argument based on facts and data—the broadly accepted gold standard if you are trying to persuade a rational, impartial judge. To compare these two approaches, we ran a series of experiments that all had the same basic structure. First, we chose a topic on which public opinion was divided and for which we could make strong factual arguments for either perspective with just a bit of online research. We then rewrote the factual arguments to make them sound like they were describing an author's personal experience.

For example, a topic we used in several studies was whether the national minimum wage should be raised to $15 an hour. Here is the factual, data-driven message that we wrote, arguing against raising the minimum wage:

> Increasing the minimum wage hurts the people it's supposed to help and drives up prices.
>
> Seattle raised its minimum wage to $15 an hour in 2015. Studies found that many businesses run on small margins, so that many have had to lay off employees. One study reported that the number of low and moderate wage jobs available decreased by 10 percent. Since the minimum wage has changed, some businesses had to raise prices for their customers. Moreover, one study estimated that it reduced the number of hours employers offered to their workers. Employers also reduced costs by cutting health insurance benefits. Many businesses have shut down because they couldn't afford the increased costs, and prices in some stores have gone up.
>
> Life for many and for their families has gotten harder as a result.

Here is a message of similar length and delivered in a similar tone that makes the opposite argument:

The minimum wage should be increased because it benefits working families who need all the help they can get.

In Chicago, the minimum wage is at $12 an hour. Studies found that workers struggle to live in a city that once was more affordable: 66 percent report having trouble paying for basic living expenses like groceries and the copays of prescriptions. Some have to resort to payday loans to pay the bills, with interest rates averaging 400 percent.

Life for them and their families is tough because the cities they live in just don't look out for working people. Nobody should have to work for a wage they can't live on.

Both arguments sound reasonably compelling, especially if you already agree with the side they are taking. Remember, though, the key to the experiment was to compare how these fact-based messages would perform relative to messages featuring a personal narrative. To do this, we tweaked the arguments slightly to present the same facts but now in the form of a first-person account. For example, here is the message arguing against the minimum-wage increase in narrative form:

Increasing the minimum wage hurts the people it's supposed to help and drives up prices.

I used to work for a small family-owned business in Seattle. The city recently raised its minimum wage to $15 an hour. The place where I worked was barely able to keep the doors open, and after the minimum wage increase they fired some longtime employees, including me. I've been looking for work and really need a job, but most businesses are not hiring because they can't pay the high wages. The jobs that are available are part-time and don't offer benefits, like basic health insurance. At the same time, prices in my neighborhood have gone up too.

Life for many and for their families has gotten harder as a result.

And here is the message in favor of the minimum-wage increase as a narrative:

> The minimum wage should be increased because it benefits working families who need all the help they can get.
> I work in Chicago, where the minimum wage is $12 an hour. Losing the fight to earn a living wage means I won't be able to afford to live in the city I grew up in anymore. I struggle to take care of living expenses like groceries and cover copay prescriptions. I have to resort to payday loans to make ends meet, paying as much as 400 percent interest.
> Life for me and my family is a constant struggle and it's all because the city I live in just doesn't look out for working people. Nobody should have to work for a wage they can't live on.

During the study, we first asked participants what they believed about the minimum wage and then sent them the argument for the opposing perspective. Importantly, we randomly assigned each person to see an opposing argument based on data and facts or an argument ostensibly based on the writer's personal experience. Notice that our study differs from the door-to-door canvassing experiment in multiple ways. First, instead of having a ten-minute conversation with a real-life trained human, our participants took about thirty seconds to read one of the messages above. Second, our "data-driven" arguments are extremely similar to our "personal narrative" arguments. The length is the same, the beginning and end are the same, even the arguments in the middle have basically the same content. The only real difference is that one is based on solid (and true) evidence and the other is a person you've never met talking about their life struggles. This setup allows us to very precisely identify whether the narrative approach is really causing any psychological effect.

The next question was figuring out what to measure. The canvassing study above asked participants about their attitudes toward immigrants, which makes sense if you are a professional canvasser and your mission is to persuade voters to think a certain way about a certain issue. As a canvasser, you generally don't care about your relationship with the voter because you will never see them again. But most of us care about what people we disagree with think of us because they are often our friends, family members, or colleagues. Their opinion on the topic is one thing; their opinion about us is another. People usually care about both, and in fact often care about the second more than the first. In our study, we asked participants separate questions regarding how they felt about the author of the message and how they felt about increasing or decreasing the minimum wage. In particular, we were interested in how trustworthy an author seemed based on whether they argued with facts and data or instead told a story about their life.

Trustworthiness is an interesting outcome to measure for several reasons: First, if a person doesn't trust you, you will never persuade them of anything, including having another conversation. If I believe you are being dishonest or if I think your motives are suspect, why should I take your arguments seriously or want to hear more of them? Loss of trust is pretty damning for persuasion. Ironically, of course, this is exactly what happens in disagreement. People don't believe each other's claims—either scientific ("That's fake news! Read some real science!") or personal ("You weren't 'just trying to help'! If you were, you wouldn't have told Mom!").

Additionally, if sharing a personal narrative makes a person come across as more trustworthy, this is more than a bit ironic. Stories about people can be easily made up and are often difficult to check. For example, some people may remember Joe the Plumber, an Ohio voter often cited by John McCain's presidential campaign as a potential victim of Democratic tax increases on small businesses. The man's actual name was Samuel Joseph Wurzelbacher, and he became a minor celebrity. That's when it came to light that "Joe the Plumber" had completed some plumbing training years ago while in the military, was not licensed to work as a plumber in Ohio, and certainly did not own a plumbing business that would be hurt by the proposed Obama tax plan. By contrast, facts and data are supposed to be verifiable: If I told you about a study, you should be able to go online, find it, and decide for yourself if the evidence is credible. If people intuitively trust personal stories more than data, we should rethink how we go about many of our persuasion attempts.

But this was exactly what we found. In experiment after experiment, a narrator was evaluated by the readers as more trustworthy and more believable if they presented their arguments in terms of a personal experience rather than bolstering their claims with facts and data. The completely made-up personal stories were seen as more credible than the real studies that provided the original foundation for those stories. Topics ranging from the minimum wage to restrictions on abortion access returned the same results: Personal stories were seen as more true than actual, true facts.

WHY IS STORYTELLING EFFECTIVE?

Why do personal narratives increase trustworthiness, and does this approach always work? Consider the stories I've included in this chapter and the ones used in our research: Dr. Sakran's story about almost dying at the age of seventeen from a stray bullet and his frustration at being unable to save every patient; the stories in our experiments about people who can barely put food on the table or have to lay off their employees; or stories of immigrants trying to make it in the United States. All of these stories share a common characteristic: They reveal the vulnerability and the humanity of the author. The person seems believable because they are revealing something intimate, possibly painful, or slightly embarrassing about themselves. People generally don't like talking about near-death experiences, losing their jobs, or being barely able to care for their families. When they do, we tend to believe them, because why would they tell us these things if they hadn't happened? The secret to successfully leveraging a narrative to build trust during a disagreement is to use the narrative to reveal your own vulnerability. That's why people believe the story more than the evidence—anyone can pull up some data online and twist it so that it comes to support their argument. But when people share something personal and slightly embarrassing, we assume they are telling the truth. Talking about dire financial problems or regretted abortions is just not something you bring up unless you feel very strongly about the point you are making and are willing to pay a psychological toll to make others take you seriously.

Understanding that the trust-boosting effects of stories arise from creating an impression of vulnerability has practical implications. First of all, if you are trying to increase trust during a disagreement, don't brag about how great you are. Imagine Dr. Sakran saying:

> When I was recently promoted to the role of executive vice chair of surgery, I decided to give myself a treat and bought a yellow Lamborghini. As one of the top trauma surgeons in the country, I really thought that I should enjoy some well-deserved fun. However, I quickly realized that I was not spending any time in my fabulous new car because of all the gunshot victims

> I am constantly operating on. The gun crisis in America is really interfering with my leisure. And that's why I came to believe that the best medical treatment is prevention.

For the record, Dr. Sakran does not have a yellow Lamborghini and is one of the most humble and dedicated people I have ever met. But my fictional example drives home the point: It's not enough to simply tell a story about how you yourself came to hold your belief. The story needs to make you seem vulnerable, and not like a braggard who wants to change national policy for the sake of their own recreation.

The recognition that trustworthiness is increased through perceptions of vulnerability has a second practical takeaway: The story has to be about you or somebody you know well and care about. If I tell you that I became an advocate for the rights of immigrants because I am an immigrant or because of the experiences of discrimination that my family lived through, that's vulnerable. If I tell you that I advocate for immigrants because I read about the plight of immigrants in *The New York Times*, I sound like a preachy liberal snowflake, disconnected from both the realities of the immigrant experience and the policy challenges involved in reforming immigration.

Could you tell a story about a third party in a way that is compelling? Probably, but you have to reveal a piece of yourself when you do it. Take my friend Chris. Chris is an older man who is deeply committed to and guided by his Christian faith. A few years ago, Chris took a leave of absence from his job to travel to the U.S.–Mexico border and minister to the new immigrants waiting in the detention centers there. He worked with kids and teens reading the Bible and leading prayer sessions and sing-alongs. Years later, when Chris sat in my living room and talked about his time at the border, he teared up describing the trauma and hopelessness he observed. Chris is not an immigrant himself, and he will likely never see most of those kids again. But when you see a grown man cry, you tend to believe his story.

WHEN AND HOW TO PUT YOUR STORY TO WORK FOR YOU

Comparing self-revealing personal narratives to arguments based on facts and data yielded a pattern of results that was highly consistent from experiment to experiment. However, we also observed some important wrinkles that need to be considered before we put personal narratives in our toolbox of conversational strategies for navigating disagreement. For example, you might be wondering whether our arguments changed participants' views on raising the minimum wage or abortion access and whether doing so in narrative form was more or less persuasive. You might say to me, "Julia, you may not think that persuasion is realistic or important, but I paid for your book, and I want to know how to be persuasive, damn it!"

Well, as is often the case when dealing with real data, there is good news and bad news. The good news is that across our studies, both kinds of arguments (those based on data and those featuring a personal narrative) shifted people's views by a tiny amount. This seems to be a pretty consistent finding in studies where participants receive messages written by expert experimenters and don't have a chance to argue back. The less good news, especially if in your mind you are now cheering for personal narratives, is that they were no more persuasive than the fact-based arguments. Unlike the results reported in the canvassing study—a manipulation featuring an in-person conversation with a trained canvasser—our laboratory experiments featuring a short written message did not show narratives to have superior persuasive effects. Although on one hand this was a bummer, the finding that personal narratives were no less persuasive than arguments based on data is good to know: It suggests that sharing a vulnerable personal narrative can make you more credible without making you less persuasive.

When I talk about this research with professional audiences, I also often get questions about what is the best rhetorical move in situations where a solid command of facts and data is expected. You can't lead every board presentation or client pitch with stories about your difficult childhood or your current financial problems. At some point, in order to be taken seriously, you need to produce some charts and graphs. Of course, to answer this question, we ran another experiment. It turns out that mixing facts and data with a personal narrative does not hurt anything. In studies where we combined personal narratives and research findings in one longer argument, the personal narrative still boosted trust, and the addition of some facts didn't seem to hurt it. If you have been paying attention, you might have noticed that this is what I've actually been doing throughout this whole book—telling you stories about my life while also supporting my conclusions with data.

Seeing somebody as trustworthy is good, but what does trust actually buy you? In the workplace, being seen as trustworthy definitely buys greater access to resources and greater freedom in using them. Many managers must constantly navigate the trade-off between trusting an employee to do the job well and not run off to Cancún on the company budget, versus closely supervising the work and endlessly validating expenses. Trust can be costly if somebody takes advantage of it, but lack of trust is also costly since constant supervision uses precious resources and creates friction. In the final experiment in the paper I wrote with David Hagmann and Catherine Tinsley, we decided to see if sharing a brief, self-revealing narrative would lead people to trust the author's word in an unrelated domain, even when real money was on the line.

In this study, we again asked participants about their attitudes toward a policy issue (abortion) and sent them two messages advocating for the opposite perspective than the one they endorsed. Both messages made arguments based on data, but one also included a personal narrative. We then asked the participants to evaluate the trustworthiness of both authors and gave them the opportunity to win an extra financial bonus. The twist was that to win the bonus, the participant had to work with a partner—a partner they had to choose from among the two people who they disagreed with and whose arguments they just read.

We then told participants about the task that would determine whether they would win the bonus: solving a difficult puzzle that most people get wrong. Participants in one group learned that if the partner they picked from the two authors *correctly solved the puzzle*, they would get a financial bonus. Participants in the other group learned that if the partner *truthfully told them whether they solved the puzzle*, then they would get a bonus. Thus, in one condition, the participants were incentivized to choose the partner who seemed smarter, whereas in the other condition the participants were incentivized to choose the partner who was both smart and trustworthy—you wanted them to solve the puzzle but also to tell you if they couldn't. Convoluted as our setup might seem, it closely mirrors many workplace contexts where, on the one hand, we are interested in hiring the most competent employee, but when the task is difficult, we also want a person who will admit to failure—a trustworthy employee.

The results were in line with what we expected based on the earlier studies. Overall, participants preferred to work with the person who included a self-revealing narrative in their argument by combining both facts and data with a story about a personal experience. However, this preference was especially pronounced when the participant bonus was tied to the chosen partner's trustworthiness. Our participants seemed to have the intuition that a person who shares a vulnerable story with a perfect stranger is less likely to lie to them about solving a puzzle and thus will increase their chances at the bonus payment. In the end, just by telling a story about themselves, people came across as both smarter and more trustworthy. What a powerful tool.

HOW TO IMPROVE YOUR STORYTELLING

It's not easy to tell a compelling and vulnerable personal story, especially when we're using it to argue for a set of important beliefs. Vulnerability is embarrassing almost by definition and is usually the last thing we want to do in the midst of a disagreement. The same barriers that prevent people from expressing curiosity—the desire to win the argument and grind our opponents' stupid beliefs into the dirt—also make us reach for the highest standard of evidence available to us while concealing our own warts and weaknesses. I am not going to try to convince you that vulnerability is good for you and will lead you toward greater self-mastery and a higher spiritual plane—this is not that book. As in prior chapters, I will simply suggest that if you wish to get good at a new approach to disagreement, it makes sense to plan in advance and practice a bit.

As an exercise, consider a belief you have in your life, one that is not shared by somebody who is important to you. Now, instead of thinking about all the reasons why you are right, think about how you came to hold that belief. Where did it come from and why does it matter? What are the specific life experiences, interactions, or influential mentors that led to your holding this view? Now explain the origins of your beliefs in a short narrative.

Here are some storytelling basics to get you started:

- Your story has to have a beginning, a middle, and an end. "When I was . . . this thing happened to me, which led me to wonder . . . and then it turned out that . . ."

- Stories usually have a conflict and the conflict gets resolved. In other words, there has to be a bit of drama. Maybe you saw something bad and it really bothered you. Or you had a problem you couldn't overcome and it left you with your current beliefs. Or somebody helped you out and now you want to pay it forward.

- There has to be a protagonist (probably you), and something has to happen to that person that the listener might want to know about.

- Your story should fit on a single typed page, so you don't lose your audience's attention.

Write out your story and read it aloud to yourself. Does it accurately represent the origin of your beliefs? Does it reveal something of your delicate emotional underbelly? Does it reveal so much that it will make people uncomfortable? Go back and edit it a few times until you feel that you can share the result with the person you disagree with. Observe their reaction, answer their questions, and then ask them to share their story. This simple but powerful approach is a far more effective strategy for conveying your beliefs than insisting that your arguments and reasoning are simply superior to theirs, and it can be adapted to almost every relationship and setting. Conversations where you share your beliefs through storytelling and learn about the events and people that shaped the beliefs of others can be interesting, heartwarming, and even humorous. Storytelling can turn disagreement from a source of dread to a source of profound connection.

CHAPTER SUMMARY

- Several lines of research point to the idea that telling a story about why and how you came to believe something (i.e., telling a personal narrative) has relational benefits over advocating for your beliefs with facts and data alone.

- Our own research finds that telling a personal story makes you come across as more trustworthy, an outcome that opens the door to most other conversational goals.

- To be maximally effective, a narrative has to show vulnerability. This makes people believe your story and reciprocate with their own trustworthy behavior. Share something personal, meaningful, or slightly embarrassing to convince your counterpart that you are being truly genuine.

- There is nothing wrong with combining a personal narrative with facts and data. The story helps and the facts don't hurt.

9

THE COURAGE TO SPEAK WITH RECEPTIVENESS

MOST PEOPLE I KNOW THINK THAT RECEPTIVENESS SOUNDS LIKE a good idea. We are all tired of conflict in our lives and we all want a way to engage with our disagreeing colleagues, friends, and neighbors in a way that, on the one hand, reflects our true views and beliefs and, on the other, avoids most of the drama. Having done countless talks, trainings, and podcasts about receptiveness over the last few years, I'm not surprised that most people react to these tools with enthusiasm and want to give them a shot.

But others are skeptical. They express a hesitancy to fully embrace the mindset and the practices developed in our research. Usually, when people are hesitant, it is because they are concerned about specific risks that they associate with behaving in a more receptive manner. They are worried about the possibility of unintended consequences in certain situations or with certain people or on certain topics. Ironically, those often turn out to be exactly the situations in which practicing receptiveness is most important. Below, I discuss some of the most common questions I've encountered and the reflections and new research they have prompted.

WHY SHOULD I TALK TO CRAZY PEOPLE?

A common reason for not wanting to invest time and effort into being more receptive is the belief that the other person's opinions are so wild and unsubstantiated that there is no point in talking to them. On the one hand, this seems reasonable. Time is a finite resource, and we should be careful about how we invest it. On the other hand, however, research suggests that our evaluations of other people's opinions are often off base. You should definitely consider whether a conversation is a good use of your time, but also question the basis on which you are making this determination. It's worth considering your evidence before you completely write somebody off.

In the late 1980s, American researchers distributed questionnaires to residents of what was then East and West Germany, two countries created after the conclusion of World War II and physically divided by the Berlin Wall. The questionnaires asked Germans on both sides of the wall to report their views on a variety of social and political issues and then to estimate the views of other Germans (both East and West) on the same issues. Not surprisingly, East Germans, living in the Soviet Union's sphere of informational influence, had different views on many topics compared to West Germans, who shared many opinions with their Western European neighbors. However, despite the real differences, the pattern that stood out the most was the extent to which people on both sides of the wall *exaggerated* their level of disagreement. In other words, although real disagreement existed, people assumed that they disagreed by a far greater amount than they really did.

This pattern of assuming disagreement to be greater than it is has come to be known as "false polarization." Whereas the term "polarization" refers to how much members of different groups *actually* disagree with one another, false polarization refers to the *exaggerated* beliefs people hold about their level of disagreement. A similar pattern of results was found across many political issues in the United States, and even among a sample of English professors who disagreed about the appropriate amount of curriculum updates to introductory literature courses.* Forty years after these studies were conducted, false polarization has reached dramatic levels in the United States and, according to many scholars, represents one of the fundamental reasons why American partisans have such a difficult time interacting with one another.

If you are interested, you can measure your own level of false polarization.† A nonpartisan think tank called More in Common has created a website where people can answer questions about their views on common topics of American policy debate and then make their best guess about the views held by the members of their own and the opposing political party. The website then uses people's self-reported views on the issues as "the truth" and creates a nice graphic showing how the truth differs from the assumptions people on both sides make about each other. The takeaway is that across a variety of issues, Republicans and Democrats wildly overestimate their level of disagreement. The gap is the largest for the strongest partisans: Committed Democrats and committed Republicans exaggerate the gap the most, while people who are closer to the middle perceive both parties in a more realistic manner. If you think you are the exception to the rule, you should take the quiz. You might be right, you might be wrong, but testing your assumptions is how you learn.

Like many other conflict-related biases and misperceptions,

---

* The professors who wanted to stick to the traditional (largely Western European) curriculum thought that the reformers wanted to scrap all of it. By contrast, the reformers merely wanted to introduce a handful of non-Western and contemporary sources but believed that the traditionalist crew was open to zero change.

† https://perceptiongap.us/.

false polarization likely has its roots in naïve realism. To the extent that people believe their own views to be an objective reaction to careful analysis, and the views of a disagreeing other to somehow stem from error, delusion, or bias, it becomes easy for them to imagine a caricatured version of those opposing views. We see our conclusions as having been derived "bottom up"—I observed a set of events and drew a set of conclusions about the world that reflect the underlying reality in all of its glorious complexity and nuance.

By contrast, we see the conclusions of people who disagree with us as "top down"—the people on the other side are motivated by dogma, self-interest, and ideology, and these influences in turn force them to see the evidence in a certain way. Because their interpretation of the evidence is being channeled toward a previously determined conclusion, they will fail to note any nuance and complexity, instead reverting to more simplistic, more extreme views. In this way, during the 2024 U.S. presidential election, all Trump voters become uneducated bigots in the minds of liberals and all Harris voters become socialist snowflakes in the eyes of conservatives.

Disagreements outside of politics are not structurally different. When designers of cutting-edge new products assume that the folks in legal are going to be extremely concerned with risk, they are likely exaggerating the amount of disagreement. Yes, lawyers tend to be concerned with liability, but likely less so than the daredevils in engineering assume they will be. When the spouse who believes in gentle and supportive parenting assumes that their disciplinarian partner will ground the kids for life, they are probably right about the likelihood of punishment (after all, they've had this fight before!), but they are exaggerating the duration of the planned house arrest. When your aging parent refuses to give up driving, even though you think they are about to commit vehicular homicide, it is not because they are oblivious to their growing limitations; it is because they don't see the decline to be quite as dramatic as you do.

The key insight of research on false polarization is that we are not as divided as we think. However, to become better calibrated about the beliefs of others, we have to talk to them, ask questions, listen to the answers, and do some work to wrap our minds around why their perspective makes sense to them. But remember, humans are "cognitive misers" and don't like to put in extra mental effort. Life is hard enough without spending precious time thinking about the minds of people who are basically wrong about the things that matter most. False polarization thus contributes to a vicious cycle: To the extent that I expect your views to be infected by bias and self-interest, I expect our disagreement to be greater than it is. The greater our disagreement, the less interest I have in discussing our differences. Why would I expect a biased extremist or a person who has simply taken leave of reality to listen to reason? The less effort I put into communicating with you, the more my opinion of you becomes a distorted caricature rather than an accurate reflection of your beliefs, gradually fueling greater and greater false polarization.

The most important point, however, is that if you do have a thoughtful conversation with a person you disagree with, you are likely to discover the truth—that you have more in common in terms of beliefs, attitudes, and goals than you probably thought. But that requires taking a leap of faith. For one awkward conversation you have to run with the assumption that the research evidence is true and that your own perceptions of the disagreement are probably biased. Then you have the conversation and let the chips land where they may.

BUT WHAT IF I AM *ACTUALLY* RIGHT?

People (psychologists included) tend to draw a distinction between facts and opinions. Most people believe that you are allowed to disagree about opinions but facts are facts, and if you can't get on the same page with me about the fact that the sky is blue or that the Earth is round, what is even the point? But it turns out that the line between facts and opinions is not as clear as people like to think, especially in the types of divisive conversations we are considering here.

You would be surprised at the number of times the topic of so-called flat-earthers comes up as an example of the sorts of folks we should definitely not be receptive to. This example is easy to reach for because the vast majority of us believe that the Earth is round and see little point in talking to somebody who is convinced that it is flat. I once saw a T-shirt that perfectly captured this sentiment: "Science doesn't care about your feelings." Right on. But then again, how many of you have actually had a disagreement with a flat-earther? Although this belief exists, and is passionately held by a small minority of people, it doesn't actually matter to your life unless you are actively engaged in planning a trip to space!

Most disagreements that people do engage in on a regular basis have to do with matters closer to home and ones on which a much larger proportion of the population happens to disagree. These arguments generally involve some mix of facts and opinions. Because most of us don't usually have direct access to the relevant data for a particular viewpoint—I can't personally go around and count how many homicides would be prevented if guns were made illegal or what number of children have experienced a side effect from the MMR vaccine—people have to choose which information sources they consider trustworthy and which of the facts being offered by those sources seem believable.

And guess what? Those are subjective judgments largely driven by the opinion we held in the first place.

One of the most well-documented phenomena in social psychology is called "confirmation bias." In short, we are more likely to seek out, pay attention to, and believe evidence that supports our views than evidence that contradicts them. When you think that the evidence for a particular stance is rock solid, it is not because you actually went through the scientific literature, critically examined the research methodology of each study, and ultimately concluded that the evidence is good. It is far more likely that it is because some information source you tend to believe (a news outlet, an expert, your parents, your high school teacher) told you that this is how it is, and you have now internalized that viewpoint. Because of confirmation bias, any new information that contradicts your established view must meet a higher bar of evidence to make a dent in your thinking, while information that supports the established view gets incorporated with no questions asked. In other words, our selection of information that gets elevated to the glorious status of being a "fact" is very much affected by a set of previously held and likely poorly vetted opinions. And what we consider to be a high-quality, reliable source is profoundly influenced by whether that source agrees with whatever we believed from the start. This means that while we would like to think that our opinions are determined by facts, in reality what we consider to be facts is also determined by our previously held opinions. To be clear, I am not saying that we live in a "post-truth world" and everything is up for debate, but I am saying that we should all be a little less high-and-mighty in how we judge people who are *obviously* clinging to positions that are *obviously* not true.

Few topics in recent history have sparked as much outrage about people failing to understand "facts" as the debate about the benefits and safety of COVID-19 mitigation measures. Almost overnight, everyone with a social media account became a health policy expert, proclaiming "scientific facts" with tremendous certainty. In retrospect, I am embarrassed to say that I was just as judgmental as everyone else when I encountered disagreement among my circle of friends and acquaintances. A particular conversation stands out in my mind as one I wish I could do over.

In the summer of 2021, soon after the COVID-19 vaccines were approved for children under sixteen, my teenage daughters restarted participating in indoor volleyball tournaments. All the kids had to show proof of vaccination to enter the gym and all had to wear a face mask. The masks were a hodgepodge of cloth masks, surgical masks, and N95s and KN95s. Some of them covered noses; some of them didn't. Most of them were probably not changed much throughout the day, and all of them were constantly adjusted mid-play as the girls sweated, yelled, jumped, and dove for volleyballs. A group of volunteers paraded through the gym displaying large posters: "Masking is mandatory."

At the time, wearing a mask in public seemed like a core responsibility of any good citizen. It was a fact that COVID-19 was deadly, it was a fact that it was transmitted through the air, and it was a fact that masks prevented such transmission. When another mom on the sidelines commented, "That's so unfortunate—those masks are so useless," a perspective that wildly contradicted what I believed to be the medical consensus, our conversation did not go well.

I did not ask about her thoughts on masking or her experience with COVID-19. All I managed to do was to lecture her on my beliefs, in what I thought was a reasonable and civil tone. In retrospect, I recognize that lecturing somebody politely is not at all the same thing as being receptive.

Of course, now we know that COVID-19, while very dangerous at the population level, is not very dangerous for fully vaccinated, healthy teenagers. We also now know that cloth masks and surgical masks worn haphazardly by kids who are sprinting, diving, and spiking balls for hours are unlikely to meaningfully prevent the spread of disease. But at the time, I could not wrap my mind around how this woman (who had a master's degree in public health and worked as a health economist) could possibly be so clueless. It was a fact that masking was necessary, and anybody who did not know that fact needed to be educated.

The moral of this story is that many facts change over time. Some things that we believe to be scientific truths stand the test of time and some don't. This is also the case for many moral convictions. Some practices that were widely accepted back in the day are now considered child abuse (e.g., spanking). Other practices that were considered a mortal sin (e.g., premarital sex) are now common practice. Again, I am not saying that there are no facts and everything is relative. However, I am saying that we should recognize that facts can change, and we just don't know if the one we are currently dealing with is an "eternal fact" or a "right now fact." Maybe we should wait for the future to unfold before destroying friendships.

BUT DO WE NEED TO BE RECEPTIVE TO IMMORAL PERSPECTIVES?

The other category of beliefs that people consider to be in a more elevated category, distinct from mere opinions, are attitudes rooted in moral values. Beliefs about fundamental human rights, beliefs about equality and dignity, and beliefs about the wrongness of certain agreed-upon actions such as murder, rape, and theft seem beyond the pale of receptive conversation. And yet, explicitly or implicitly, we (and our elected representatives) debate these matters all the time. A conversation about immigration is a conversation about whether people who are born in one country are more entitled to a good life than people who are born in another. A conversation about abortion regulation is for many a conversation about the murder of babies, while for others it is a conversation about the murder of women. A conversation about gender fluidity among teenagers is always a conversation about protecting children from harm—with the two sides disagreeing on which harm we are trying to protect them from.

It is tempting to categorically declare that you do not condone conversations with racists, homophobes, nazis, religious zealots, anti-Semites, or misogynists. Talking to such folk, especially *listening* to them, often feels like you are tacitly elevating their perspective to one worthy of consideration, which feels, simply put, gross. By being receptive, you are engaging with ideas that should instead be locked in a dark vault and thrown into the ocean, never to be surfaced again. The far more appealing move is to walk away with your head held high, wrapped in the cloak of moral superiority. But what are the actual costs and benefits of this approach?

The first issue, suggested by our earlier discussion of false polarization, is that your label of the other person as a bigot might simply be wrong. The coworker who does not agree with policies designed to hire more women in engineering roles might not actually be a misogynist. Maybe instead they believe that such affirmative action policies put into question the qualifications of the existing female engineers who attained their positions prior to the newly proposed policies. Or maybe they believe that the culture of the company is so toxic to women that you would not be doing anyone any favors by increasing female representation before other changes are made. Or maybe they believe that real change will come from better preparing women for leadership positions rather than simply hiring them in greater numbers. You might disagree with this individual's interpretation of events, their beliefs about the causes of the problem, or their predictions about the likely consequences of different approaches, but their fundamental disagreement with your policy views does not come from a lack of regard for women. In fact, it may be the opposite. Assuming that it does is likely to cause offense to your colleagues if your thinking were to become known to them. By contrast, if you keep your judgment to yourself and simply refuse to discuss issues of workplace diversity with somebody you judge to be a sexist jerk, you will be the one walking around angry and disdainful, wondering what the hell is wrong with the world at large and people you work with in particular.

But let's consider a situation where a person's disparagement of women (or some other group or important value) is on pretty clear display. Is there any reason to strive for receptive dialogue with this person? It depends.

Remember my friend Hawk, the mediator from Chapter 6. Hawk is a six-foot-five Black man who has both witnessed and experienced many examples of racism in his life. The combination of his soothing personal style and his life history regularly leads to awkward situations where people feel so at ease around him that they state opinions that he has cause to strongly disagree with. Each of these situations then forces him into a difficult choice: Say something or let it go? Put a person in their place or turn the other cheek? Let another racist claim hang in the air or correct the record?

A couple of years ago, Hawk was invited to watch an NHL hockey game by a friend whose brother-in-law worked for a company that had a fancy VIP suite at the hockey rink. Hawk is an avid sports fan and was thrilled to join. During the intermission, while the guests in the suite were enjoying the catering and the free alcohol, somebody turned the television to a news channel. In a perfect example of how conflict can crop up anywhere at any time, a commentator on the news channel just happened to make a statement critical of President Trump. That statement, which might have gone unnoticed by many people, elicited a strong reaction from the host of the gathering, one of the executives of the company. The host thought that the television comment was unfair to the president and that instead the fault lay with all the "woke" people ruining America with their affirmative action policies, which were clearly designed to let unqualified minorities attain high-level positions above other, more qualified candidates. As Hawk politely told me, the resulting rant made him "feel some kinda way."

As a Black man who has spent his career working in corporate HR and labor-management mediation, Hawk knows a whole lot about affirmative action policies: what they are, what they are designed to do, and what they are definitely not designed to do. Furthermore, he does not think of being "woke" as a bad thing and certainly doesn't think that woke people are out to ruin America. So, here he was, an invited guest facing a hard choice: try to express his feelings, correct his host, and possibly start a scene, or swallow his feelings and "let it go."

The first thing he considered was who would be affected by his choices: certainly the host and him, but also his buddy who had invited him, his buddy's brother-in-law who worked for the company, as well as the other people in the suite who were now looking around a little nervously. Hawk also felt strongly that something had to be said—he was not okay just letting it go. He then considered what he was hoping to accomplish. His goal, he realized, was to understand why his host would make the statements he did and where and how he had come to form his opinions. So instead of making a challenging retort, Hawk started asking questions. "What does 'woke' mean to you?" "Why do you feel this way about it?" "What is the point of affirmative action in your mind? Why do you think it was started?" Having been in these sorts of conversations more than once, Hawk also knew that he had to be careful about not being too instructive. First and foremost, his questions had to convey curiosity. Any information or personal perspective he shared had to be added in moderation. He felt that the best he could do was to leave his counterpart with some food for thought.

In the course of the conversation, Hawk learned that his host mostly listened to conservative talk shows, which is where he got his views on wokeness and affirmative action. He had also had the experience of being shut down and "canceled" for his conservative views by people who claimed to be woke. The man was resentful of the phrase "white privilege" because, in his mind, it negated his decades of hard work and made it sound like he had been handed all his success on a silver platter.

In turn, Hawk shared that to him, "'woke' means that I have been awakened, that my eyes have been opened. That I am seeing things in a greater scope than I have seen before because I have more knowledge." However, he also added, "It doesn't mean I let it get in the way of my relationships or prevent me from being able to connect with people." Hawk also shared that he has some very conservative views because of his deeply held Christian beliefs and that he also doesn't appreciate being judged for holding those views.

As they talked, the intermission ended. People went back to the food, the drinks, and the hockey. At the end of the evening, the host pulled Hawk aside. "I want to shake your hand, and I wanted to thank you for the conversation," he said. "And any time you want to join us in the suite, you are always welcome."

Hawk said that even in the context of his long mediation career, this experience was an important personal lesson. "We often want to fix someone's Little Red Wagon, set them straight, kill them with all the facts, show them how wrong they are . . . and I think people just need to be understood. The most I can do is get them to examine the merits of their own perspective."

Was Hawk's host a racist? Or was he just a guy who watched too many talking heads on TV? Or was he somebody who was ticked off about other people telling him how to think and talk one too many times? I don't really know and neither does Hawk. But if Hawk had decided the topic was beyond the pale and walked away from the conversation, he would have lost the opportunity to influence this person's thinking and behavior. And he never would've been able to start building a relationship with this man.

In making the choice between speaking up and "turning the other cheek," we often imagine that the threat of being ostracized by us will eventually bring the other person around to our superior way of thinking. However, the reality is that for every individual shunned for not thinking or speaking the correct way, there is a community of like-minded folks who are willing to embrace them and forge a common bond around what a judgmental jerk *you are* for shunning them. When we decide that somebody is not worth listening to, they are unlikely to sit alone in the corner and reflect on the error of their ways. Instead, they will probably come to see your judgment as further evidence of your unreasonableness, lack of intelligence, and bigotry (against them). Nothing good is likely to follow.

WHAT IF BEING RECEPTIVE MAKES PEOPLE THINK I MIGHT CHANGE MY MIND?

One of the most common concerns about receptiveness is that people see being receptive as a form of capitulation or at least compromise. And if you have no intention of doing that, why bother?

It stands to reason that more receptive people do change their minds more often than less receptive people. If you are regularly exposing yourself to multiple perspectives, thinking about them deeply, and evaluating them fairly, you are likely to sooner or later come across something that makes you reconsider your beliefs. But that's not such a bad thing, is it? Although receptive people might change their minds more frequently than unreceptive people *on average*, in any one encounter receptiveness does not obligate you to be open to persuasion. You could listen to someone's point of view, think about it hard, show them that you heard them through your questions and your behavior, and then still walk away unconvinced. Hopefully, you will also walk away better informed about the nature of the disagreement and having a stronger relationship with your counterpart.

Even if you're confident you won't be persuaded, you may still worry that receptiveness might make you *look* persuadable to disagreeing counterparts and that they will somehow take advantage of this apparent weakness. People put a high premium on appearing stalwart in their beliefs, even when facing arguments and evidence that should be raising questions in their minds. It is as if we forget that continuing to believe what you do is only a virtue when you are correct—not 100 percent of the time. However, even if appearing stalwart is your goal, this is not incompatible with receptiveness. The secret to looking firm in your convictions and being receptive at the same time is, again, language. For example, one might say: "I am very confident in the fact that the flu vaccine is more beneficial than harmful and therefore should be taken. It would take very strong evidence to change my beliefs. But I understand that you disagree, and I am curious about what you have heard. Can you tell me about your thinking?" The above phrasing makes it clear that although you are open to hearing another person's opinion, it is not for lack of having a well-informed opinion of your own. You are signaling receptiveness without signaling wishy-washiness. If you have no interest in having your mind changed and it is important to you that the other party understands this, you can just say so.

Another related concern has to do with the reactions of third-party observers. For example, imagine you are a leader dealing with a difficult employee. Wouldn't it be better to assert your authority than listen and ask questions? Or imagine that you are an elected official dealing with unruly protesters. Will your constituents see you as a pushover if you enter into discussions with protest leaders? This concern was recently addressed by a set of studies conducted by University of British Columbia psychologist Kristin Laurin and her student Gordon Heltzel. When looking at in-group judgments of people who asked questions seeking to understand the out-group perspective, the researchers found that these "perspective seekers" were better liked than those who asked no questions and were also seen as more tolerant, cooperative, and rational. In a recent series of studies, Molly Moore, a faculty member at Washington University, and I corroborated these findings using different scenarios that focused specifically on the receptiveness of leaders. We asked participants to evaluate doctors who were receptive to vaccine-hesitant patients, city council members who were receptive to belligerent protesters, and executives who were receptive to resentful employees. Across the board, we consistently found that people prefer the receptive leaders to unreceptive ones. Despite the concerns about how receptiveness among leaders might be perceived, the data consistently demonstrated that people prefer their leaders to engage with multiple perspectives rather than shut them out. It seems that although some people are concerned about receptiveness having reputational costs, on average, people mostly see the benefits.

That said, sometimes even having a conversation with somebody who holds derogatory beliefs about another person or group of people can be hurtful to the members of the group in question. To the extent that even one or two members of a disempowered or marginalized group feel that your engagement with somebody who holds prejudiced views against them is a sign of your potential agreement with those people, you have a set of questions to ask yourself.

For example, imagine you are a CEO of an athletic apparel company, about to release a line of colorful leggings and tops with slogans celebrating Pride Month. However, the head of your workers' union approaches you with a concern. Some of the factory workers have stated that they do not feel comfortable producing apparel that "celebrates gayness" and believe that their religious beliefs demand that they refuse to work on the new product line. You think you could work something out with the union, but you are afraid that your LGBTQ+ employees and their allies will see your efforts as tacitly caving to a bigoted mindset.

In this situation, as the CEO, you might consider a set of questions in order to decide the pros and cons of engaging in discussions with the disgruntled workers. Do you and your leadership team have a reputation for being strong allies of marginalized groups? In other words, do the LGBTQ+ workers have prior evidence of your support that will help them interpret your engagement with the union workers in a positive manner? Can you make your own stance on the issue clear (as discussed above), while also highlighting that in a pluralistic society people are free to believe whatever they want, and it is your job as a leader to make every employee feel heard? Can you minimize the attention and visibility around these discussions by engaging lower-level managers to dialogue with smaller groups of employees? Do you have clarity regarding the roots of this issue? Is it really about Pride Month?

Leaders of governments as well as professional and civic organizations are often faced with choices that initially seem binary. Talk to the protesters or shut the protest down? Listen to grievances or cite precedent and move on? I am not saying that receptive dialogue is always the answer, but I am saying that the choices are almost never binary. Carefully considering why you are concerned about engaging in a conversation often points toward specific and actionable ways of mitigating that concern.

WHAT IF I AM RECEPTIVE TO THEM, BUT THEY ARE REALLY COMBATIVE BACK?

False polarization research focuses on what we think of others. But a similarly important driver of conflict is what we think others think of us—a set of beliefs that psychologists have (extremely confusingly) labeled "meta-perceptions." Meta-perceptions are perceptions about perceptions—what I think other people think of me. And it turns out that in disagreement, people's meta-perceptions are systematically off base.

Many studies have demonstrated that people believe that opponents in conflict hold more negative beliefs about them and their actions than they really do. One of the most striking demonstrations of this phenomenon involves measuring "dehumanization"—the extent to which people think another individual or members of another group are not sufficiently "evolved" or "civilized." Dehumanization is often measured with the "Ascent of Man" scale—an image with an apelike silhouette on the far left that changes gradually to a fully erect human silhouette on the far right.

According to this research, groups in conflict often see the other side as less human (i.e., more animalistic, unevolved, and uncivilized) than the members of their own contingent. Perhaps more troubling, however, is that both sides *imagine* that their opponents dehumanize them twice as much as they do in reality. In other words, as much as we actually dislike and disparage our opponents, in their minds that level of negativity is doubled.

Like false polarization, biased meta-perceptions feed a negative cycle. The less experience we have interacting with disagreeing others in a fruitful manner, the more we expect the interaction to be negative when it happens. As we observe our counterparts seemingly wishing to avoid interacting with us, we interpret their (reasonable) reluctance as a sign of dislike and even enmity. As a result, we come to dislike them, and the cycle continues. But remember, people tend to reciprocate each other's interpersonal style. Receptiveness begets receptiveness, not escalating hostility. When you are extremely receptive to a person who is ready to rumble, you often witness a moment when your counterpart awkwardly reevaluates the situation as if they just realized that they showed up at church wearing a scary Halloween costume. Your receptiveness gives them license to de-escalate their own behavior, to the benefit of everyone involved.

A few years ago, I was at a concert with my older daughters and one of their friends. Imagine supervising two fifteen-year-olds and a thirteen-year-old in a crowded nightclub for an indie-pop concert, with standing room only. Trying to get a better view, I took the girls upstairs where the four of us got to look out over the stage from a balcony surrounded by an iron railing. Unfortunately, other people figured out this trick too, and our little balcony began filling up. Some guys shoved in next to my daughters, who awkwardly backed into me. I tried to make space for them, which made me take a step backward and brought me closer to some other woman who also had a teenage daughter. Next thing you know, the woman behind me was complaining to her daughter about how rude I was for pushing her and stepping on her stuff. I looked back and apologized, but there was nothing

I could do, because the guys were still pushing my kids, and the three of them were practically lying on me, while I held on to the balcony railing for balance. I physically couldn't hold up everybody's weight, so I took another step back, which produced a full-on rant from the lady behind me. There was no moving and no leaving, so I spent the entire first set trying not to breathe too much, because every time I did, I heard the woman behind me audibly cursing under her breath.

Intermission came, and the girls wanted to go buy drinks. That's when it dawned on me: I turned to the woman who I had been mentally telling off for the past forty minutes, smiled, and said, "I am going to go get a drink. Can I buy you a glass of wine?" The look on her face was well worth the overpriced nightclub booze (which she turned down). She got flustered, thanked me profusely, asked me if I wanted to put my coat with hers, and then proceeded to complain about the club, the parking, the weather, and the traffic. Clearly, the lady had been through it that evening, and being crowded in by me was the last straw. Offering to buy her a drink instantly flipped the dynamic from spiraling mutual irritation to two moms of teenage daughters commiserating over our common woes.

Next time you come across a person who is being obnoxious, try this as an experiment. Buy them a coffee and see what happens next. I suspect you will be surprised at the speed and magnitude of the reaction. If enough of you do it, maybe Starbucks will one day give me a free latte for my services!

WHAT IF I JUST DON'T WANT TO HAVE A MISERABLE TIME?

One obvious consequence of the fact that people systematically exaggerate the extent of their disagreements and how poorly their counterparts think of them is that they expect any conversation with holders of opposing views to go badly. But because our expectations of the conversation are based on our faulty assumptions about the degree of disagreement and our counterparts' attitudes about us, the expectations turn out to be faulty as well. Simply put, listening to someone's opposing views is often much less unpleasant than we expect it to be, a pattern we documented in a set of experiments with Charlie Dorison and Todd Rogers, a colleague at the Harvard Kennedy School.

In our studies, we asked participants to imagine watching a two-minute video featuring a politician from the opposing party and then to consider a list of five positive and five negative emotions. The participants' task was to imagine how much of each emotion they thought they would feel if they had to watch the video. We then recruited a different group of participants and asked them to *really* watch the video that we had only described to the other group and report the *actual* emotions they felt. The politicians we picked were Ted Cruz and Bernie Sanders because at the time they were the most extremely conservative and extremely liberal members of the United States Senate. Yet, in our study, Democrats who watched Ted Cruz and Republicans who watched Bernie Sanders had one thing in common: When watching the videos, both sides had a less negative experience than their counterparts who only imagined the videos and anticipated their emotions. Although listening to arguments for the opposing perspective was unpleasant, it was much less unpleasant in practice than in the participants' imaginations.

Of course, this is not always the case. An important feature of our experiment was that people were watching a video—they could not actually get into a fight with Senators Cruz and Sanders because the senators were not there in the flesh. In the real world, engagement with opposing perspectives always carries the risk of conflict escalation because real live people might say something stupid, or hurtful, or both. Furthermore, although engagement with opposing perspectives turned out to be more positive on average than expected, "more positive than expected" is not the same thing as "delightfully wonderful." Conversations on topics of deep disagreement are still likely to be emotionally and cognitively exhausting. The question is whether any given conversation is worth it.

It depends. If a random stranger wants to debate politics at a holiday party, especially if alcohol is involved, I would try to politely change the topic. However, if your beloved spouse keeps spending every weekend golfing with his friends rather than spending time with you and your children, it may be worth asking some questions around his choices, preferences, and perceptions of your family dynamic. It is not likely to be a pleasant conversation, especially if you have had it before, but making the effort to practice the tools in this book will increase your chances of shifting the dynamic in a more fruitful direction. Improving important relationships often requires engaging in many, many unpleasant conversations.

Finally, if a relationship is important and yet the conversation you need to have is likely to be extremely uncomfortable, your ticket to success may be a third party. Simply put, this is why the universe provided us with therapists, mediators, ministers, rabbis, and wise old aunts. You might not be surprised that I often play this role in my family. I jokingly call it "shuttle diplomacy"—a term professional diplomats use for shuttling back and forth between different heads of state until a deal that is acceptable to all parties emerges. Shuttle diplomacy (both the professional and the home-spun version) works because a third party who is not directly involved in the conflict has more ability to be receptive and find areas of understanding than the individuals who are directly involved and thus emotionally affected by the issue. Sometimes you can gain a better understanding of somebody's perspective if you can call on a third party who will be able to listen to them with receptiveness and no judgment and then convey the message back to you.

SHOULDN'T THIS ADVICE DIFFER FROM CULTURE TO CULTURE?

Many of the tools and recommendations in this book were developed and tested with English-speaking Americans, a group of people that share a set of cultural norms around communication and conflict management. So, it is reasonable to ask about the extent to which these recommendations apply in different cultural or linguistic contexts. However, in answering this question, we should go beyond a blanket concession that all cultures are different and consider what we actually know from the research. Although human cultures vary in myriad ways, there are also many things we share.

One way to think about receptiveness and how it varies culturally is to compare it to the familiar construct of politeness. Every culture in the world prizes politeness. In any given place there exists a cultural consensus around appropriate and inappropriate ways to treat others. Paying attention to politeness norms usually matters more when a lower-status person is interacting with a higher-status person (i.e., child to parent or subordinate to manager) than vice versa. You can give your sibling a wedgie, but you probably should not try it with Grandma. That is pretty universally true. But cultures also differ on how strict the rules are. You'd never give Grandma a wedgie, but in some countries, it is okay to stick your tongue out. In other countries, you would only stick your tongue out at a younger sibling but not an older one.

Unless you happen to live in Tibet, in which case sticking your tongue out is a sign of respect and you should definitely do it to Grandma!

We all have some idea of politeness, and we all think it's a good thing, but we express it differently in different cultures, and different cultures care about it to different degrees. You should think of receptiveness in a similar way. Extensive research has demonstrated that people across the globe care about feeling heard and value disagreement counterparts who seem to be engaging with their views. These findings come from different labs and have been replicated in many countries, and the results make intuitive sense: It is hard to imagine why a person would voice an opinion if not to have their counterpart understand and engage with that opinion.

But how exactly you express your willingness to hear and engage with the other person will differ from culture to culture and will have a lot to do with norms around communication. For example, in some countries interruption when another person is speaking is considered extremely rude. In other countries, it is not what you would call polite, but everyone does it and most people don't care too much. Yet in others, everybody interrupts all the time and if you are not interrupting, others will wonder if you are even awake. So, if people everywhere want others to show that they care about their opinions, but different cultures enact receptiveness in different ways, the question becomes: How do you enact it according to the norms of the place where you happen to be? This formulation of the question gives us a more concrete process for identifying culturally appropriate behaviors than simply throwing up our hands and saying that everything is culturally variable. However, when in doubt, I suggest that you err on the side of more receptiveness rather than less. As my mother-in-law, wife of a retired army officer, would say, you can never be too polite.

BEHAVING RECEPTIVELY SEEMS "FAKE." ISN'T THAT A PROBLEM?

Beyond concerns about receptive behavior being difficult, unpleasant, and just not as satisfying as telling people exactly what you think of them, there are concerns about the idea that performing receptiveness if you don't actually feel it is somehow inauthentic. People (especially people from Western cultures) are obsessed with authenticity. We want to be authentic ourselves, demand authenticity from our life partners and friends, and punish inauthentic-sounding leaders. Considered from this perspective, expressing receptiveness through language, even if you don't feel it, sounds like a bad idea. Won't people know that you don't truly want to understand them and are just performing receptiveness because you read about it in a book?

There are two answers to this question: "No they won't" and "It's fine if they do."

Like the research on failures of perspective-taking that we discussed in earlier chapters, many other studies have documented that people are terrible at detecting when others are deceiving them. People have a "truth bias"—meaning that we generally assume that others are being truthful with us even if they aren't. The truth bias is in turn exacerbated by wishful thinking and confirmation bias. In other words, people are much more likely to believe the things that they wanted to believe in the first place. When it comes to someone who disagrees with us asking us thoughtful questions and showing curiosity about our perspective, we are pretty eager to believe that these expressions of receptiveness reflect a genuine interest. We *want* to believe that others are interested in us and value our views, and, when offered the slightest evidence, we do.

Importantly, however, such eagerness to believe in the receptiveness of other humans based on their outward expressions is not really a mistake in the same way that believing a lie is a mistake. Anyone using receptive words to demonstrate engagement with opposing views is at least *trying* to have a thoughtful conversation. Yes, they are relying on a set of techniques that they learned in a book or a workshop, but they are not faking their desire to at least try to make their counterpart feel heard—they just realize that they need a little help.

In this way, receptiveness resembles all the other behaviors that psychologists refer to as posing a "want-should" conflict. I want to eat cake, but I know I should eat apples. I want to sit on the couch, but I know I should go to the gym. I want to fly off the handle and yell at my business partner, but I know I should try to be receptive. And what do we do when we know that our short-term desires are not in line with our long-term interests? We create structures and processes to make us more likely to succeed. We don't buy the cake because cake is less tempting when it's not in the house. We commit to only watching trashy TV on the treadmill to give ourselves a reward for exercising. We memorize the H.E.A.R. framework so that the right words are easier to say.

Learning and applying the techniques in this book are to receptiveness like taking lessons is to making music. Yes, you could learn to play piano by independently rediscovering music theory, but you are much more likely to be successful if you learn the notes from a professional and practice consistently. When a person takes lessons and then performs the piece with sheet music in front of them, nobody calls them a fake musician. Whether they do or do not feel the melody in the depth of their soul, they still get respect for making the effort to learn and giving pleasure to their audience. Similarly, when a person puts in the effort to learn to perform receptiveness, they should get credit for the effort they are putting in to make life easier for those around them. Fake it till you make it, as my immigrant mother used to say.

WHAT DOES "COURAGE" HAVE TO DO WITH IT?

I titled this chapter "The Courage to Speak with Receptiveness" because, in the end, engaging with opposing views in order to learn about other people, improve your mastery over your own emotions, and improve your relationships does take courage. Several steps are involved and almost all of them are uncomfortable, producing a strong temptation to simply ignore the topic of disagreement, the threat that this disagreement might pose to your personal relationships or professional success, and to look the other way.

Yet, the very recognition that a disagreement exists presents us with the question of how to deal with it. If you consider that question honestly, you might come to identify which of the considerations discussed in this chapter are dictating your behavior. Do you think this person is likely to be unreasonable? Do you think their perspective is so abhorrent as to be unworthy of consideration? Are you afraid of yelling, crying, or hearing things you don't want to know about yourself? Are you afraid of being judged by others for having the conversation or causing them harm?

Considering which concerns prevent you from behaving in a receptive manner often means facing unpleasant realities about yourself or your relationship with the other person. Strategizing how to have the dialogue in the face of these concerns takes more courage still. So, in the end, despite all the benefits to be reaped, receptiveness is not for the faint of heart. It is for people who have enough faith in their ideas and perspectives to want to share them but also recognize the importance of engaging with the ideas of others and considering them with an open mind. Gaining the confidence that you can have such conversations and not walk away bruised and battered takes both commitment and practice. Nevertheless, the potential benefits to your relationships, your decision-making, and the world we live in are enormous. In the next chapter, we will talk about the concrete steps you can take to build your receptiveness muscle.

CHAPTER SUMMARY

- There is a common set of concerns that often prevent people from taking a receptive approach to disagreement. These include our assumptions about the actual substance of the disagreement as well as assumptions about what our counterparts think of us and how they are likely to treat us. Sometimes, the concerns have to do with how we'll be perceived by observers—coworkers, members of our political in-group, or vulnerable individuals we want to protect from harm.

- Research suggests that many of these concerns are exaggerated. Although disagreement on difficult topics is often emotionally taxing and people do view disagreeing negatively, the state of affairs is generally not as bad as we imagine it to be.

- Carefully considering whether a conversation with a particular relationship partner is worth it to you and what exactly is holding you back from engaging in it can often help you identify an approach that allows you to address the disagreement without incurring the costs that worry you.

10

BUILDING YOUR RECEPTIVENESS MUSCLE

I HAVE SPENT MY ENTIRE ADULT LIFE TEACHING. AS A TEENAGER, when most of my friends got jobs waiting on tables and delivering pizzas, I began to teach dance lessons. I taught dancing through high school and most of college, to supplement my student stipend and make a bit of extra money for our first mortgage and then while getting my PhD. Teaching dancing to bride-and-groom couples and large classes of eager singles came surprisingly handy when I later had to face teaching large lectures on negotiations and decision-making to college students and executives. Besides preparing me well for hours of standing in heels while projecting my voice and maintaining a high level of energy, it has also made me think long and hard about how adults acquire new skills.

Acquiring a skill is not the same thing as learning new information. It is often the case that learning information helps a person with enacting a particular skill. For example, understanding some music theory generally makes a person a better musician. Understanding some geometry makes a person a better pool player. But there are plenty of people who are talented musicians who know very little music theory, and lots of people who understand some music theory (yours truly included) who can't sing a note to save their life. In other words, information is helpful for skill acquisition, but it is not strictly necessary and is definitely not sufficient.

The thing that is absolutely necessary for developing a skill is practice. No matter how much information you know, you will not excel at a skill (music, a sport, drawing, science writing, data analysis, present wrapping) unless you practice it. You can read all the books available on the topic, but sooner or later you have to actually try to perform the activity. And then, if you want to get better, you have to do it again and again and again. Even if you are immensely talented and are already naturally better than most other people, you will still only get better if you practice.

I think of receptive communication as a skill that must be acquired through practice, just like learning the foxtrot or driving a car. Remember that the goal is not to change your thoughts, feelings, or level of personal maturity but rather your concrete, observable, and measurable behaviors. Most of the book up to this point has been devoted to giving you information about receptiveness to help you understand the underlying psychological theory and offer some ideas about approaches you could try, as well as knowing what success looks like. But now, we need to figure out how to actually execute these behaviors habitually. We need to build a new skill.

People read self-help books all the time and vow to behave differently. Usually, after reading a book about conflict, we commit to being more empathetic, becoming better listeners, and reading more media representing opposing ideological perspectives. But just like our commitment to go to the gym, these good intentions often dissipate within a couple of weeks. This book is no different. As much as I appreciate that you stuck with me this far, the simple fact of the matter is that reading this book and vowing to try harder is not enough to change behavior. More likely than not, the next time you face disagreement, your old habits will take over. To make a difference in your life, you must become skilled enough at receptiveness so that it becomes your most comfortable, default response to disagreement. This chapter is about how to go from good intentions to developing a skill. It's not rocket science, but it will take some concerted effort and won't be quick.

THE KEY TO EFFECTIVE PRACTICE IS FREQUENCY

Everyone from kindergarten teachers to Olympic coaches will tell you that practice frequency is crucial to skill acquisition. The most common mistake of new learners is getting obsessed with a new hobby, practicing for hours on end, and then burning out either because of exhaustion and frustration or because no family can put up with six hours of beginner violin a day. Practicing in small amounts but with greater regularity will get you much farther than deciding to change how you approach disagreement by talking to every person whose views you abhor in the span of a single week.

The problem with practicing receptiveness all the time, however, is that nobody likes to seek out disagreement. No matter how good you get at the skills in this book, engaging with opposing views is still more taxing than simply avoiding difficult conversations. So, to increase practice frequency, you need to think of how to make the task easier on yourself.

One way to do this is to start small. Pay attention to the smallest, most innocuous disagreements and try to correct how you engage in those before you reach for the big conflicts. When your spouse wants to set the alarm for six a.m. and you would really like to sleep until six-thirty, you could use this as an opportunity to practice receptiveness: "I am curious why you want to get up at six? I was hoping that maybe we could both sleep a little later."

When your unmotivated coworker wants to use the same bland slide template that you know makes clients snooze, lead with: "I remember you mentioned that keeping the slides looking clean is important to you. I am wondering if we might be able to think of a way to keep the clean look while adding a little more color?"

See if you can be so over-the-top receptive that's its laughable. Try it with your family, your friends, your coworkers, and your mechanic. When the waitress asks you if you want French fries or salad with your sandwich, reply with "Thank you for asking! I generally prefer French fries, but I would love to know what you would recommend." When receptiveness becomes a practice that you are so comfortable with that you can turn it into satire, then you know you've mastered the flavor.

MAKE A PLAN AND (AT LEAST TRY TO) STICK TO IT

An important component of any regular practice is making a plan for how and when it will actually happen. A few years ago, my friend and former Wharton colleague Katy Milkman conducted an experiment to test a new approach for increasing flu vaccine uptake. Many companies offer free vaccine clinics because having people take twenty minutes off work to get a shot is far cheaper than having people out with the flu for days. Yet, although most people think that free flu shots at work are a great idea, these clinics are often underutilized. People have a vague intention of getting vaccinated, but as they keep rushing from meeting to meeting and email to email, that intention never quite turns into action.

Katy's intervention was brilliant in its simplicity. She partnered with a company that sent out fliers advertising the free vaccine clinics. All the fliers provided employees with the necessary information (dates, times, locations) and words of encouragement about the importance of vaccination. However, for some of the employees, the flyers were slightly modified to also include a small box where the employee was encouraged to write down the date and time when they themselves would go to get vaccinated. The flyers arrived by mail to employees' homes and were never collected by the researchers. We have no way of knowing how many people in the treatment condition actually filled out the little box or how many of them showed up at the time when they said they would. However, we do know that, on average, the people who received the flyers encouraging them to make a concrete plan were more likely to get the vaccine. Making a plan, no matter how simple, helps.

With receptiveness, I would recommend the following: Find a time on your calendar where you can schedule in ten to fifteen minutes to work on your receptiveness. This could be weekly, twice a week, or even daily if you feel ambitious. The key is that you actually write it down, instead of assuming that you will be able to find the time spontaneously. Use that ten to fifteen minutes to engage in any one of several activities that could increase your level of receptiveness over time:

- Listen to or read a perspective from the opposite side of the political aisle.

- Think about a disagreement you had in the last few days (at home, at work, or with a friend) and write down your reflections. What did you do well? What gave you trouble? What could you have done differently to have come across as more receptive to the other perspective?

- Think about a disagreement you might not have engaged with yet and review your goals in that relationship or upcoming conversation. What are your goals and what do you think your counterpart's goals are?

- Consider some questions you would like to ask a person you disagree with. It could be a person in your life now (like your spouse, your father-in-law, or one of your employees); a person from your past (a high school friend, a former colleague, or an ex); or a person you've never met who you imagine holds a view you disagree with. How can you ask your question so that it communicates minimum snark and maximum learning goals?

- If you feel particularly ambitious, schedule a conversation with a real-life 3D human you disagree with and try talking about something you have avoided. (This exercise will likely take more than fifteen minutes.)

The activities above are examples to get you started, but they are certainly not a comprehensive list. They should help you recognize that there are many ways to actively hone your receptiveness skills: You can work on exposing yourself to opposing perspectives. You could think about how to express particular ideas. You could actively interact with a counterpart. All of these activities will give you some insight into where you struggle and lead you to consider new approaches that might be a good fit for your life and your particular disagreement.

In building your receptiveness practice, take it easy on yourself. You won't manage to practice during every time you had put down on your calendar because life will inevitably get in the way. However, making a commitment to yourself to work on a skill and figuring out how that commitment actually fits in among work, kids, chores, and other activities makes it much more likely that you will actually follow through on your intentions. The plan does not have to be ironclad—you can change your calendar as much as you want—but having any kind of plan is vastly better than not having one at all.

PRACTICE IN WRITING SO YOU HAVE TIME TO CONSIDER YOUR WORDS

One benefit of focusing on your language is that you can improve a lot just by practicing receptiveness in writing.

When engaging in real disagreements, there are trade-offs between writing and live conversation. On the one hand, the human voice can convey a lot of information through tone, pitch, speed, and what psychologists call "paralinguistic cues."* On the other hand, spoken language is more difficult to control, and it happens much faster. As a result, it's easier to get yourself into trouble. There is a Russian saying I remember from my childhood: "A word is not a sparrow. Once it escapes, it can't be caught." In other words, poorly chosen words, once spoken, cannot be unsaid. An email, however, can be written and rewritten a dozen times, until you are happy with the tone. This is especially true when you are first trying to master receptive communication. Responding in writing to a perspective you disagree with gives you a chance to edit your words as many times as you want and to respond only when you are finally pleased with your choices. It also gives you an opportunity to respond when you feel mentally and emotionally ready. You just need the self-control to not send the first draft.

Another good way to focus on your language is to write out responses that you never plan to send. For example, imagine you get a piece of unsolicited advice from a colleague. You might decide that you don't care enough to get into a disagreement and that it is easier to follow your colleague's plan, even if you don't

---

* Recent research by my colleagues Mike Yeomans and Juliana Schroeder (a professor at UC Berkeley) showed that if you randomly assign some people to communicate in writing and others through spoken conversation, people naturally adopt a more receptive tone when speaking than when writing.

think it's optimal. But, for the sake of your own practice, you could write an email receptively pushing back on the advice you don't like. Does writing the email in a way that communicates receptiveness actually help you understand where you colleague is coming from? Do you now have genuine questions you want to ask? You don't have to send the email, but you should hold on to it and review it a few days later. Can you improve it with some time and distance?

HAVE A RECEPTIVENESS BUDDY (OR SEVERAL)

Most behavioral changes, from exercising more to drinking less, are easier with a partner who is committed to taking the journey with you and helping you succeed. This person can be a friend, a colleague, a family member, or a trusted mentor. In fact, it doesn't even have to be the same person for every disagreement. Your receptiveness buddy needs to be a person who understands the general principles of receptive communication (feel free to buy them a copy of this book!) and someone who is eager to help you succeed in *your* goals rather than insisting that you take their advice. This person can help you in several ways.

For example, when I am boiling mad, I often have my husband read and edit my emails. When I am too mad to even write a decent first draft, I ask my best friend, who is also a mediator, to do it for me. I don't have to send what they wrote. I can edit it and make it sound like me, which may at that moment be less receptive than what they came up with. But usually, seeing my point of view expressed in receptive terms flips a switch in my head so that I can proceed with the conversation in a more constructive manner.

Beyond having people supporting your receptiveness efforts in different disagreements, you could also have more than one person give you advice in a particularly tricky situation. For example, my husband and my best friend have very different personalities. Sometimes when I am all tied up in knots about how to handle a disagreement, I will sit them both down together and listen to them offer completely contradictory advice on what I should do. Listening to them disagree about my disagreement helps me understand it from different points of view. All of us are human, and we all fall prey to strong emotions. What years of experience in research and coaching have given me is the wisdom to know when I need help.

Yet another way that a receptiveness buddy can help is to offer a sounding board so that you can reflect on what about a particular situation made it easier or more difficult to be open-minded. For example, together you can think about the topic or the person that made you want to run for the hills or yell, and whether that reaction was justified. You can also make plans for how to deal with things better when a similar situation arises in the future. Talking these reactions through with someone who understands your goals and is familiar with the tools of receptiveness will help you be more honest with yourself and more articulate with your thoughts. The process of dissecting your reactions and mistakes is certainly not easy. Often, I hesitate to review my receptiveness failures because I am simply too embarrassed. But time tends to dull most emotions, including embarrassment. After a few days or a week, I am usually ready to sit down and consider what I could have done differently.

NOTE GOOD EXAMPLES OF RECEPTIVENESS AND EMULATE THEM

There are many ways to elegantly execute the suggestions in this book. Some of them will feel natural to you, and some of them will feel weird. There are other approaches you will not have thought of on your own until you see somebody else navigate a disagreement in an artful way. When you see such examples, take note and think about how you could apply them in your own life. Such observations are especially useful because if you see a colleague or a relative respond to a disagreement in an effective manner, their approach is likely to be one that fits your workplace or your family. Not every approach works everywhere, so look for people around you who seem to be executing receptiveness in a way that's appropriate for the context.

For example, I was recently in an academic seminar where a visiting researcher was presenting a statistical approach he had developed. A Harvard colleague wasn't buying the speaker's argument and asked a question that amounted to "I don't think your approach would work in XYZ circumstances, and I think that's a real problem for your claims." The speaker listened to the question—a question that was clearly challenging and had been posed in front of a room full of other researchers—and responded with the following: "Okay, so let me talk through an example of the worst-possible-case scenario that might give rise to what you are concerned about. And then I will explain why I don't believe it's really a problem."

Sitting in the audience, I thought this was a brilliant execution of receptiveness because the speaker demonstrated not only that he heard the questioner's critique of his work but also that he was willing to engage with the worst, most severe version of it. At the same time, by foreshadowing that he ultimately thought the concern was not particularly damning to his idea, the speaker demonstrated command of the content and basically "won" the exchange without sounding defensive or dismissive. Given that academic seminars can get pretty contentious, I tucked this approach away in my brain for the next time somebody has a big issue with research *I* am presenting.

Different contexts have different norms for how receptiveness is most appropriately expressed. Now that you understand the basic principles, keep an eye out for people in your environment who are very good at applying them. We can all learn a lot from observing each other and thinking about why certain approaches are effective, how and where they might fit, and how they might be modified for our own use.

GOING FROM PRACTICE TO IMPLEMENTATION

At some point, you will have to go from just practicing receptiveness on relatively innocuous topics ("Which one of Taylor Swift's albums is her strongest work?") to topics that matter deeply to you and the people you care about. In making this leap from practice for the sake of self-improvement to putting your new skills to work for you, it is worth thinking through all the steps and structures that will make you the most likely to succeed. What can you do before, during, and after an interaction to make sure that at the end you understand your partner and your partner understands you better than you did before the interaction? How can you ensure that as a result of your efforts, both of you want to talk to each other again?

Before the Conversation

The first step to engaging in a conversation about a disagreement is to carefully consider the assumptions that have likely taken root in your mind.

- How confident are you that you and the other person in fact disagree? And are there some areas of agreement? (Remember, people tend to exaggerate their degree of disagreement.)

- How much do you know about what exactly you disagree on? For example, do you disagree about the details of a specific course of action? About the appropriate reasons to support this course of action? Or about how hard or easy it will be to execute it? Disagreeing about "vacation" or disagreeing about "abortion" can take on a hundred different flavors. It's good to think through where the fault lines really are.

- What are you assuming about the source of the disagreement and especially about your counterpart? What do you think they think and where did those views come from? (If you are about to tell yourself a story about how their bad upbringing or lackluster education has led them to the incorrect conclusion, you should reread the naïve realism chapter.)

- How do you expect the conversation to go? Have you attempted discussing this topic with this person in the past? Do you think it will be emotional? Will it take a long time? Does raising this topic risk damaging your relationship? Having some idea of what you are in for will help you avoid "unforced errors" such as starting on a difficult topic late at night or in front of an audience of rowdy relatives.

After thinking through what you know (or what you think you know), you will want to do some concrete planning. Is this conversation going to be on the phone? In person? Over coffee? After dinner? On a walk? The setting matters because you generally want to avoid:

- Times when people are already tired and cranky;

- Running out of time and having to rush;

- Having an audience whose mere presence will shape the behavior of the conversation participants.

With a loose plan in your mind, it's time to invite the other person into the conversation. This is where things can sometimes go in unexpected ways. Your counterpart might not realize that there is an issue at all and be surprised that there is something to discuss; or they might dread talking to you and try to avoid the conversation; or they might say, "Yeah . . . I wanted to talk to you about that as well. Our last conversation made me realize that there are *other* things that also concern me about our relationship."

So, the first part of talking about a disagreement becomes an exercise in joint goal setting. For example, you might say: "You know, I was thinking through what you said the other day about our finances, and I had some thoughts I wanted to share. Is that something you would be interested in talking through with me? Do you have time for coffee on Wednesday?"

Notice a few things about the way I phrased my invitation:

1. I named the topic. (Instead of ominously announcing, "We need to talk," and letting my counterpart marinate in their own anxiety, I said it was about the finances.)

2. I signaled that the conversation was prompted by me listening to something they said earlier. (I get some points for good listening!)

3. I asked the other person about their willingness to participate instead of just jumping into the conversation at a time that may be bad for them.

4. I kept control over the date and setting by suggesting coffee on Wednesday, which they are likely to agree to because agreeing is usually easier than coming up with an alternative.

During the Conversation

We have already spent most of the book on what to do (and what not to do) during a conversation about opposing views. But here is a quick summary if you want to copy these pages and tape them to your wall for easy reference:

1. Stay focused on your goals. You might go into a conversation with the desire to learn, ask questions, or simply express your views, but those goals can be easy to forget in the heat of the moment. If you start feeling like you are trying to win an argument, convince your counterpart that they are wrong, or just land a clever zinger, you might want to ask yourself if these new goals are realistic or in line with your long-term interests.

2. Demonstrate receptiveness by:
    - Asking questions that telegraph your strong interest in learning about and understanding your counterpart.
    - Listening to the whole answer, even if it's stupid, wrong, infuriating, hurtful, inarticulate, or too long.
    - Restating your counterpart's views until they have verbally confirmed that you truly understand where they are coming from.

3. Use the H.E.A.R. framework to communicate your receptiveness when it's your turn to talk.
   - Hedge your claims
   - Emphasize agreement
   - Acknowledge the other perspective
   - Reframe to the positive
   - Avoid explanatory words ("because," "therefore") and minimizing words ("just," "simply") that make you and your argument sound condescending.

4. Share the personal experiences that led you to hold your belief:
   - Talk about your own experiences and convictions (not some other person's).
   - Show a little vulnerability so your story doesn't sound like bragging or lecturing.

Finally, remember that no matter how hard you try, some conversations will just go badly. It may be that the other person is not ready to talk, or it's a bad time for them, or they are simply a jerk. It could be that the topic is too hard, and the wounds are too deep. It may be that despite your best intentions and thoughtful planning, you find yourself too uncomfortable hearing the other person's point of view.

In any of those cases, it's okay to take a pause either for a while or forever. Stopping a conversation that's not going well does not have to be done abruptly or angrily. Nobody needs to storm out and doors need not be slammed. You can again use words to clearly explain why the conversation is not working for you and suggest a path forward. For example, you might say: "I don't think this is going the way I expected it to. Can we take a break and talk about this some more tomorrow?" Or: "I want to take some time to consider what you said. Can we table this discussion and start again later?" The point is that you have control over the timing of the conversation, and if you feel yourself getting in trouble, there is no reason to continue. The opportunity to talk again is very likely to be there tomorrow as well as next week, unless, that is, you destroy the relationship by perseverating in a conversation that's not doing anyone any good.

After the Conversation

Remember my definition of a constructive disagreement from the beginning of this book:

> A constructive disagreement is any disagreement that increases the parties' willingness to talk to each other again.

When you conclude a conversation about a difference of opinion, whether one that went fabulously well or one that was just one snide remark short of a complete dumpster fire, remember that your goal is to build a bridge to the next conversation. To this end, you need to show appreciation and care for your counterpart so that they are eager to talk to you again. You could give them a casual hug in the kitchen along with, "Thanks for talking through that with me." Or you might send a more formal email expressing appreciation for their time and perspective. In either of these versions, it is again helpful to demonstrate receptiveness. For example, you might highlight something that made an impression on you: "I keep thinking about the argument you made for the value of investing in some new drafting software. I'll look into the costs of that." Or "I've never heard about your experiences in Wyoming. That was really thought-provoking. Thanks for sharing!" Notice that, like all other expressions of receptiveness in this book, these statements demonstrate your appreciation for and interest in someone's point of view without obligating you to change your mind. A person can be made to feel heard and seen without anyone budging an inch.

Finally, reflecting on a conversation afterward might make you realize that you are not done. You may have new thoughts or new questions, or have simply realized that the person who you dreaded talking to is sort of interesting. Extending or restarting a discussion that feels unfinished is just as much under your control as ending one that's dragging on too long. The best possible ending to a conversation between people in disagreement is when one party invites the other to talk some more.

THROUGHOUT THIS BOOK, I have tried to make the case that receptiveness is the Swiss Army knife of conflict communication. In casual interactions with flight attendants and baristas, in professional disagreements with hundreds of thousands of dollars on the line, and in your daily efforts to coexist harmoniously with your family, expressing greater receptiveness can help you achieve more understanding with less drama. But of course, there is a price to pay—you have to put in the work to master the tools if you want them to work for you consistently. You don't want to be in the middle of a major disagreement with your boss and suddenly realize that you need to run back to your office to look up the phrases that make up the H.E.A.R. framework. However, if you put in the time to work on your receptiveness when you don't really need to, when your mind is relatively at peace and you have some energy to devote to self-improvement, the tool kit will be there for you when you find yourself under stress and struggling to find the right words. When that time comes, you will be grateful that you spent a few minutes a week mastering the functions of your new Swiss Army knife so that you don't accidentally poke yourself in the eye.

CHAPTER SUMMARY

- Learning to disagree receptively is a trainable skill that improves with consistent practice and thoughtful feedback. In this way, it is not that different than learning to play a musical instrument or performing most professional activities—the more work you put in to improve in advance, the better prepared you will be when it's "showtime."

- To help you improve, create a practice plan with specific activities and structure. Consider other people whose example you can emulate or who can offer support and guidance when you need it.

- Think about how you can make your behavior more receptive at three time points in a conversation with somebody you disagree with: before, during, and after. Dividing disagreement into these discrete segments makes skill-building more manageable.

11

BUILDING RECEPTIVE RELATIONSHIPS, TEAMS, AND COMMUNITIES

IT'S A TUESDAY MORNING AND I AM ON MY WAY TO WORK. LIKE most people, I started my morning at home—in my case, an environment of relatively easy receptiveness. I then arrived at work at the Harvard Kennedy School, a community of hundreds of extraordinarily smart people who try a little too hard not to make waves or hurt anybody's feelings. And I walked into my office suite where, because my research assistants, grad students, and postdocs are passionate, underpaid, and constantly stressed, disagreement is frequent and can escalate dramatically depending on who is involved. As days go, it's a pretty laid-back one, but even this relatively mundane morning takes me on a journey across the multiple "disagreement cultures" that shape my daily life.

Most of us spend our lives shuttling between disagreement cultures—different social settings in which people over time have developed norms and habits around how they navigate opposing views. Some of these cultures are as small as a relationship between two people—a friendship, a romance, or the conversational habits of a parent and child. Some cultures are of medium size—a work team, a classroom, or a homeowners' association. And some comprise thousands or millions of people employed in one company or living in one country. But all groups of people eventually develop habits and norms, ways of acting that are expected, appropriate, and familiar. When it comes to opposing perspectives, do the people in this social group hide their disagreement? Voice it clearly? Get easily angered? Engage in receptive exploration? Rush to compromise? No matter how good you get at enacting receptiveness on your own, you will still be affected (for better or for worse) by what people are doing around you. Thus, the question we want to consider in this chapter deals with how you can shape the way disagreement is approached across the different disagreement cultures you belong to so your efforts are not completely overwhelmed by the influence of others.

IF THERE IS one question that comes up in every single talk or training I do, it is: How can a person make the other people around them be more receptive to them? In general, folks are all for the idea of learning and using receptiveness. What they would really love, however, is to be on the receiving end of some receptive behavior!

This is not surprising. Psychology boasts a long list of "self-enhancement biases"—ways in which people think that they are somehow better, wiser, and more attractive than objective reality suggests. Receptiveness is no exception. Our studies show that when two people interact and then rate their own and their partner's receptiveness, both think they are a little more receptive than the other—a mathematically impossible result! So, if I am already doing an excellent job being receptive to you, it is only fair that you should do your part and be receptive back.

Naïve realism also plays a part in our desire for others to be more receptive. If I believe that I am basically correct in my views on any given topic of disagreement, you should also be open to engaging with my perspective and be willing to understand my reasoning. After all, being receptive to me will only help you benefit from my wisdom. If I am being generous enough to make the effort to listen to your wrongheaded ideas, the least you should do is be equally receptive to my clearly superior ones.

The question most people have, when we ask them about what they think of receptiveness, is: How can they change the mindsets and behaviors of other people? How can they get their spouses, children, coworkers, and country mates—people who populate the various disagreement cultures they belong to—to realize that they need to do more to express curiosity and engage with their perspectives? What can we do to make others listen to us thoughtfully and consider our arguments with no prejudice?

There are two answers to this question. First, you can buy ten copies of this book and give a copy to every person in your life you wish were more receptive. Together, we can launch a campaign teaching the world about receptiveness, one disagreeable relative or coworker at a time. This approach would do wonders for my book sales and fund a whole lot of new studies. Personally, I like this plan a lot.

However, as much as the approach above would benefit me, scientific integrity demands that I also share some other ideas that I believe to be effective, as well as highlight common pitfalls that prevent people from creating the receptiveness cultures they seek. Not every idea below will apply to every setting, but even considering why certain ideas feel like a "fit" and others don't is likely to give you new insights into your own situation.

RECEPTIVENESS IS CONTAGIOUS

The first tip for improving the receptiveness of others is simply being receptive to them! We can get a lot of mileage out of the fact that receptiveness is contagious, especially in one-on-one conversations. Rather than telling you how I want you to treat me, I can treat you that way myself and rely on the natural human tendency toward mimicry to do the work for me. Of course, this approach requires considerable self-control: When a disagreement crops up, you have to model receptiveness instead of pouring gasoline on the fire. However, the major upside is that the human tendency toward mimicry gives you agency over the flow of all your future conversations. You don't have to go around the world preaching receptiveness (that's my job!), you just have to worry about controlling your own behavior.

When you are about to face a discussion with a person whom you have little control over and you are thinking about how to get through it with minimal collateral damage, modeling receptiveness in a way that is transparent and consistent is a great place to start. When you do this over and over again, your counterpart will come to expect conversations with you to have a particular flavor. Those expectations will shape how they approach you and begin to feed a self-reinforcing cycle. You can shift the culture of a particular relationship by committing to be unfailingly receptive to the other person and letting mimicry do the rest.

RECEPTIVE BEHAVIOR IS TRAINABLE

If we have seen one thing in our studies, it is that receptiveness is readily trainable. Giving people simple instructions on what to say and what not to say, along with incentives to follow those instructions, is an incredibly effective way to change behavior. Receptiveness is trainable precisely because it is simple, concrete, and transparent. This simplicity and concreteness yields better results than seemingly more sophisticated (but also more opaque) attempts at changing people's mindsets around disagreement on contentious topics.

You may remember a study I described in Chapter 7 where

one group of participants received training in conversational receptiveness and another group received instructions to be empathetic, to take the other side's perspective, and to exercise intellectual humility. In algorithmically measuring the level of receptiveness that participants exhibited in their writing to a disagreeing counterpart, we saw that receptiveness training resulted in messages that were twice as receptive as the messages that were written by participants who were told to think different thoughts and feel different feelings.

One implication of this study is that if you are going to train people, train them in exactly what you want them to do and make it as easy as possible for them to do it. If you wanted to teach a kid to drive, you wouldn't first teach them to play basketball to improve their hand-eye coordination. You would instead put them into a car, preferably with an automatic transmission and antilock brakes, to make progress happen faster and more safely. The idea here is the same: If you want to improve a particular behavior, train that behavior, but try to make it easy and safe.

But of course, all of us have been in both good training and bad training—how a particular idea is presented can make a huge difference. Here are a couple of ideas on how to make your attempts at training people in receptiveness the most effective:

Connect the training to pressing challenges: Think about the disagreement challenges in the setting you are trying to improve. What do people disagree about and why do they struggle? Think about vignettes and examples that apply to the setting you are in.

If you are training a team of surgeons in being more receptive, don't ask them to think about disagreements among race car drivers. People's time is precious, and the training will benefit them more if they can see how it will make their daily life immediately better.

Create an active experience: The most challenging aspect of teaching people to disagree receptively is giving them the experience of applying the tools so they can see how easy or difficult it is for them. Receptiveness sounds great in concept, but people need to try it on in an actual disagreement to formulate good questions and identify areas that most desperately need work. Any training you create should give participants the opportunity to talk to each other about disagreements that matter to them and consider that experience as a larger group. Did receptiveness help? Did it feel weird? Were the words hard to say? When would it be helpful? When would it not? Having a thoughtful discussion based on a shared experience is key to internalizing the lessons.

Provide portable reminders of desirable behaviors: Most classes in educational institutions or in the workplace are accompanied by a PowerPoint deck or a booklet of key takeaways that learners are supposed to refer to in order to refresh their memories. In the midst of a disagreement, nobody is going to fire up the PowerPoint to recall what they are supposed to be saying and not saying. By contrast, small posters, wallet cards, or swag such as mugs or mouse pads can serve as environmental cues to remind members of a community about what they learned. If you are going to spend time and money training people in receptiveness, order some water bottles with the H.E.A.R. framework on them—it'll be worth it!

BEHAVIOR CHANGE REQUIRES FOLLOW-THROUGH

A key mistake that thwarts most change efforts, be it in families, workplaces, or community organizations, is lack of follow-through. In most cases, attempts at changing behavior begin and end with a book, a keynote, or a class. Immediately afterward, people go back to their real lives and real problems, and their hard-won skills and insights fade into the background. Even if the delivery was fantastic, the information valuable, and the motivation to improve high, it is simply impossible to change the way people behave in one attempt. An approach that is far more likely to succeed is to incorporate receptiveness and related follow-up activities into recurring events and processes, so that the topic of how to disagree more effectively comes up with some regularity.

To begin, consider where and how receptiveness can be integrated into regular, repetitive events and processes that happen in your setting. For example, most teams in most organizations have weekly check-ins or staff meetings. However, little thought is normally put into how those are structured to ensure that everyone in the room is comfortable clearly articulating their beliefs and ideas, particularly if those ideas differ from the majority consensus. How can every meeting be subtly reorganized so that colleagues are comfortable voicing their genuine perspectives and can expect to be greeted with receptiveness?

Families also have regular touchpoints that lend themselves to the practice of receptiveness. Meals and long drives to and from kids' activities are great opportunities to invite disagreement and model receptiveness. Disagreeing with adults, while being respectful and thoughtful, is a key life skill that most of our kids lack. To be fair to the kids, though, the adults don't do a great job of teaching them. Most parents I know hide their disagreements from their children, intentionally choosing to "present a united front." However, one might imagine a different philosophy that emphasizes respectful disagreement as a useful skill to be modeled. "I understand that Dad doesn't want you to get a new fish because you've killed the prior three. But I do think that you are older now and may be more ready for a pet. Dad, what would make you more comfortable with Joya getting a new fish?" Fish or no fish, conversations like these might teach your kids something valuable that will help them comfortably withstand more serious parental disagreements and will also make them better at navigating disagreement in their own relationships.

When people are new to a setting or hold a position of relatively lower status, they are not likely to trust a sudden emergence of a culture of constructive disagreement. It will take time for them to come to believe that divergent perspectives are truly welcome. By contrast, it takes very little time to shut down fledgling attempts at thoughtful debate. This should make people in positions of power and authority think hard about how their behavior contributes to shaping the environment around them. When a person of lower status is nervously trying to voice disagreement, work like hell to encourage it. It only takes one unreceptive response to shut them down. Initially, you might hear a lot of goofy and poorly articulated ideas, but it will pay off in the long run. That's why considering how disagreement can be practiced in repetitive interactions is so important: It takes many encounters to convince somebody that they won't get shut down or fired for disagreeing with an authority figure.

A key job of a leader hoping for change is finding opportunities and processes to promote and model the behaviors they want to see. Remember the point about receptiveness being contagious—this point is especially important for people in positions of leadership to remember because their behavior is observed and attended to by more people. If you are leading a meeting with ten people in the room, your behavior is ten times more influential than your behavior in a one-on-one interaction. If that meeting happens every Tuesday, it represents a weekly opportunity to shape your team's culture for better or for worse. Exhausted managers and harried parents rarely consider the fact that in every interaction they are modeling the norms of how disagreement will later be handled by everyone else in the room, during every future interaction. Given that most organizations large and small have repetitive interactions, leaders should consider the impact that those interactions have for shaping the organizational culture.

RECEPTIVE BEHAVIOR SHOULD BE INCENTIVIZED

I spent the first years of my professional life after college working as a management consultant. In retrospect, considering that at twenty-one all my work experience consisted of teaching ballroom dancing, I am surprised I was hired. But my peers were similarly clueless, so it is possible that dancing helped—after all, I could speak confidently in front of groups and walk in heels without tripping.

My first manager was a guy named Jim Parise, a Vietnam veteran who built his career in large manufacturing companies in the Midwest. In our group of mostly female, mostly psychology or conflict resolution–trained change-management consultants, Jim's brash takes were sometimes jarring. For example, after we would spend an hour debating whether a focus group, a listening circle, or a team-building activity was most likely to foster change on a client team, Jim would often put an end to the debate by simply declaring: "People do what they get paid for." He meant: Quit talking about feelings and figure out how to measure and incentivize the behavior that the client wants to see more of. Two decades later, I realized that Jim was right—people do all sorts of things because they get paid for them. Behaving in a receptive manner is no exception.

So how would you incentivize receptiveness?

Like most things, the answer depends on the context. Look around and consider what types of incentives are available to you and are appropriate to the situation. For example, every organization of any size requires people to evaluate their own performance and the performance of their subordinates and managers on a regular basis. Employees have annual and biannual reviews, which often measure a battery of "soft skills." People regularly evaluate each other's leadership ability, oral and written communication skills, capacity for teamwork, and even creativity. If an organization is serious about changing the way employees engage with disagreement, these evaluations could include questions about how a particular individual or team handles such interactions and what concrete behaviors they demonstrate that show their skills in this area. Promotions and placement on particular projects could (and should) take these evaluations into account. Given that we have established that receptiveness is largely in the eye of the beholder, it makes sense to use peer evaluations to judge whether a person can deploy this skill effectively and then reward them for doing so.

Even outside of organizational hierarchies that run on financial incentives, there are multiple ways to reinforce desirable habits. There are many contexts where rewarding people for their ability to handle disagreement is more useful than rewarding them for their ability to write an essay about why they want the job. Team captains, camp counselors, youth pastors, and nannies should be hired at least in part based on receptiveness. Spouses, children, and friends should be praised for disagreeing effectively, so they know that their interpersonal risk-taking is appreciated rather than resented and consequently become more willing to do it again.

A few years ago, my best friend told me that I should write a book about conflict. I told her that it was a goofy idea, and I had no interest in book-writing. She kept bringing it up, and I kept resisting. Eventually, I started exploring the idea. Then I sat down and wrote this book. My life has radically changed for the better because a person cared enough to disagree repeatedly but graciously. Now, I take every opportunity to give her credit for coming up with the book idea. I am hoping that my encouragement will make her disagree with me more often.

CHOOSE TO BE AROUND RECEPTIVE PEOPLE

The ideas for increasing the level of receptiveness in your social groups that we discussed above all deal with changing the behavior of the people who are already there. However, another point of leverage is considering the kinds of people you invite into your disagreement cultures in the first place. It's hard to replace unreceptive family members with more receptive ones, but some social groups are more fluid, and as you bring new people in, it is worth considering how their level of receptiveness will contribute to the culture you are trying to create.

One beauty of working in academia is that everyone around me is smart. So, when I think of who I want to write my next paper with, I don't look for the biggest genius; rather, I look for people I want to spend time with. Who is going to push back on my ideas but not make me feel bad? Who can take some amount of pushback from me and not need to be consoled afterward? Who can stick to receptiveness even under stress, in the face of journal rejections, or when the statistical software crashes for no apparent reason? The people whose names appear over and over again on my list of publications usually fit these criteria.

Obviously, not everyone has the freedom to choose their colleagues, but many of us do have some say in who gets to join the team. When you begin selecting new hires, new teammates, or new admits, consider whether they can engage with opposing views in a receptive manner. By bringing in receptive people, you can dramatically shift the disagreement culture of an organization. People who already belong to the organization will observe the updated selection criteria and realize that receptiveness is a value that you take seriously. The new wave of recruits will also recognize that receptiveness is valued and will show up ready to prove that they belong. Gradually, this shift will shape the norms among the existing group members while continuing to drive who gets brought on in the future.

A simple way to screen for receptiveness is to use the receptiveness survey in Chapter 2. The survey can be administered to potential new recruits and the results discussed during the interview process. Building a discussion of receptiveness right into an interview will send a strong message about the values and priorities in your organization. Another way of approaching this task is to simply to ask people about how they would handle a real or hypothetical disagreement. The more ways you evaluate receptiveness, the clearer it will become to your new recruits that this is something you care about.

SCALING RECEPTIVENESS

Whenever I mention that I am writing a book on receptiveness to opposing views, people nod thoughtfully and say something to the effect of "Yeah . . . we sure need that right now . . ." Of course, they are not referring to their family disagreements or the arguments at work. Instead, they are reflecting on the state of political discourse in the United States and around the world, where scholars have noted a troubling increase in political polarization and a growing disdain for holders of opposing views. The question becomes: Can we scale receptiveness? Are there approaches that might bear more fruit than training millions of people one at a time? Can we speed this up a little?

If that's something you are interested in, here are a couple of ideas worth considering.

Start earlier: In most American schools, children from preschool onward receive instructions in socio-emotional skills: how to be kind, deal with bullies, ask for help, and engage with a variety of identity characteristics that kids from different families and backgrounds bring to every classroom. But somewhere in middle school and high school we have an opportunity to teach our soon-to-be young adults to talk about the things that matter most with peers who may disagree.

The skills of receptive communication planted in middle school can be reinforced throughout the years of secondary education using classroom norms and repeated practice. Courses from social studies to biology could include intentional instruction preparing students to be more engaged citizens and more engaged colleagues. Imagine if a group project for a high school English class included a requirement that students describe a facet of the project on which their group disagreed and how they handled the disagreement effectively. Or if every time a student had to make a class presentation, a peer was appointed to play "devil's advocate." Experiencing disagreement as a normal occurrence and being coached on how to handle it with receptiveness would, over the years, form different habits and expectations. If exercises like these happened in every classroom, our teenagers would leave school far more prepared for the diversity of backgrounds and views they are likely to encounter as adults.

Hundreds of nonprofits around the United States are working to bridge our ideological divide. However, most of them work with adults. These adults, in turn, are the sorts of people who show up to bridging workshops. In some sense, they are the people least in need of help. Starting with kids and making training in constructive disagreement widely available are likely to save us millions of dollars down the road as we prevent arguments, physical fights, and the resultant disciplinary action. Beyond saving money, we might end up with a generation of adult voters who are able to discuss issues thoughtfully and thoroughly in the public square, at work, and in their homes.

Use technology to cross distances: Training millions of kids in constructive disagreement is first and foremost prohibitively expensive. However, technology can help. Live, synchronous instruction can be combined with asynchronous online learning and practice. Indeed, training people in receptive communication using a video platform can actually be easier and more effective than trying to facilitate live practice because platforms like Zoom and Microsoft Teams make it easy to bring together people with different views, from different parts of an organization, in different geographical locations.

When I first came to the United States from Russia, I tried to organize a "pen pal" program between my new American middle school and my old Russian one. Given that a handwritten letter took a couple of weeks to get from Denver, Colorado, to Ekaterinburg, Russia, the program fizzled almost immediately. No middle school kid has the patience to wait a month for a reply from a pen pal when Mario Brothers is calling. These days, with just a few clicks we can get hundreds of people who disagree to talk in groups of any size, from anywhere in the world. We should use this opportunity to connect kids from Texas with kids from New York, and kids from Montana with kids from Virginia. This work could be done in classrooms, but also in church groups and as preparation for national sporting events. For all the talk about technology dividing us, it can also serve to unite us if we use it wisely.

Embrace the power of an artificial intelligence coach: As I write this, we are experiencing the first wave of what is likely to be a tectonic shift in how we live, brought about by artificial intelligence. It will take decades to know whether AI ends up doing more good than harm for humanity, but what is already apparent is that it can be used to great effect in educational settings. At the Harvard Kennedy School we are developing chatbots that can coach students in statistics, economics, and yes, constructive disagreement.

The availability of AI removes two of the most important barriers to robust receptiveness training: the fact that people don't like disagreeing because they might offend their counterpart, and the fact that in our polarized world people are surrounded by like-minded others. The beauty of disagreeing with a chatbot is that there is no risk of real conflict, and your "counterpart" can argue any side of any issue with equal facility. As a learner, you can try to be more receptive or less receptive. You can practice in English, Spanish, or Mandarin. You can try the same conversation seven different ways—and the chatbot will never get fed up and never run out of arguments.

Indeed, a recent paper by one of my coauthors, Stanford professor Zak Tormala, and his coauthors demonstrates that people are more receptive to opposing perspectives from AI counterparts than they are from humans. Why? Because they don't think that AI is trying to persuade them—a stance that most humans seem to find very difficult to execute!

In sum, while training any skill can get very expensive, especially at scale, technology can help. With a bit of creativity, almost any organization or community can find a way of teaching people about receptiveness that fits their size, resources, and manner of working together.

Celebrate people who model receptiveness: Receptiveness is not sexy. It is not quick-witted or cutting. It does not humiliate its opponent, drop the mic, and swagger offstage. Because receptive discussions don't amass millions of clicks, receptive leaders toil in relative anonymity. Consequently, societal discourse is dominated by the loud, the dogmatic, and the snarky.

If we want change, we need to reverse this trend. Instead of telling employees to be more confident, let's start promoting them for being more thoughtful. Instead of electing leaders who are the most fiery, let's elect the leaders who are best at fostering understanding. Let's offer college admissions and prestigious jobs to young people who have organized the most dialogue groups, not the ones who attended the most protests. Doing this at the local level—in our schools, town councils, and synagogue boards—will show our values to other members of our communities. Let's create little bubbles of peace around ourselves and model what we want to see in others. Remember, receptiveness is contagious.

CHAPTER SUMMARY

- Beyond improving our own receptiveness, the tools in this book can be applied to shifting the receptiveness cultures we belong to. Members of families, classrooms, and workplaces can come to interact in a more habitually receptive manner with some thoughtful design and effort.

- Making other people around you more receptive by creating processes that build good habits is worth the effort because it will directly benefit you in your next disagreement!

- To shift the receptiveness culture around you, consider how you might bring in more receptive people, increase the receptiveness skills of the people who are already there, and incentivize everyone to keep putting in consistent effort.

- To foster receptiveness at a societal level, think about early adulthood education and using technology to cut costs and bridge distances.

Conclusion

IT'S GOOD TO END WHERE WE BEGAN—BY THINKING ABOUT OUR goals. I wrote this book because, despite the thousands of pages of advice on handling disagreement and conflict, people continue to struggle every day with how to express their views without damaging their relationships. It is my hope that by sharing the research and translating it into actionable takeaways, I can help readers get one step closer to mutual understanding with their families, their coworkers, and maybe even their fellow citizens. By focusing our energy on approaches that work and largely ignoring ones that are not supported by the data, I wanted to help people achieve their goals faster and with fewer missteps. As more people try on an evidence-based approach to disagreeing better, new ideas will emerge that will need to be tested. The research apparatus will continue to crank along, moving us closer and closer to a more complete and more *useful* understanding of disagreement.

Now think back to what made *you* pick up this book. There is a good chance that, like most of us, you have a problem with disagreement. It could be that you have a sense that your life has too much conflict, with every disagreement turning into a heated argument, and many arguments contributing to a later feeling of unease and resentment. It could be the opposite: Your mind is filled with unspoken objections and frustrations that you are reluctant to voice because you anticipate the drama that is likely to emerge out of any attempt at sharing your ideas. People say you are "conflict averse," and although you suspect that this is not a compliment, for you, maintaining the peace is worth it. You continue to keep quiet, hoping that things will be okay in the end.

My hope is that by this point in our journey you have come to realize that both kinds of disagreement problems stem from the same source. Being in a constant state of conflict and keeping silent in order to prevent blowups are both caused by a lack of skill in effectively voicing your point of view and receptively engaging with opposing perspectives. Some people who lack the skill get by with avoiding disagreement and keeping silent until they no longer can. When they finally decide to speak up, they often handle the conversation badly due to lack of practice. Their more conflict-seeking counterparts do the opposite: They jump into every argument with gusto and are frequently surprised at the negative reactions of others. After enough spats, they learn to keep their thoughts to themselves, retreating into a sullen posture of "not my problem." The solution to both issues is the same: We don't need to disagree less or disagree more, we need to disagree better. I hope that you now have some ideas about how.

Throughout our discussion, I've argued that many disagreement-related problems start with a lack of clarity regarding our goals in any given conversation or, alternatively, setting goals that are fundamentally unattainable (like changing a person's lifelong beliefs about abortion policy or about their relationship with their sister). As you look forward to putting the ideas in this book to work for you, go back to reviewing your goals. Do you want to ask better questions? Learn to more successfully voice your opposition to your coworkers' worst ideas? Or avoid parenting spats with your spouse? Concrete goals lead to concrete plans, which ultimately lead to measurable results.

Because our disagreement outcomes are impacted by both how we think and how we act, as well as the environment we are in, the overall problem of improving your disagreement practice can be approached from several different angles. Pick a chapter that speaks to you the most and start there. You may be the sort of "steady as she goes" person who wants to begin by reflecting on the results from your receptiveness assessment (Chapter 2) and considering why certain aspects of processing information in a receptive manner feel particularly challenging. You may be the sort that wants to see a quick improvement in your very next conversation and put the H.E.A.R. framework into immediate use (Chapter 7). You may have realized that many of your beliefs are grounded in personal experiences that you rarely share, and you are excited about sitting down and crafting an argument for a core belief supported by a story from your life (Chapter 8). It doesn't matter where you start as long as you make a plan and put in the work. In fact, now that you have a sense of what the various chapters are about, you can work through the guidance and exercises in any order you like, repeating some and putting off others until you are ready.

Expect to stumble at least a few times. In your next team meeting, you might formulate a question that sounds thoughtful in your head but will sound snarky out loud. When talking to your landlord, you might find yourself unable to follow through on the H.E.A.R. framework because you are just too fed up with their pathetic attempts at snow removal. You might go visit your family, execute all the tools in this book perfectly, and then realize that the tremendous emotional effort of engaging with their craziness is just not worth it. You might be really receptive at work, and then lose patience with your kids when you come home. As with any practice, the key is to observe the result, consider the causes, focus on the ones that are under your control, and try again when you are ready. No approach to any human problem works 100 percent of the time, but trying again after some reflection and adjustment generally gets you further than not trying!

Receptiveness is not easy. Consistently deploying these skills in every disagreement, no matter how long-running or bitter, takes quite a bit of both analytical reasoning and emotional self-control. Nevertheless, if you live and work with other humans, the effort is well worth it. After decades of studying and teaching receptive communication, I walk through life pretty confident that if I have an idea that I need to express, I can find a way of communicating it without getting into an argument. To be honest, occasionally my confidence turns out to not be entirely justified and some encounters still leave me a little frayed. But by and large, my conversations are both more informative and more peaceful because I have taken the time to cultivate a skill set grounded in evidence.

As we wrap up our exploration of disagreement, it is worth considering that there has never been a world without conflict, and chances are you don't remember a day in your life that did not feature a disagreement of some kind. Given that the planet keeps spinning and most of us are doing okay putting one foot in front of the other, it is also reasonable to ask why one should bother to do anything different now. Aren't there bigger issues to worry about than how we talk (or don't talk) to people we disagree with? What about immigration, the economy, AI regulation? Shouldn't we be focusing our mental efforts there?

Yes and no. You have probably heard about the growing problem of political polarization in the United States. Democrats and Republicans dislike and distrust each other more than ever before. Many people now consider that it would be worse for a child to marry somebody from another political party than somebody from another race. And although this statistic can be seen as a testament to improved race relations, it also suggests that people's prejudices have found a new target—those who disagree with us. Importantly, polarization is growing not only in the United States but also globally. Most political systems, including ones that do not revolve around two parties, feature a continuum between a more liberal (left) and more conservative (right) set of attitudes and policies, and in many the left and the right are becoming less and less tolerant of each other. With political division reaching new heights on a seemingly daily basis, many researchers and policymakers have raised an alarm about the related dangers. If people can't have civil conversations across the political divide, how are we to make wise policy decisions, pass legislation, or even retain relationships with our neighbors? Framed in this way, our ability to debate issues honestly and receptively is literally a matter of life and death that will determine our ability to survive climate change, the next pandemic, and the next election.

Importantly, our ideological debates have permeated almost every aspect of life, far beyond the political sphere. For example, many hotly contested workplace debates have a grounding in political ideology: Should we strive to hire more people of color and members of other disadvantaged groups? Should we offer employees a health plan that includes abortion benefits? Should we mandate vaccines? Should we limit travel to decrease our carbon footprint? Disagreements in families are similarly politicized, with people accusing members of the opposite sex or a different generation or living in a different state of being too or not sufficiently woke, or too naïve, or too uncaring. Political ideology and the divisions it has created are now truly everywhere.

Yet, even as we continue to battle over policies and parenting approaches, the world continues to grow more complex, demanding greater and greater levels of information sharing, coordination, and creativity to navigate. The technologies that have brought us together have also enabled both misinformation and viruses to easily traverse the globe. The scientific advances that have made our lives easier, healthier, and more pleasurable also demand that we work together when systems fail because no single person has all the knowledge needed to get things up and running again. Online access to an endless number of differing perspectives on literally any topic puts us at risk of being paralyzed by contradiction unless we learn to tolerate each other long enough to thoughtfully examine both sides.

In this world of ever-accelerating change, countries, organizations, and families that fail to come together and communicate about their differences effectively will do so at their own peril. As both complexity and risk mount, the groups that succeed will be composed of people who know how to speak their mind without shutting others down, how to telegraph learning goals without giving up on their convictions, and how to wield influence without resorting to coercion. Thus, we need solutions that are grounded in rigorous research (so they are more likely to work), are relatively easy to implement (so people actually try them), and can be scaled at low cost (so more than a handful of us get to benefit from them).

I hope that this book has offered you a set of principles for designing such solutions. If you disagreed with something, I would love to hear from you about it and put the tools in this book toward learning from each other.

Acknowledgments

A CORE TENET OF SOCIAL PSYCHOLOGY IS THAT NO SUCCESS OR failure belongs to any one person. Instead, all outcomes arise out of the combined currents of social and situational forces that buffet all of us throughout our lifetimes. Whether you did well or poorly in life, don't take yourself too seriously—your personal contribution was likely pretty minor compared to the much larger influence of everyone and everything else involved.

In my case, my mom, my favorite aunt, and my stepfather were all psychologists—a family environment that encouraged my early fascination (read "obsession") with human behavior. Of these, the greatest influence was my mother, whose fiery energy convinced all around her that anything was possible. Hers was not a Pollyannish belief in the power of positive thinking, but a bone-deep faith that if she tried hard enough, she could move mountains. On the rare occasions when someone got in her way, her biting wit usually made them retreat in a hurry. That mindset, which she intentionally cultivated in me, sustained me through dozens of dancing injuries, brutal academic rejections, and almost every marital and parenting freak-out you can imagine.

My grandmother was a journalist and an author—not an easy feat for a Jewish woman in the Soviet Union of the 1960s. I remember coming home from elementary school and being allowed to help her "edit" manuscripts. In retrospect, she was probably letting me play with Wite-Out to keep me out of her hair while she worked. However, in my mind, I was becoming a writer like her. Into her nineties she still read my papers, was eager to hear about all my successes and failures, and constantly affirmed the value of my work. In her mind nothing was more important—except the kids and Ryan.

My in-laws, David and Rosanne Minson, accepted me and my crazy immigrant family with wide-open arms and constant offers of food and cocktails. Our lifestyle (too codependent), our arguments (too loud), and our parenting (too permissive) were all probably very strange to them, but I would not have finished my PhD, or raised my girls, or written this book, without their unfailing support. Nothing makes me more proud to be an American than thinking of the family that produced my husband.

And speaking of the husband. There are few more potent reminders of the power of sheer dumb luck than knowing that almost all of your life outcomes were determined at seventeen, when a lanky boy wearing a purple T-shirt (stamped with multicolored dinosaurs) walked into a dance studio and asked to learn the foxtrot. For nearly thirty years, that boy has been my most consistent supporter, disagreement partner, critic, and admirer. Out of love, faith, and a healthy fear of standing in my way, he has agreed to several cross-country moves, job changes, and home purchases. He supported me through graduate school, helped nurse my mom through cancer, and welcomed my grandmother into our home after she became a widow. There would be no PhD, no research, no Harvard professorship—hell, no "me"—without Ryan.

Beyond the blood family, there is the extended intellectual

clan that inspired, encouraged, and contributed to the research and its translation into meaningful, teachable insights. My mentors and colleagues at Stanford, Penn, and Harvard gave me a chance to spend years pursuing ideas, some of which made it into this book and some of which turned out to be spectacular failures. I am grateful for their faith, their encouragement, their warnings, and their criticism. I am the researcher I am today because lots of people who had absolutely nothing to gain have spent hundreds of hours mentoring me.

First among those was Lee Ross, who taught me to love social psychology, and its potential for making the world a better place. He also modeled being the kind of adviser I sought to become—fully engaged, endlessly available, intellectually exacting, more of a parent than a teacher.

Later, my own students and coauthors made the years of work fly by. Academia is largely fueled by competition, criticism, rejection, and uncertainty. The people whom you choose to spend years coauthoring with become family, and their successes and failures come to be your own. In the best collaborations, you don't remember who came up with any given idea, you just remember that the jokes you told at the time were really funny.

Heather Sulejman is the sister I chose for myself. She convinced me that the world needed to know about the research and that pointing people to academic journals wasn't going to do the trick. Her passion for giving people everywhere useful tools for navigating conflict gave her the patience to listen to me talk about research details for hours and hours—far longer than anyone besides Ryan ever has. Over time, we began intentionally extracting practical insights from the experimental results and translating those insights into teaching materials, exercises, and ultimately the idea for this book.

Celeste Fine and Tracy Behar, and their respective teams at Park, Fine & Brower and Penguin Random House, made this book happen. Through months of brainstorming, editing, and coaching, they taught me how to communicate my ideas in a way that made them clear and practical. I am so grateful for the opportunity to learn from the best in the business and see these ideas liberated from academic journals and shared with the world.

Notes

INTRODUCTION

xvii **Participants read a list describing a variety of different activities:** Charles A. Dorison, Julia A. Minson, and Todd Rogers, "Selective Exposure Partly Relies on Faulty Affective Forecasts," *Cognition* 188 (2019): 98–107.

xxiii **as "receptiveness to opposing views":** Julia A. Minson, Frances S. Chen, and Catherine H. Tinsley, "Why Won't You Listen to Me? Measuring Receptiveness to Opposing Views," *Management Science* 66, no. 7 (2020): 3069–94.

xxiv **more diverse social networks:** Brian P. Reschke, Julia A. Minson, Hannah Riley Bowles, Mathijs de Vaan, and Sameer B. Srivastava, "Friends on the Other Side: Receptiveness to Opposing Views Predicts Formation of Politically Heterogeneous Relationships," *Personality and Social Psychology Bulletin* (2025), forthcoming.

xxviii **dieting doesn't work for weight loss:** T. Wu, Xiang Gao, M. Chen, and Rob M. Van Dam, "Long-Term Effectiveness of Diet-Plus-Exercise Interventions vs. Diet-Only Interventions for Weight Loss: A Meta-Analysis," *Obesity Reviews* 10, no. 3 (2009): 313–323.

xxviii **being out in the cold does not cause colds:** Ronald Eccles, "Common Cold," *Frontiers in Allergy* 4 (2023): Article 1224988.

CHAPTER 1

4 **phenomenon "naïve realism":** Robert J. Robinson, Dacher Keltner, Andrew Ward, and Lee Ross, "Actual Versus Assumed Differences in Construal: 'Naive Realism' in Intergroup Perception and Conflict," *Journal of Personality and Social Psychology* 68, no. 3 (1995): 404–17; Lee Ross, "Perspectives on Disagreement and Dispute Resolution," in *The Behavioral Foundations of Public Policy*, edited by Eldar Shafir (Princeton University Press, 2013), 108–23; Lee Ross, Mark Lepper, and Andrew Ward, "History of Social Psychology: Insights, Challenges, and Contributions to Theory and Application," in *Handbook of Social Psychology*, 5th ed., edited by Susan T. Fiske, Daniel T. Gilbert, and Gardner Lindzey (John Wiley & Sons, 2010), 3–50; Lee Ross and Andrew Ward, "Psychological Barriers to Dispute Resolution," in *Advances in Experimental Social Psychology*, vol. 27, edited by Mark P. Zanna (Academic Press, 1995), 255–304.

4 **Northern Ireland and the Middle East:** Ross et al., "History of Social Psychology"; Lee Ross, "From the Fundamental Attribution Error to the Truly Fundamental Attribution Error and Beyond: My Research Journey," *Perspectives on Psychological Science* 13, no. 6 (2018): 750–69.

7 **"making an attribution":** Ross et al., "History of Social Psychology."

10 **doggedly attached to their convictions:** Lee Ross and Andrew Ward, "Naive Realism in Everyday Life: Implications for Social Conflict and Misunderstanding," in *Values and Knowledge*, edited by Edward S. Reed, Elliot Turiel, and Terrance Brown (Psychology Press, 2013), 103–35; Ross, "Perspectives on Disagreement and Dispute Resolution"; Ross et al., "History of Social Psychology."

11 **read arguments for the opposing perspective:** Julia A. Minson and Charles A. Dorison, "Why Is Exposure to Opposing Views Aversive? Reconciling Three Theoretical Perspectives," *Current Opinion in Psychology* 47 (2022): Article 101435.

12 **consider the emotions they and their opposing counterparts feel:** Charles A. Dorison and Julia A. Minson, "You Can't Handle the Truth! Conflict Counterparts Over-Estimate Each Other's Feelings

of Self-Threat," *Organizational Behavior and Human Decision Processes* 170 (2022): Article 104147.

13 **"the bias blind spot":** Emily Pronin, Daniel Y. Lin, and Lee Ross, "The Bias Blind Spot: Perceptions of Bias in Self Versus Others," *Personality and Social Psychology Bulletin* 28, no. 3 (2002): 369–81.

14 **people are "cognitive misers":** Susan T. Fiske and Shelley E. Taylor, *Social Cognition* (Addison-Wesley, 1984); Daniel Kahneman, *Thinking, Fast and Slow* (Macmillan, 2011).

14 **disagreeing parties struggle to live and let live:** Julia A. Minson and Charles A. Dorison, "Toward a Psychology of Attitude Conflict," *Current Opinion in Psychology* 43 (2022): 182–88.

17 **clinch the win for their team:** J. L. Logg, L. Berg, and J. A. Minson, "Everybody Argues and Nobody Loses: Overestimation of Success as a Driver of Debate" (working paper, 2015).

CHAPTER 2

21 **called "receptiveness to opposing views":** Julia A. Minson, Frances S. Chen, and Catherine H. Tinsley, "Why Won't You Listen to Me? Measuring Receptiveness to Opposing Views," *Management Science* 66, no. 7 (2020): 3069–94.

26 **This is called "selective exposure":** William Hart, Dolores Albarracín, Alice H. Eagly, Inge Brechan, Matthew J. Lindberg, and Lisa Merrill, "Feeling Validated Versus Being Correct: A Meta-Analysis of Selective Exposure to Information," *Psychological Bulletin* 135, no. 4 (2009): 555–88.

28 **watch two senators make speeches about the law:** Minson et al., "Why Won't You Listen to Me?"

29 **"social networks" of students:** Brian P. Reschke, Julia A. Minson, Hannah Riley Bowles, Mathijs de Vaan, and Sameer B. Srivastava, "Friends on the Other Side: Receptiveness to Opposing Views Predicts Formation of Politically Heterogeneous Relationships," *Personality and Social Psychology Bulletin* (2025), forthcoming.

34 **Need for Cognition:** J. T. Cacioppo, R. E. Petty, and C. F. Kao, "The Efficient Assessment of Need for Cognition," *Journal of*

Personality Assessment 48, no. 3 (1984): 306–7, https://doi.org/10.1207/s15327752jpa4803_13.

34 **Actively Open-Minded Thinking:** Jonathan Baron, "Actively Open-Minded Thinking in Politics," *Cognition* 188 (2019): 8–18.

34 **and Intellectual Humility:** S. M. Bowes, T. H. Costello, C. Lee, S. McElroy-Heltzel, D. E. Davis, and S. O. Lilienfeld, "Stepping Outside the Echo Chamber: Is Intellectual Humility Associated with Less Political Myside Bias?" *Personality and Social Psychology Bulletin* 48, no. 1 (2019): 150–64.

39 **psychologists call "situational factors":** Richard E. Nisbett, Joshua Aronson, Clancy Blair, William Dickens, James Flynn, Diane F. Halpern, and Eric Turkheimer, "Intelligence: New Findings and Theoretical Developments," *American Psychologist* 67, no. 2 (2012): 130–59.

40 **partly determined by your biology:** Kerry L. Jang, W. John Livesley, and Philip A. Vernon, "Heritability of the Big Five Personality Dimensions and Their Facets: A Twin Study," *Journal of Personality* 64, no. 3 (1996): 577–92.

CHAPTER 3

51 **anonymous online chat:** Michael Yeomans, Julia Minson, Hanne Collins, Frances Chen, and Francesca Gino, "Conversational Receptiveness: Improving Engagement with Opposing Views," *Organizational Behavior and Human Decision Processes* 160 (2020): 131–48.

58 **animals also imitate each other's utterances:** Elisabetta Palagi, Ivan Norscia, Serena Pressi, and Giada Cordoni, "Facial Mimicry and Play: A Comparative Study in Chimpanzees and Gorillas," *Emotion* 19, no. 4 (2019): 665; Luigi Baciadonna, Cwyn Solvi, Flavia Del Vecchio, Cristina Pilenga, David Baracchi, Francesca Bandoli, Valentina Isaja et al., "Vocal Accommodation in Penguins (*Spheniscus demersus*) as a Result of Social Environment," *Proceedings of the Royal Society B* 289, no. 1978 (2022): 20220626.

61 **series of muted commercials:** H. K. Collins, J. A. Minson, A. Kristal, and A. W. Brooks, "Conveying and Detecting Listening

During Live Conversation," *Journal of Experimental Psychology: General* 153, no. 2 (2024): 473–92.

62 **if they were listening, they would have agreed with us:** Zhiying Ren and Rebecca Schaumberg, "Disagreement Gets Mistaken for Bad Listening," *Psychological Science* 35, no. 5 (2024): 455–70.

63 **nonverbal signals are often interpreted differently by different people:** Miles L. Patterson, Alan J. Fridlund, and Carlos Crivelli, "Four Misconceptions About Nonverbal Communication," *Perspectives on Psychological Science* 18, no. 6 (2023): 1388–1411.

CHAPTER 4

70 **research on conversational goals:** Michael Yeomans, Maurice E. Schweitzer, and Alison Wood Brooks, "The Conversational Circumplex: Identifying, Prioritizing, and Pursuing Informational and Relational Motives in Conversation," *Current Opinion in Psychology* 44 (2022): 293–302.

72 **an "inquiry mindset":** David A. Garvin and Michael A. Roberto, "What You Don't Know About Making Decisions," *Harvard Business Review* 79, no. 8 (2001): 108–16; Charles M. Judd, "Cognitive Effects of Attitude Conflict Resolution," *Journal of Conflict Resolution* 22, no. 3 (1978): 483–98; Douglas Stone, Bruce Patton, and Sheila Heen, *Difficult Conversations: How to Discuss What Matters Most* (Penguin Books, 2023).

73 **list the goals they anticipated:** Hanne K. Collins, Charles A. Dorison, Francesca Gino, and Julia A. Minson, "Underestimating Counterparts' Learning Goals Impairs Conflictual Conversations," *Psychological Science* 33, no. 10 (2022): 1732–52.

74 **approach their disagreements with the goal of learning:** Collins et al., "Underestimating Counterparts' Learning Goals Impairs Conflictual Conversations."

75 **show the participants a fake questionnaire:** Collins et al., "Underestimating Counterparts' Learning Goals Impairs Conflictual Conversations."

76 **Biden and Trump supporters:** Collins et al., "Underestimating Counterparts' Learning Goals Impairs Conflictual Conversations."

77   **feeling heard and understood generates positive emotions:** Guy Itzchakov, Netta Weinstein, Dvori Saluk, and Moty Amar, "Connection Heals Wounds: Feeling Listened To Reduces Speakers' Loneliness Following a Social Rejection Disclosure," *Personality and Social Psychology Bulletin* 49, no. 8 (2023): 1273–94; Hiroaki Kawamichi, Kazufumi Yoshihara, Akihiro T. Sasaki, Sho K. Sugawara, Hiroki C. Tanabe, Ryoji Shinohara, Yuka Sugisawa et al., "Perceiving Active Listening Activates the Reward System and Improves the Impression of Relevant Experiences," *Social Neuroscience* 10, no. 1 (2015): 16–26.

78   **two sentences at the beginning:** Hanne K. Collins and Julia A. Minson, *Expressing Learning Goals: A Conflict Want-Should Conflict* (unpublished manuscript submitted for publication, 2025).

82   **"Overconfidence," by contrast:** Don A. Moore, *Perfectly Confident: How to Calibrate Your Decisions Wisely* (HarperCollins, 2020).

83   **overconfident in their ability to persuade disagreeing counterparts:** Jennifer L. Logg, Lindsey Berg, and Julia A. Minson, *Everybody Argues and Nobody Loses: Overestimation of Success as a Driver of Debate* (unpublished manuscript, 2025).

CHAPTER 5

90   **questions serve to communicate information:** Julia A. Minson, Eric M. VanEpps, Jeremy A. Yip, and Maurice E. Schweitzer, "Eliciting the Truth, the Whole Truth, and Nothing but the Truth: The Effect of Question Phrasing on Deception," *Organizational Behavior and Human Decision Processes* 147 (2018): 76–93.

92   **This is called "self-perception":** Russell H. Fazio, "Self-Perception Theory: A Current Perspective," *Social Influence* (2014): 129–50.

92   **the power of question-asking:** Frances S. Chen, Julia A. Minson, and Zakary L. Tormala, "Tell Me More: The Effects of Expressed Interest on Receptiveness During Dialog," *Journal of Experimental Social Psychology* 46, no. 5 (2010): 850–53.

94   **a set of comprehensive exams:** Chen et al., "Tell Me More."

96 **that asking more questions:** Karen Huang, Michael Yeomans, Alison Wood Brooks, Julia Minson, and Francesca Gino, "It Doesn't Hurt to Ask: Question-Asking Increases Liking," *Journal of Personality and Social Psychology* 113, no. 3 (2017): 430–52.

98 **what psychologists call "responsiveness":** Harry T. Reis and Shelly L. Gable, "Responsiveness," *Current Opinion in Psychology* 1 (2015): 67–71.

99 **Mike Yeomans calls "boomerasking":** Alison Wood Brooks and Michael Yeomans, "Boomerasking: Answering Your Own Questions," *Journal of Experimental Psychology: General* 154, no. 3 (2025), 864–93.

104 **sensitive and nonsensitive questions:** Einav Hart, Eric M. VanEpps, and Maurice E. Schweitzer, "The (Better Than Expected) Consequences of Asking Sensitive Questions." *Organizational Behavior and Human Decision Processes* 162 (2021): 136–54.

CHAPTER 6

109 **the phenomenon of "perspective-taking":** Tal Eyal, Mary Steffel, and Nicholas Epley, "Perspective Mistaking: Accurately Understanding the Mind of Another Requires Getting Perspective, Not Taking Perspective," *Journal of Personality and Social Psychology* 114, no. 4 (2018): 547–71.

118 **leveraging the Listening Triangle:** Moshe Cohen, *Collywobbles: How to Negotiate When Negotiating Makes You Nervous* (The Negotiating Table, Inc., 2020).

CHAPTER 7

130 **government executives discussed:** Michael Yeomans, Julia Minson, Hanne Collins, Frances Chen, and Francesca Gino, "Conversational Receptiveness: Improving Engagement with Opposing Views," *Organizational Behavior and Human Decision Processes* 160 (2020): 131–48.

133 **natural language processing:** Yeomans et al., "Conversational Receptiveness."

137 **discussion threads from Wikipedia talk pages:** Justine Zhang, Jonathan Chang, Cristian Danescu-Niculescu-Mizil, Lucas Dixon, Yiqing Hua, Dario Taraborelli, and Nithum Thain, "Conversations Gone Awry: Detecting Early Signs of Conversational Failure," in *Proceedings of the 56th Annual Meeting of the Association for Computational Linguistics*, vol. 1, 1350–1361. Melbourne, Australia, 2018.

143 **Reflection step in the Listening Triangle:** Moshe Cohen, *Collywobbles: How to Negotiate When Negotiating Makes You Nervous* (The Negotiating Table, Inc., 2020).

145 **components of the H.E.A.R. framework:** Yeomans et al., "Conversational Receptiveness"; Julia A. Minson, David Hagmann, and Katherine Luo, "Beyond Persuasion: Improving Conversational Quality Around High-Stakes Interpersonal Disagreements" (unpublished manuscript, Harvard University, 2025); Julia A. Minson, Michael Yeomans, Hanne K. Collins, and Charles A. Dorison, "Conversational Receptiveness Transmits Between Parties and Bridges Ideological Conflict" (unpublished manuscript, Harvard University, 2025).

146 **people who learned the "receptiveness recipe":** Michael Yeomans, Julia Minson, and Hanne Collins, "Commentary on 'Belief in the Utility of Cross-Partisan Empathy Reduces Partisan Animosity and Facilitates Political Persuasion': Conversational Receptiveness and the Effects of Empathy on Disagreement Outcomes" (unpublished manuscript, Imperial College London, 2025).

149 **that receptiveness is contagious has several important implications:** Minson et al., "Beyond Persuasion."

CHAPTER 8

153 **these two arguments about gun violence and gun regulation:** Simar Bajaj, "He Was Shot in the Throat. Now He Saves Gun Victims as a Trauma Surgeon in Baltimore," *The Guardian*, June 20, 2024.

159 **different versions of a "canvassing script":** Joshua L. Kalla and David E. Broockman, "Reducing Exclusionary Attitudes Through Interpersonal Conversation: Evidence from Three Field Experiments," *American Political Science Review* 114, no. 2 (2020): 410–25.

162 **personal narratives on conversation about opposing views:** David Hagmann, Julia A. Minson, and Catherine H. Tinsley, "Personal Narratives Build Trust Across Ideological Divides," *Journal of Applied Psychology* 109, no. 11 (2024): 1693–1715.

167 **"Joe the Plumber":** "'Joe the Plumber,' Who Challenged Obama on Taxes in 2008, Dies Aged 49," *The Guardian*, August 28, 2023, https://www.theguardian.com/us-news/2023/aug/28/joe-plumber-dead-obama-campaign.

167 **completely made-up personal stories:** Hagmann et al., "Personal Narratives Build Trust Across Ideological Divides."

172 **the trustworthiness of both authors:** Hagmann et al., "Personal Narratives Build Trust Across Ideological Divides."

CHAPTER 9

178 **divided by the Berlin Wall:** Dacher Keltner and Robert J. Robinson, "Extremism, Power, and the Imagined Basis of Social Conflict," *Current Directions in Psychological Science* 5, no. 4 (1996): 101–5.

179 **called More in Common:** More in Common, "The Perception Gap" (2019), https://perceptiongap.us/.

181 **humans are "cognitive misers":** Susan T. Fiske and Shelley E. Taylor, *Social Cognition* (Addison-Wesley, 1984); Daniel Kahneman, *Thinking, Fast and Slow* (Macmillan, 2011).

192 **receptiveness having reputational costs:** Molly Moore and Julia A. Minson, "A Conceptual Model of the Reputational Consequences of Engagement with Opposing Views" (unpublished manuscript, Washington University, 2025); Gordon Heltzel and Kristin Laurin, "Seek and Ye Shall Be Fine: Attitudes Toward Political-Perspective Seekers," *Psychological Science* 32, no. 11 (2021): 1782–1800.

194 **"Ascent of Man":** Nour Kteily, Emile Bruneau, Adam Waytz, and Sarah Cotterill, "The Ascent of Man: Theoretical and Empirical Evidence for Blatant Dehumanization," *Journal of Personality and Social Psychology* 109, no. 5 (2015): 901–31; Samantha L. Moore-Berg, Lee-Or Ankori-Karlinsky, Boaz Hameiri, and Emile Bruneau, "Exaggerated Meta-Perceptions Predict Intergroup Hostility

Between American Political Partisans," *Proceedings of the National Academy of Sciences* 117, no. 26 (2020): 14864–72.

197 **imagine how much of each emotion they thought they would feel if they had to watch the video:** Charles A. Dorison, Julia A. Minson, and Todd Rogers, "Selective Exposure Partly Relies on Faulty Affective Forecasts," *Cognition* 188 (2019): 98–107.

200 **sticking your tongue out:** Norine Dresser, "On Sticking Out Your Tongue," *Los Angeles Times*, October 8, 1997.

200 **care about feeling heard:** E. G. Bruneau and R. Saxe, "The Power of Being Heard: The Benefits of 'Perspective-Giving' in the Context of Intergroup Conflict," *Journal of Experimental Social Psychology* 48, no. 4 (2012): 855–66; E.-S. Forsgärde, M. F. Attebring, and C. Elmqvist, "It Is Like Mental Pain: Patient Perspectives on Patient–Provider Communication in Emergency Care for Chest Pain in Sweden," *Cambridge Journal of Education* 48, no. 3 (2016): 371–89.

201 **People have a "truth bias":** Charles F. Bond, Jr., and Bella M. DePaulo, "Accuracy of Deception Judgments," *Personality and Social Psychology Review* 10, no. 3 (2006): 214–34.

202 **posing a "want-should" conflict:** Katherine L. Milkman, Todd Rogers, and Max H. Bazerman, "Harnessing Our Inner Angels and Demons: What We Have Learned About Want/Should Conflicts and How That Knowledge Can Help Us Reduce Short-Sighted Decision Making," *Perspectives on Psychological Science* 3, no. 4 (2008): 324–38.

CHAPTER 10

208 **flu vaccine uptake:** Katherine L. Milkman, John Beshears, James J. Choi, David Laibson, and Brigitte C. Madrian, "Using Implementation Intentions Prompts to Enhance Influenza Vaccination Rates," *Proceedings of the National Academy of Sciences* 108, no. 26 (2011): 10415–20.

211 **writing and live conversation:** Burint Bevis, Juliana Schroeder, and Michael Yeomans, "Speaking Makes Disagreement More Constructive Than Writing" (unpublished manuscript, Department of Management and Entrepreneurship, Imperial College London, 2025).

CHAPTER 11

226 **receptiveness is readily trainable:** Michael Yeomans, Julia Minson, and Hanne Collins, "Cross-Partisan Empathy Reduces Partisan Animosity and Facilitates Political Persuasion': Conversational Receptiveness and the Effects of Empathy on Disagreement Outcomes" (unpublished manuscript, Imperial College London, 2025).

236 **chatbots that can coach:** Louise Lu, Zakary L. Tormala, and Adam Duhachek, "How AI Sources Can Increase Openness to Opposing Views," *Scientific Reports* 15, no. 1 (2025): Article 17170.

CONCLUSION

242 **Democrats and Republicans dislike and distrust each other:** Eli J. Finkel, Christopher A. Bail, Mina Cikara, Peter H. Ditto, Shanto Iyengar, Samara Klar, Lilliana Mason et al., "Political Sectarianism in America," *Science* 370, no. 6516 (2020): 533–36.

243 **somebody from another political party:** Shanto Iyengar and Sean J. Westwood, "Fear and Loathing Across Party Lines: New Evidence on Group Polarization," *American Journal of Political Science* 59, no. 3 (2015): 690–707.

Index

A
acknowledging other perspectives, 142–44
active experiences, 227–28
adverb limiters, 145
affirmative action, 186–87, 188–89
agreeableness, 40
agreement, emphasizing, 141–42
anger, 12
anxiety, 12, 34, 70, 217
artificial intelligence (AI), 236–37
Ascent of Man, 194, 194*fig*
assumptions, careful consideration of, 215–16. *See also* bias
attention, receptiveness and, 23, 28
attitude-change, 24–25
attributional process, 7–10, 18
authenticity, 201
Avastin, 47–49

B
ballroom dancing, 1–5, 15
behavior
    follow-through for change in, 228–30
    importance of, 57–58
    incentivizing receptive, 231–32
    language as, 55–56
    nonverbal, 59–64
Berlin Wall, 178
bias
    bias blind spot and, 13
    cognitive, 6
    confirmation, 183, 201
    congeniality, 26–28
    cultivating awareness of, 16
    self-enhancement, 224
    truth, 201
body language, 59–64
boomerasking, 99–103, 106
Broockman, David, 158–61
Brooks, Alison Wood, 70, 96

C

canvassers, 158–62
Caruso, Moira, 113–14, 115–17
chatbots, 236–37
Chen, Frances, 20–24, 26, 34, 91–94
children, teaching receptiveness to, 229, 234–35, 238
cognitive biases, 6
Cohen, Adar, 119
Cohen, Moshe, 118
Collins, Hanne, 72–73, 140n
combativeness, 194–96
compassion, 160
computational linguistics, 132–34, 162
condescension, avoiding, 145
confirmation bias, 183, 201
conflict
  ballroom dancing and, 1–4
  disagreement versus, xviii–xix
  naïve realism and, 4–6, 8, 10–18
  psychological causes of, 4–10
  testing approaches to, xxviii
congeniality bias, 26–28
constructive disagreements, xxv–xxvi, 220
conversational goals, 70–78
conversational receptiveness, 70–78, 136–40, 150. *See also* H.E.A.R. framework
COVID-19, 183–85
Cruz, Ted, 197
cultural differences, 199–200
curiosity
  expressing, 91
  intellectual, 35–36, 41–42

D

dehumanization, 194–95
disagreement cultures, 223–24, 233
disagreements
  conflict and, xviii–xix, xxviii, 1–18
  constructive, xxv–xxvi, 220
  costs of, xviii–xix
  dynamics of, xix–xxi, xxii–xxiii
  exaggerated beliefs regarding, 178–81, 204
  examples of, xiii–xv
  impact of, xii
  importance of, xvi
  science of, xxvi–xxix
  typical number of, xi
dispositional factors, 39–40
Dorison, Charlie, 11–12, 140n, 197

E

elaboration questions, 106–7
Emotional Equanimity, 33–35, 41
emotional reactivity, 40
emotional self-control, 41
empathy, 56–57
emphasizing agreement, 141–42
engagement, 91
evaluations, 231–32
exaggerated beliefs regarding disagreement, 178–81, 204
Executive Education students, 50–56, 132
expectations, faulty, 196–99. *See also* false polarization
experiences, active, 227–28
extraversion, 40

F

facts versus opinions, 182–85
fair-mindedness, 28–29
false polarization, 142n, 178–81, 194
fear, 12
Federal Mediation and Conciliation Service (FMCS), 113–14
flat-earthers, 182
flu vaccine clinics, 208–9
follow-through, behavior change and, 228–30
follow-up
    after conversations, 220–21
    questions for, 97–99, 106–7

G

Germany, 178
goals
    conversational, 70–78, 136–40, 150
    joint setting of, 217–18
    reviewing, 240–41
    signaling learning, 67–87
    staying focused on, 218
Golden Rule, 59

H

Hagmann, David, 162–63, 171–72
Hart, Einav, 103
Hawkins, Kevin "Hawk," 113–14, 187–90
H.E.A.R. framework, 140–51, 144*fig*, 219
hedging, 140–41
Heltzel, Gordon, 192

I

immigration examples, 158–62, 168, 169–70
immoral perspectives, 185–90
impatience, 81–82, 85
implementation, going from practice to, 215–21
inappropriate questions, 103–6, 107
incentivizing receptive behavior, 231–32
influence, receptiveness and, xxiv–xxvi
inquiry mindset, 72
Intellectual Curiosity, 35–36, 41–42
Intellectual Humility, 36
interventions, kitchen sink, 161–62
irritation, 12

J

Jacobs, Charlotte, 48–49
Joe the Plumber, 167

K

Kahneman, Daniel, 14
Kalla, Josh, 158–61
kitchen sink interventions, 161–62

L

language
    as behavior, 55–56
    body language versus, 63–64
    computational linguistics and, 132–34

language (*cont.*)
   as "contagious," 58–59, 148
   conversational receptiveness and, 136
   perceptions of receptiveness and, 65
   perspective-getting and, 111
   practice and, 211–12
laugh tracks, 58
Laurin, Kristin, 192
leadership positions, 230
learning goals, signaling, 67–87
learning orientation, 72
LGBTQ+ community, 193
linguistic mimicry, 58–59
listening
   difficulty of evaluating, 61–63
   Listening Triangle and, 118–27, 121*fig*, 128, 143–44
   mediators and, 112–18
   with your words, 109–28
Logg, Jennifer, 83
lung cancer, 47–49

M
McCain, John, 167
mediators, listening and, 112–18
meta-perceptions, 194–95
Milkman, Katy, 208
mimicry
   linguistic, 58–59
   receptiveness and, 58–59, 225–26
mindset
   inquiry, 72
   for receptiveness, 19–45
minimum wage arguments, 163–66, 167–68
Moore, Molly, 192

moral values, 185–90
More in Common, 179

N
naïve realism
   conflict and, 4–6, 8, 10–18
   desire for receptiveness and, 224–25
   emotions and, 34–35
   false polarization and, 180
   judging listening quality and, 62
   overconfidence and, 83
   research on, 19–20
   Respect Toward Opponents and, 37
   stereotypes and, 77
natural language processing (NLP), 133–34
negative features, 134–36, 135*fig*, 139–40
nonjudgmental exchange of personal narratives, 159–62. *See also* storytelling
nonverbal behavior, 59–64

O
opinions versus facts, 182–85
overconfidence, 82–83, 85, 110–11, 112, 119

P
paralinguistic cues, 211
Parise, Jim, 231
personal narratives, nonjudgmental exchange of, 159–62. *See also* storytelling

perspective-getting, 111
perspectives, immoral, 185–90
perspective-taking, 109–12
persuasion
   as goal, 73–75, 77
   as ineffective strategy, 16–17, 18
   perceptions of openness to, 191
   receptiveness versus, 24–25
planning
   for implementation, 216–18
   for practice, 208–9, 222
polarization
   false, 142n, 178–81, 194
   political, 234, 242–43
politeness, 199–200
political polarization, 234, 242–43
portable reminders, 228
positive, reframing to the, 144
positive features, 134–36, 135*fig*, 139–40
practice
   frequency of, 207–8
   going to implementation from, 215–21
   importance of, 206
   planning for, 208–10, 222
   receptiveness buddies and, 212–13
   using examples, 213–15
   in writing, 211–12
pride, 84–85
Pride Month, 193
problem-solving process, ix
Pronin, Emily, 13

Q
questions
   asking the right, 89–107
   boomerasking and, 99–103, 106
   elaboration, 106–7
   follow-up, 97–99, 106–7
   inappropriate/sensitive, 103–6, 107
   Listening Triangle and, 121–22, 123–26
   messages conveyed by, 90–92
   number of, 96–97

R
reasoning words, avoiding, 144–45
receptive people, choosing to be around, 233–34, 238
receptiveness
   benefits of, 44
   building with others, 223–38
   celebrating, 237–38
   as "contagious," 55, 65, 148–49, 225–26, 230, 238
   conversational, 136–40, 150
   courage to speak with, 177–204
   defining, 21–24, 44
   demonstrating, 218
   features of, 134–36, 135*fig*, 139–40
   four factors of, 30–38. *See also individual factors*
   H.E.A.R. framework and, 140–51, 144*fig*, 219
   improving, 205–22
   incentivizing, 231–32
   increasing, 39–44, 45
   influence and, xxiv–xxvi
   mimicry and, 58–59, 225–26
   mindset for, 19–45
   people displaying, 26–30

receptiveness (*cont.*)
   perceptions of, 52–55, 65
   persuasion versus, 24–26
   practicing, xxi–xxiv
   research on, 50–56
   scaling, 234–38
   score, 30–38
   storytelling and, 153–75
   survey on, 21
   taking breaks and, 219–20
   as trainable behavior, 226–28
   using technology to teach, 235–36, 238
receptiveness buddies, 212–13
"receptiveness recipe," 146
reflection, 120–22, 124, 126–27, 143–44
reframing to the positive, 144
reminders, portable, 228
Ren, Bella, 62
Respect Toward Opponents, 36–37, 42–43
responsiveness, 98–99
Rogers, Todd, 197
Ross, Lee, 4–5, 19, 25

S
Sakran, Joseph, 153–57, 167, 168–69
Sanders, Bernie, 197
sarcasm, 64n
Schaumberg, Becky, 62
Schroeder, Juliana, 211n
Schweitzer, Maurice, 70
scores, understanding, 39–44
selective exposure, 26–28
self-enhancement biases, 224
self-perception, 92

sensitive questions, 103–6, 107
shuttle diplomacy, 198
sincerity, lack of, 100–101
situational factors, 39–40
skill acquisition, 205–6
social networks, 29–30
soft asks, 105
stereotypes, 77
storytelling
   combining with facts, 171–72, 175
   effectiveness of, 167–70
   improving, 173–74
   Sakran and, 153–57
   science of, 157–67
   using, 170–73

T
testing for understanding, 115–18, 121
third-party observers
   as mediators, 198–99
   reactions from, 191–92
threat, 34
Tinsley, Catherine, 162–63, 171–72
Tolerance of Taboo Issues, 37–38, 43–44
Tormala, Zak, 237
trust/trustworthiness, 60, 166–69, 171–72, 175
truth bias, 201

U
understanding
   of receptiveness scores, 39–44
   testing for, 115–18, 121

V
vulnerability, 168–69, 173, 175

W
want-should conflicts, 202
Wikipedia, 136–38
wishful thinking, 201

wokeness, 188–89
Wurzelbacher, Samuel Joseph, 167. *See also* Joe the Plumber

Y
Yeomans, Mike, 70, 99, 100, 131–32, 137, 211n